Advertising and the European City

Historical Urban Studies

Series editors: Richard Rodger and Jean-Luc Pinol

Titles in this series include:

Capital Cities and their Hinterlands in Early Modern Europe
edited by Peter Clark and Bernard Lepetit

*Power, Profit and Urban Land: Landownership in Medieval and
Early Modern Northern European Towns*
edited by Finn-Einar Eliassen and Geir Atle Ersland

*Water and European Cities from the Middle Ages to the
Nineteenth Century*
edited by Jean-Luc Pinol and Dennis Menjeot

The Built Form of Colonial Cities
Manuel Texeira

Advertising and the European City
edited by Clemens Wischermann and Elliott Shore

*Cathedrals of Urban Modernity:
The First Museums of Contemporary Art, 1800–1930*
J. Pedro Lorente

*Body and City: A Cultural History of
Urban Public Health*
edited by Helen Power and Sally Sheard

The Artisan and the European Town, 1500–1900
edited by Geoffrey Crossick

*Urban Fortunes: Property and
Inheritance in the Town, 1700–1900*
edited by Jon Stobart and Alastair Owens

Advertising and the European City:

Historical Perspectives

Edited by

**CLEMENS WISCHERMANN
and ELLIOTT SHORE**

Ashgate

Aldershot • Burlington USA • Singapore • Sydney

Published by
Ashgate Publishing Ltd
Gower House
Croft Road
Aldershot
Hants GU11 3HR
England

Ashgate Publishing Company
131 Main Street
Burlington
Vermont 05401–5600
USA

ISBN 1-84014-237-5

Ashgate website: http://www.ashgate.com

British Library Cataloguing in Publication Data

Wischermann, Clemens
  Advertising and the European City. – (Historical urban
  studies)
  1. Advertising – Europe – History
  I. Title   II. Shore, Elliott, 1951–
  659.1'094

Library of Congress Cataloguing-in-Publication Data

Advertising and the European City/[edited by] Clemens Wischermann, Elliott Shore.
      p.   cm. – (Historical urban studies)
    Includes bibliographical references
    1. Advertising – Europe.   I. Wischermann, Clemens.   II. Shore, Elliott,
  1951–   III. Series.

  HF5813.E79 A364   2000
  659.1'094–dc21
                                                            00–020651

Typeset in Sabon by Manton Typesetters, Louth, Lincolnshire, UK and printed in Great Britain by TJ International Ltd, Padstow, Cornwall.

Contents

General Editors' Preface   vii

List of Figures   ix

Notes on Contributors   xiv

Preface   xvii

1 Placing Advertising in the Modern Cultural History of the
  City   1
  Clemens Wischermann

2 Advertising as *Kulturkampf* in Berlin and Vienna   32
  Elliott Shore

3 Visual Discourse and the Metropolis: The Importance of
  Mental Models of Cities for the Emergence of Commercial
  Advertising   54
  Stefan Haas

4 The Advertising and Marketing of Consumer Goods in
  Eighteenth Century London   79
  Claire Walsh

5 French Court Society and Advertising Art: The Reputation
  of Parisian Merchants at the End of the Eighteenth Century   96
  Natacha Coquery

6 Commercial Immanence: The Poster and Urban Territory in
  Nineteenth-Century France   113
  Aaron J. Segal

7 Display Windows and Window Displays in German Cities of
  the Nineteenth Century: Towards the History of a
  Commercial Breakthrough   139
  Uwe Spiekermann

8 Surrounding the Consumer: Persuasive Campaigns and
  Dutch Advertising Theory of the 1920s and 1930s   172
  Esther Cleven

Select Bibliography   206

Index   219

Historical Urban Studies
General Editors' Preface

Density and proximity of buildings and people are two of the defining characteristics of the urban dimension. It is these which identify a place as uniquely urban, though the threshold for such pressure points varies from place to place. What is considered an important cluster in one context – a few hundred inhabitants or buildings on the margins of Europe – may not be considered as urban eldewhere. A third defining characteristic is functionality – the commercial or strategic position of a town or city which conveys an advantage. Over time, these functional advantages may diminish, or the balance of advantage may change within a hierarchy of towns. To understand how the relative importance of towns shifts over time and space is to grasp a set of relationships which is fundamental to the study of urban history.

Towns and cities are products of history, yet have themselves helped to shape history. As the proportion of urban dwellers has increased, so the urban dimension has proved a legitimate unit of analysis through which to understand the spectrum of human experience and to explore the cumulative memory of past generations. Though obscured by layers of economic, social and political change, the study of the urban milieu provides insights into the functioning of human relationships and, if urban historians themselves are not directly concerned with current policy studies, few contemporary concerns can be understood without reference to the historical development of towns and cities.

This longer historical perspective is essential to an understanding of social processes. Crime, housing conditions and property values, health and education, discrimination and deviance, and the formulation of regulations and social policies to deal with them were, and remain, amongst the perennial preoccupations of towns and cities – no historical period has a monopoly of these concerns. They recur in successive generations, albeit in varying mixtures and strengths; the details may differ but the central forces of class, power and authority in the city remain. If this was the case for different periods, so it was for different geographical entities and cultures. Both scientific knowledge and technical information were available across Europe and showed little respect for frontiers. Yet despite common concerns and access to broadly similar knowledge, different solutions to urban problems were proposed and adopted by towns and cities in different parts of Europe. This comparative dimension informs urban historians as to which were systematic factors and which were of a purely local nature: general and particular forces can be distinguished.

These analytical frameworks, considered in a comparative context, inform the books in this series.

Jean-Luc Pinol
Richard Rodger
2000

Université de Tour
University of Leicester

List of Figures

1.1   Metamorphosis: The shops past and present
       (contemporary caricature; the shop's name on the left is
       'Heirs of late J. Bimmel', on the right the name has
       changed to 'J. Bimmel, private limited liability company')   2
       Source: Fliegende Blätter 136 (1912), S. 54–55
1.2   An architectural view of a contemporary store front in
       mid-nineteenth-century Paris   5
       Source: M. Viollet-Le-Duc, *Entretiens sur L'Architecture.*
       Atlas (Paris: A. Morel, 1863), plate 36
1.3   The 'Bon Marché', the prototype for the store in Zola's
       Au Bonheur des Dames. This view is of the Paris store in
       1874, a copperplate by Ch. Fichot   6
       Source: Grands magazins oder Die Geburt des
       Warenhauses im Paris des 19. Jahrhundert. Photographs
       by Dieter Sawatzki, with an introduction by Siegfried
       Gerlach (Dortmund, 1989), 25
1.4   *Litfaßsäule* (advertising pillar) in Berlin, 1855   8
       Source: Walter von zur Westen, *Reklamekunst aus zwei*
       Jahrtausenden (Berlin, 1925), 243
1.5   An English building wall from 1830 covered with
       advertising   9
       Source: United Sates Patent Office, *The Growth of*
       Industrial Art (Washington: Government Printing Office,
       1892), 41
1.6   The latest craze from America: a display window fitted
       out with an electric reflecting device, patented in the USA
       in 1884   11
       Source: As for Figure 1.5
1.7   'Cheap Substitution': Mr Wamperl is sly! When his
       relatives came from the country to the city to see the art
       exhibit, he directed them to the closest walls of
       advertisements – in order to avoid spending money on
       admission tickets!   14
       Source: Fliegende Blätter 98 (1893), 79.

1.8   Photograph, taken in 1851, of the west end of building
        for the Great Exhibition of the Works of Industry of all
        Nations, 1851. The term 'Crystal Palace' was first
        applied by *Punch* in 1850 and immediately became the
        popular name of the building   23
        Source: C.H. Gibbs-Smith, *The Great Exhibition of 1851*
        (London, 1950, reprint 1964), 51.
1.9   The transept of the 'Crystal Palace' looking North with
        the Fountain of Glass in the middle   24
        Source: As for Figure 1.8

3.1   First artificial light, then the illuminated advertisement
        conquered the city. Friedrichstraße in Berlin, 1909   58
        Source: *Mitteilungen des Verbandes der Reklamefachleute*
        (July 1914) 253
3.2   Advertising tried early on to evoke new possible
        meanings, playing with the imagination of its recipients.
        'What is happening? Half and Half.' Advertising for a
        liqueur   59
        Source: *Propoganda* (3 May 1900), 253–4.
3.3   The *Litfaßsäule*, or advertising pillar, in Berlin in the early
        twentieth century   61
        Source: *Mitteilungen des Verbandes der Reklamefachleute*
        (1915), 212
3.4   During the First World War the language of advertising
        was reworked in order to make it fit contemporary
        circumstances   63
        Source: *Mitteilungen des Verbandes der Reklamefachleute*
        (December 1914), 355
3.5   Advertising becomes architecture. A 12-meter-high
        advertising tower in Budapest with four stores   64
        Source: *Die Reklame* (1927), 19
3.6   The highest illuminated advertisement in Europe in the
        late 1920s on top of the White House of Rotterdam   67
        Source: As for Figure 3.6

4.1   Newspaper advertisements for Briscoe's, goldsmith and
        jeweller   86
        Source: *Public Advertiser* (20 March 1760) *General
        Advertiser* (2 January 1750), British Library, Burney
        Collection
4.2   Trade card for Masefield's, wallpaper and papier mâché
        seller, *c.* 1758   90
        Source: British Museum, Heal Collection

5.1   Letterhead of the fashion merchant Baeulard, 1772   100
       Source: Archives Nationales, T 166.35
5.2   Letterhead of the silk fabrics merchant Le Normand,
       1780   101
       Source: Archives Nationales, T 166.3–5
5.3   Letterhead of the silk merchant Buffault, 1769   102
       Source: Archives Nationales, T 220. 5–7
5.4   Letterhead of the fabrics merchant Hayet, 1788   103
       Source: Archives Nationales, T 186.50
5.5   Letterhead of the furrier Arson, 1780   104
       Source: Archives Nationales, T166.3–5
5.6   Letterhead of the merchant Vaugeois, purveyor of toys,
       undated   105
       Source: Archives Nationales, T 186.52
5.7   Brochure for the glover Chafanel Dupon, 1777   106
       Source: Archives Nationales, T 186.36

6.1   Bonnard-Bidault   117
       Source: Bibliothèque Nationale de France, Print
       Collection
6.2   Carnaval   120
       Source: Lucy Broids, *The Posters of Jules Chéret* (New
       York: Dover Publications, 1997), plate XVII
6.3   *Parti pour l'école*   125
       Source: *La France Íllustrée*, 15 March 1890, 180,
       Bibliothèque Nationale de France

7.1   Shop windows in Hamburg (*Alter Jungfernstieg*),
       1846/47   144
       Source: *Hamburgs Neubau. Sammlung sammtlicher
       Fassaden der Gebäude an den neubebauten Strassen*,
       Hamburg: Charles Fuchs (reprint 1985): Th. Schäfer:
       Hannover, folio 39
7.2   Display window in Hamburg (*Bohnenstrasse*), 1846/47   144
       Source: *Hamburgs Neubau*, folio 17
7.3   Façade of the Karlshof in Aachen, 1869   147
       Source: *Deutsche Bauzeitung 3* (1869), 496.
7.4   Façade of Rosipal department store in Munich, 1884   150
       Source: 'Waaren- und Kaufhaus des Herrn C. Rosipal
       Rosengasse 3 in München', *Zeitschrift für Baukunde 7*
       (1884), 147–8

7.5 Upper floors of the department store Ascher &
Müchow in Berlin (1886/87) 151
Source: 'Kaufhaus Ascher & Müchow in Berlin,
Leipzigerstr. 43', *Blätter für Architektur und
Kunsthandwerk* 4 (1891), 14, illustration 27

7.6 The department store Kander in Mannheim in 1900 152
Source: Barbara Kilian, *Die Mannheimer Warenhäuser
Kander, Schmoller und Wronker: Ein Stück Mannheimer
Wirtschafts- und Architekturgeschichte, Mannheimer
Geschichtsblätter* 1 (1994), 336

7.7 Window display of a south German butcher's shop in
1877 154
Source: 'Mißdeuteter Schönheitssinn', *Fliegende Blätter*
66 (1877), 207; see also the caricature 'Ein Zartes Herz',
Fliegende Blätter 76 (1882), 46

7.8 A frosted-over shop window 157
Source: *Fliegende Blätter*, 88 (1888), no. 2230, Suppl., 5

7.9 Salesrooms of the Berlin firm H. Esders & Dyckhoff,
1901 160
Source: *Der Manufacturist* 24, no. 23 (1901), 9

7.10 Salesrooms of the Berlin firm Kersten & Tuteur in 1914 161
Source: *Berliner Architekturwelt* 16 (1914), 148

7.11 Salesrooms of the firm of H.C. Weddy-Pönicke in Halle in
1901 161
Source: *Der Manufacturist* 24, no. 25 (1901), 13

8.1 Amsterdam, Utrechtsestraat in 1898. Photograph by
Jacob Olie 173
Source: Gemeentearchief Amsterdam

8.2 The Hague, Spui, 1979 173
Source: P. Nijhof, *Buitenreclame in beeld. 50 jaar
Alrecon Medea 1946–1996* (Zwolle: Waanders, 1996)

8.3 1920s mural for Blue Band margarine in Amsterdam on
Van Eeghenstraat 175
Source: E. van Ravensberg, Amsterdam

8.4 The model Norah Walters poses in the Blue Band girl
outfit in front of a chalk board with the text 'The Low
Country's quality standard' in the early 1920s. Notice on
the top right the efforts made to emphasize the (blu) scarf.
Insert: Painting of the Blue Band girl. 176
Source: K. Sartory et al., *De Vierde Vrijheid, zijnde een
blik in de historie van het reclamebureau delamar*
(Amsterdam: 1955)

8.5   Early 1920s poster for Blue Band margarine by Rie
      Cramer   177
      Source: Van den Bergh, Nederland, Rotterdam
8.6   A poster for the Calvé company by Jan Toorop, c. 1894–5   180
      Source: M. Le Coultre
8.7   A poster by Cassandre on the side of a lorry of the Van
      Gend & Loos transportation company, 1939   181
      Source: Nederlands Spoorwegmuseum
8.8   Advertisement for Coppens' Advies-Bureau, 1914 by J.
      Proper   186
      Source: Paul Ruben (ed.), *Die Reklame: Ihre Kunst und
      Wissenschaft* (Berlin: Hermann Paetel Verlag, 1913–14)
8.9   Example of a slide used in an experiment on the
      perception of advertising, published 1938   190
      Source: Franciscus Roels, *Psychologie der Reclame*
      (Amsterdam: H.J.W. Brecht, 1938)

Notes on Contributors

Esther Cleven is an art historian, currently at Utrecht, where she is working in Dutch mass media history, concentrating on the use of images in commercial graphic design after the Second World War, with support from the Dutch Organization for Scientific Research. Her most recent publication is on the history of the relationship between the term 'image' and advertising in the Dutch journal on the history of representation, *Feit & Fictie*, in which she has published other work, in addition her dissertation at the University of Utrecht *Image bedeutet Bild : eine Geschichte des Bildbegriffs in der Werbetheorie am Beispiel der Niederlande, 1917–1967*. She has written as well for *Akt-over Kunst, Groniek* and *Jaarboek mediageschiedenis*.

Natacha Coquery is an assistant professor of the history of the eighteenth century at the University of Tours. Among her recent publications are those concerned with both economic and administrative history: 'La conversion de l'hôtel aristocratique en bureaux au XVIIIe siècle' in *L'alchemie du patrimonie: Discours et politiques* (Talence: éditions de la Maison des sciences de l'homme d'Aquitaine, 1996); 'Administration et ségrégation: l'émergence des quartiers administratifs de l'ouest parisien à la fin du XVIIIe siècle' in *La Ville divisée, les ségrégations urbaines en question, France, XVIIIe, XXe siècles* (Paris: Créaphis, 1996); 'Hôtel, luxe et societé de cour: le marché aristocratique parisien au XVIIIe siècle', *Histoire et Mesure* 10, nos 3/4 (1995), 339–69. Her current research deals with small retail business and with the merchant élite in eighteenth-century Paris.

Stefan Haas is an assistant professor of history at the University of Münster. His first major work was on the discourse of cultural history in Germany between 1880 and 1930, *Historische Kulturforschung in Deutschland, 1880–1930: Geschichtswissenschaft zwischen Synthese und Pluralität* (Cologne: Böhlau, 1994). He has been working on the question of visualization in modern culture and the structures of urban lifestyles, and his current work encompasses the political culture of Prussian reforms in the early nineteenth century. He is also an associate of a firm that produces historical multimedia applications.

Aaron J. Segal teaches modern European history at East Carolina University. He received his A.B. from Princeton University and his Ph.D. from the University of California, Los Angeles. He has written on artistic property rights, French cultural history and the history of consumption. His current project, 'Marketing the Nation', traces the relationship between national advertising and national political culture in France in the late nineteenth century and the early twentieth century.

Elliott Shore is the Constance A. Jones Director of Libraries and a professor of history at Bryn Mawr College. A historian of journalism and political movements of the United States, he is now working on German American history, translating and preparing for republication a novel published in Philadelphia in German in 1850 and a comparative history of advertising in the US and Germany between 1850 and 1920. His most recent books are *The German American Radical Press: The Shaping of a Left Political Culture, 1850–1930* (Bloomington: University of Illinois Press, 1992) and *Talkin' Socialism: J.A. Wayland and the Role of the Press in American Radicalism, 1890–1912* (Lawrence, Kan.: University of Kansas Press, 1988, 1992).

Uwe Spiekermann is a research fellow at the Dr Rainer Wild Foundation, Heidelberg. He is the author of numerous publications dealing with the history of retailing, food and advertising in nineteenth- and twentieth-century Germany, including *Neue Wege zur Nahrungsgeschichte* (co-editor; Frankfurt a.M.: P. Lang, 1993), *Warenhaussteuer in Deutschland* (Frankfurt a.M.: P. Lang, 1993) and *Basis der Konsumgesellschaft: Geschichte des Kleinhandels in Deutschland* (Munich: 1998).

Claire Walsh is at the European University Institute in Florence where she is completing her work on a doctorate in cultural history, comparing London and Paris as shopping centres in the seventeenth and eighteenth centuries. Her publications include 'Shop Design and the Display of Goods in Eighteenth-Century London', in *The Journal of Design History* (December 1995) and chapters in David Michell (ed.), *Goldsmiths, Silversmiths and Bankers: Innovation and the Transfer of Skill, 1550–1750* (Stroud, Gloucestershire: Sutton, 1995) and G. Crossick and S. Jaumain, (eds), *Cathedrals of Consumption: the European Department Store, 1850–1939* (London: Scolar Press, 1997).

Clemens Wischermann has taught social and economic history at Münster, Bielefeld, Munich and Düsseldorf Universities, and during 1987–88 held a scholarship at the Maison des Sciences de l'homme in Paris. He is now Professor of Economic and Social History at the University of Konstanz. He has published on nineteenth- and twentieth-century social, urban and business history and his current research interests include the role of institutional change in economic and cultural history. His recent publications include *Preußischer Staat und westfälische Unternehmer zwischen Spätmerkantilismus und Liberalismus* (Cologne: Böhlau, 1992), *Bilderwelt des Alltags: Werbung in der*

Konsumgesellschaft des 19. und 20. Jahrhunderts, edited with Peter Borscheid (Stuttgart: Steiner, 1995).

Preface

Since the middle of the nineteenth century the influence of advertising has spread throughout Europe and indeed the rest of the world. Yet there has been only very limited research into the nature, context and historical development of advertising and its relationship to contemporary society. Most historians refer to advertising at best for illustrative purposes. The treatment of advertising in terms of a theory of manipulation dominated our view for a long time, but now the notion of the 'grand manipulator' and his bag of ever-increasing refinements has largely lost its explanatory power, replaced instead with models drawn from the field of communications theory. What we are beginning to understand at the start of the twenty-first century is the ability of the receiver of the messages to filter, select and recombine the meanings from the myriad transmissions of commercial culture. The assumptions inherent in the old theories about the possibility of influencing individual behaviour have been reduced to a sense that advertising can only reinforce existing behavioural dispositions. Instead of focusing almost solely on the creators of advertising, the newer explanatory models describe an interaction between the message and the receiver of that message. The consumer of advertising and the perceptions of that consumer have moved to the centre of our research interests. We hope, in this work, to begin to reinsert advertising into the historical context from which the theories of manipulation have removed it and help to provide our own model of how the history of advertising might be studied.

This book analyses the breakthrough of the modern 'world of advertising' from the eighteenth to the twentieth centuries, locating its origins in large cities and metropolitan centres. In each European country and each large city, the pace and kind of change varied considerably, with Paris and London leading, in separate and distinct ways, in the eighteenth century. In most countries, though, the period between 1850 and 1930 saw the most obvious crystallization of early advertising strategies. This period encapsulated the transition from advertising as suggestion to systematic and explicit attempts to influence consumer behaviour. The first three essays in the volume are an attempt to frame the five case studies that follow; all the essays try to deal with advertising in context.

Advertising should not be understood solely as an adjunct, a phenomenon accompanying industrialization. Advertising created new kinds of urban perceptions and experiences, leading to new patterns of consumption which changed the face of cities while altering or perhaps helping to create the idea of urban 'lifestyles'. We see it historically as an innovation in the way the individual arranges, perceives and understands the world, a new way of attaching a specific sense to words and things. Advertising creates new principles of signification and is hence always already 'representation' in the cultural studies sense. In the age of electronic, visually dominated media, advertising functions as a central coordinating point for organizing perceptions. Images used or reused for advertising have turned into a global code of 'visual culture'. In the context of urban history, advertising is the metaphor for the making of an urban identity in a new competitive world and in the history of advertising, where transferring messages from one culture to another is one of advertising's goals, a perfect stage for comparative urban research.

Advertising and the European City: Historical Perspectives had its origins in a session entitled 'Advertising and Urban Culture' at the Third International Conference on Urban History in Budapest in August 1996. The participants in that session, many of whom are represented in this volume, were largely unknown to one another before they met at the conference, but found that they had similar ideas about how one could approach advertising historically. The conference received its impetus from Peter Clark and was organized by Vera Bacsksai. We wish to thank both for their encouragement, and Richard Rodger and Jean Luc-Pignol for their warm invitation to publish in their series on urban history. Support from the University of Münster, the Institute for Advanced Study in Princeton, New Jersey, from Bryn Mawr College in Bryn Mawr, Pennsylvania and from several friends, students and colleagues helped to make this volume a reality. The editors wish to thank Regine Wieder for translating an essay from German, Jennifer Tobias for her help in securing illustrations, Alison Cook-Sather for help with editing several essays, and Maria Sturm for her help with German and French translations and the overall editing of the volume. Two students from the University of Münster and four at Bryn Mawr College provided editorial assistance: Dagmar Lach, Anja Ingenbleek, Srijana Chettri, Marlee Leveille and Sam Foster helped throughout this project; Elizabeth S. Hill was crucial to the completion of the volume and the editors wish to thank her especially for her work.

Elliott Shore and Clemens Wischermann
Bryn Mawr and Konstanz

CHAPTER ONE

Placing Advertising in the Modern Cultural History of the City

Clemens Wischermann

The beginnings of advertising

Most commentators believe, based on such evidence as inscriptions on the walls of Pompeii or the traditional signs of pubs, that advertising has existed since the dawn of human history.[1] However, in a pre-industrial world, before the establishment of a modern market economy, advertising could be understood as little more than a means of providing the public with information necessary to find certain people or places, for example a particular craftsman or pub, in keeping with the moral underpinnings of most European economies, which posited that an 'honourable' artisan or merchant did not strive to maximize his profit, but rather to earn a reasonable living in keeping with his station. Thus the rules that governed behaviour in a pre-industrial economy did not tolerate such practices as enticing customers, poaching on the territory of others and open competition. Poaching was thought to be especially unchristian and even immoral. The height of commercial indiscretion would have been to claim that one had set prices lower than those of one's competitors. For example, in 1745, the editors of the fifth edition of the *Complete English Tradesman* noted that 'This underselling practise is grown to such a shameful height, that particular persons publicly advertise that they undersell the rest of the trade.' To some extent the situation was comparable with that of eighteenth-century France, where we find in a 1761 ordinance that such manipulation of the market seemed to signal an act of despair by an unreliable tradesman. The ordinance emphatically forbade all retail tradesmen, merchants and shopkeepers, in both Paris and its suburbs, to undercut one another in order to corner a market for their commodities and particularly prohibited the distribution of advertising leaflets to promote their wares.[2]

But during this same period, strictures aside, commercial advertisements were being published, perhaps as an indirect effect of the rising influence of the middle class. Bourgeois society was a child of the Enlightenment. Its most important means of communication was the

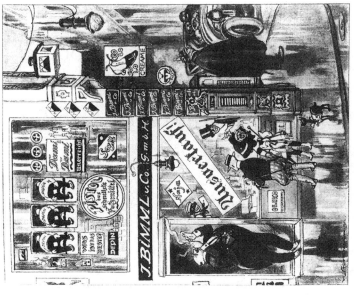

1.1 Metamorphosis: The shops past and present (contemporary caricature; the shop's name on the left is 'Heirs of late J. Bimmel', on the right the name has changed to 'J. Bimmel, private limited liability company')

Source: Fliegende Blätter 136 (1912), 54–5

press. Beginning in the seventeenth and eighteenth centuries, we find advertisements in newspapers and journals, but they are usually restricted to advertisements for books and patent medicines. Just as the *Feuilles du bureau d'adresse* followed the French model of state organization, advertising was also officially controlled and a state monopoly. It was 'an attempt of mercantile politics to realize institutionalization of market rules in branches where the corporate economic sector was not dominant, to establish means of communication to improve economic exchange and at the same time to maintain control by the government'.[3] State control of advertising in Europe continued well into the nineteenth century. In the case of Germany, Homburg argues 'that the transition to a market economy and the controversies accompanying advertising in Germany since the late nineteenth century cannot be properly understood without taking into account its long pre-history and the complex learning process involved in the formation of a domestic market and related commercial practices'. In a case study of Leipzig she demonstrates that the 'practice of, pioneers in, and promoters of commercial advertising in the *Leipziger Zeitung* between 1750 and 1850 and the subsequent responses of members of traditional retail establishments, as well as municipal and state authorities, to the innovative methods of marketing and competition were at odds with the traditional guild system and established patterns of supply and demand'.[4] The older European economy – with its tradition-bound morality and its state-controlled media of communication – was reformed in the late eighteenth and early nineteenth centuries, in an era of radical changes in economic thought. A liberal market economy, along with its notions of competition, arose. The crucial question for us is how modern advertising was established.

The relationship between new forms of advertising and consumption was formed in the great European capitals. It has usually been assumed that modern advertising began in Europe in the middle of the nineteenth century, but Natacha Coquery and Claire Walsh draw our attention back almost one hundred years to the second half of the eighteenth century. London was then the hub of the world economy, and Paris its cultural centre. To find the origins of economic change in the distribution sector we must first go to London, where Walsh finds them among the shopkeepers of the eighteenth-century city. She locates advertisements placed by shopkeepers in the city but does not find any evidence for a 'consumer revolution', the existence of which older research had inferred from these same newspaper announcements:

> Newspaper advertising increased steadily from the mid-seventeenth century onwards, rather than peaking in a revolution at the end of the eighteenth century. At the same time, however,

> newspaper advertising had very little importance for the sale of
> domestic products, and hence cannot be held as an indicator of a
> consumer revolution ... In the retailing context of the eighteenth
> century, where non-standardized goods were selected by the con-
> sumer based on verbal, tactile and visual information, there was
> little point in using newspaper advertisements to try to lure dis-
> tant customers.[5]

In Paris, the centre of urban culture of the eighteenth century, certain
forms of luxury consumption had political repercussions. The life of
French court society was centred on the king, who resided at Versailles.
Access to the sovereign was a form of power, but that access did not
guarantee a role in policy-making, so, to gain an extra advantage, the
society of the court constantly flaunted its connections to power. Court
society tried to replace openly displayed political and economic power
with prestige and taste as indicators of influence. A complicated system
of social distinctions came into being at the French court, especially
manifest in styles of clothing. It was not the fabric itself, but its social
value that was decisive: the parties concerned had a need to invent new
visible signs of prestige at every turn to keep imitators at bay. This
produced an incredible demand for novelty which made Paris into the
magasin universel du royaume. Coquery believes this to be the beginning of consumer society in the original sense of the word: the tradesmen
were the contemporary *consommateurs*.

What exactly did the tradesmen do? They seized the opportunity
provided by the specific demands of consumers for novelty and reacted
to the needs of these consumers in a dynamic relationship, both causing
and caused by changing fashions. The tradesmen reinvented the notion
of publicity, and modern advertising was born. The great tradesmen of
the Palais Royal, the centre of luxury consumption in the capital, were
the first to develop invoices, letter-heads and brochures, and, after
1750, fashion magazines which were filled with praise for the *nouveauté*.
But the tradesmen did not only fulfil wishes. They became purveyors,
and even inventors, of particular necessities, for they too designed styles
and created fashions. It is difficult to separate cause and effect here, the
needs of the aristocracy and the existence of shops with changing
fashions: who was influencing whom? The shopkeepers were the producers of both public taste and advertising:

> Far from being confined to the role of passive agents between
> manufacturers and consumers, merchants of the eighteenth century
> became designers of their products, revealing themselves as active
> influences in the changing tastes of the times. Very skilful in detect-
> ing and sparking trends, they were instigators of the new,
> accelerating the evolution of style through the subtle changes that
> they imprinted upon their wares. Powerfully challenged by their

1.2 An architectural view of a contemporary store front in mid-nineteenth-century Paris

Source: M. Viollet-Le-Duc, *Entretiens sur L'Architecture. Atlas* (Paris: A. Morel, 1863), plate 36

1.3 The 'Bon Marché', the prototype for the store in Zola's *Au Bonheur des Dames*. This view is of the Paris store in 1874, a copperplate by Ch. Fichot

Source: *Grands magazins oder Die Geburt des Warenhauses im Paris des 19. Jahrhundert*. Photographs by Dieter Sawatzki, with an introduction by Siegfried Gerlach (Dortmund, 1989), 25

> clientele's requirements, they created the fashions of the times and were the inventors of commercial advertising.[6]

Some decades later, a young and simple country maid, Denise Baudu, the heroine of Zola's novel *Au Bonheur des Dames* (*The Ladies' Paradise*), arrived in Paris. In great detail, Zola tries to describe both the overwhelming quantity and variety of the merchandise available and the girl's reactions upon seeing this commercial cornucopia for the first time (Figure 1.3):

> The high plate-glass door, facing the Place Gaillon, reached the mezzanine floor and was surrounded by elaborate decorations covered with gilding. Two allegorical figures, two laughing women with bare breasts thrust forward, were unrolling a scroll bearing the inscription *The Ladies' Paradise*. The shop windows stretched along the Rue de la Michodière and the Rue Neuve-Saint-Augustin, where, apart from the corner house, they occupied four other houses which had recently been bought and converted, two on the left and two on the right. With its series of perspectives, with the display on the ground floor and the plate-glass windows of the mezzanine floor, behind which could be seen all the intimate life of the various departments, the spectacle seemed to Denise to be endless ... There, outside in the street, on the pavement itself, was

a mountain of cheap goods, placed at the entrance as a bait, bargains which stopped women as they passed by. It all cascaded down: pieces of woollen material and fabric, merino, cheviot, flannelette, were falling from the mezzanine floor, flapping like flags, their neutral tones – slate grey, navy blue, olive green – broken up by the white of the price cards. Close by, framing the doorway, strips of fur were hanging down, straight bands for dress trimmings, the fine ash of squirrel, the pure snow of swansdown, imitation ermine and imitation sable made of rabbit. And below this, on racks and tables, in the middle of a pile of remnants, there was a profusion of knitted goods being sold for a song, gloves and woollen scarves, hooded capes, cardigans, a whole winter display of many colours, mottled, dyed, striped, with bleeding stains of red ... It was a giant fairground display, as if the shop were bursting and throwing its surplus stock into the street.[7]

Nothing embodied the new world of advertising better than the department stores of Paris in the middle of the nineteenth century.[8] These stores divided their shopfloors into discrete areas, each devoted to a particular type of merchandise; the prototype for this arrangement came from the clusters of specialized shops lining the streets of eighteenth-century London:

Growth in the number of shops and increased expenditure on shop fronts and elaborate window displays changed the profile of the street. Shopping became an activity which could be carried out every weekday rather than just on market days, and the street, with its array of shops, replaced the street market as the mental focus of consumers ... London had always been a thriving commercial centre with a rich supply of goods, but by the early eighteenth century shopping had become a much more pleasant experience as pavements were laid, street lighting introduced, streets cleared of hawkers and foul-smelling wastes, and semi-permanent 'bulks', or makeshift wooden shops, removed. In some places markets were even relocated so that the more refined activity of shopping in shops would not be hindered. Shopping in fixed retail shops was associated with the cleaner, healthier and wealthier lifestyle of new developments in city centres. Permanent shops became part of the urban identity; in London, fast becoming the commercial capital of Europe, they were a potent symbol of economic stability and fashionability that in tourist accounts clearly rivalled Paris by midcentury.[9]

We do not need to decide which of these commercial rivals – Paris or London – was ahead at a given time. Our interest here lies in the fundamental changes to the shop and the urban environment that London and Paris helped bring into being.

In pre-industrial cities the majority of consumer goods were, if not made on site, purchased locally. The integrity of the proprietor determined the product range of the manufacturers. The quality of the

1.4   Litfaßsäule (advertising pillar) in Berlin, 1855

Source: Walter von zur Westen, *Reklamekunst aus zwei Jahrtausenden* (Berlin, 1925), 243

available goods depended on their place of origin and the season, and their price had always been negotiated directly with the merchant based on the visual and tactile appeal of the product. In this world of consumption, standardized goods assumed more importance in the rise of industrial production methods designed for an anonymous market. With the introduction of new and formerly unknown goods into the market a need arose for advertising which provided the customer with information about the product, not just where it could be found. The increasing competitiveness of the economy mandated a new type of business advertisement. Early advertising served primarily to give information about a product's characteristics such as quantity, quality, price and so on. The invention of fashion and the standardization of clothing production combined to produce standardized fashion for a large group of urban buyers. This synthesis became especially apparent both at the ready-made clothier's and in the fashion journals of the big cities where, in the first half of the century, changing collections were already being

1.5   An English building wall from 1830 covered with advertising

Source: United States Patent Office, *The Growth of Industrial Art* (Washington: Goverment Printing Office, 1892), 41

described. Ready-made clothing, itself a new idea, first appeared in Berlin based on a Parisian model, the so-called *prêt-à-porter*.

The growth of the urban, regional and national markets in the middle of the nineteenth century was linked both to the expansion of the bourgeois realm and to the 'communications revolution' of the nineteenth century. A greater demand for 'public-ness' and the economic situation in general required new ways of disseminating information. Advertising, therefore, came increasingly to the fore from the middle of the century and its standard form became the column in the newspaper. The decades from the 1850s until the 1880s were a breakthrough period for advertising as a force in competition and consumption throughout Europe while, at the same time, industrial mass production of consumer goods became much more common. One innovation quickly succeeded another, and these had to be made public as rapidly as possible to as wide an audience as possible, usually by means of advertisements. Almost anything seemed possible; the atmosphere was exuberant: the more sensational an advertisement, the greater its effect was expected to be.[10] Within a few years, economic considerations induced the bourgeois daily press to print advertisements, although it had previously carried few or none. In addition to the cultural influences exerted upon it, advertising changed as art and science became an integral part of it, ensuring that some portions of society would adamantly reject modern advertising. In the late nineteenth century, this process was accelerated (in terms of quantity as well as quality) not least by the urbanization of society, because the manifestations of and innovations in advertising were concentrated in the cities (posters, shop windows, illuminated advertisements and so on).[11]

> Until 1835 or so, the display window was a means of presentation for only a few shops with luxury goods; between then and the 1870s, it caught on everywhere in the larger cities of the German Empire. Subsequently, the display window and its decoration changed fundamentally. 'Glass palaces' and window display art peaked and reached a turning-point at the start of the twentieth century. Finally, advertising extended into the shop and has now become emblematic of how merchandise is generally presented.[12]

There it catered to the needs of a growing middle class increasingly oriented towards consumption. The location of the synthesis of strictly commercial space with the more abstract perception of commerce and marketing (and of course advertising) was doubtless the department store:[13]

> Architecture became subordinate to advertising ... The first visible sign of this development was the department store ... Architecture and city planning lost their independence: these ceased to be autonomous arts, and thus buildings became more nearly purely functional, subordinate to the needs of advertising and selling. Department stores and display windows were only the first step in the process of the takeover of the whole city by advertising.[14]

Let us go back to Paris. Half a century later, what had become of the young girl in Paris whom we met in Zola's novel? The French capital city

> became a sort of pilot plant of mass consumption. The period of its most rapid change was just beginning when Denise Baudu is supposed to have disembarked there. By the time she reached middle age, a quarter of a century later, she would have seen the transmutation of Paris from the cramped city of Victor Hugo to a modern capital of consumption, a city of boulevards, cafés, electric lights, apartments, advertising posters, the Métro, cinemas, restaurants, and parks, with production largely exiled to an outer belt while the heart of the city was devoted to commerce. If the North of England is the landscape that symbolizes the industrial revolution, the Île de France can well claim to serve as the emblem of the consumer revolution.

1.6 The latest craze from America: a display window fitted out with an electric reflecting device, patented in the USA in 1884

Source: As for Figure 1.5.

French initiative in creating the new style of mass consumption was crowned by the Paris expositions of 1889 and 1900. There was revealed for the first time a planned environment of mass consumption; there thoughtful observers realized, in a confused and uneasy way, that they were immersed in a strange new world of consumer behaviour. They saw crowds milling around displays of luxurious automobiles and around glass cages displaying couturier-clothed mannequins; taking imaginary voyages via cinematic techniques to the floor of the sea or the craters of the moon; and, at night, staring at displays of lighted fountains or at voluptuous belly dancers wriggling in a reproduction of a Cairo nightspot. The expositions and similar environments (such as department stores and automobile trade shows) displayed a novel and crucial juxtaposition of imagination and merchandise, of dreams and commerce, of collective consciousness and economic fact.[15]

The fascinating world of goods and advertising has influenced our mental image of everyday life since the late nineteenth century, but this key point has not received attention in the literature on the increase of

consumption in society.[16] 'Although the concept of a consumer revolution is far less familiar than that of the industrial revolution, they are
really two facets of a single upheaval that decisively altered the material
basis of human life.'[17]

A hundred years of debating advertising in Europe

At the turn of the twentieth century advertising suddenly became prominent in European cities. It became a symbol of modernity, linked in the
minds of its opponents to the urban growth[18] which seemed to sprawl
unplanned throughout the German-speaking world.[19] The traditional
European city was filled with houses and buildings which lacked space
for advertising in their small windows and narrow house gables. This
need for advertising space spurred the changes wrought by modern
architecture as well as the rapid expansion of 'landscape advertising' or
'billboard advertising' alongside roads, rivers, lakes and railways. The
driving force behind the debate over the 'defacing' of Europe's cities
and towns was prominent representatives of the bourgeoisie, who thought
it their duty to take an interest in the protection of the landscape and
the preservation of monuments and townscapes in an admixture of
incipient environmental awareness and anti-modern hostility to the city.

Out of this intellectual movement grew contemporary advertising
criticism. One of its more prominent exponents was Werner Sombart,
who, with his old-fashioned refusal to regard advertising as anything
more than an abomination, defined an advertisement as a manifestation
of modern culture, which he found intrinsically objectionable.[20] He
pointedly expressed the belief that 'culture' and advertising should not
share the same social space. Elliott Shore demonstrates in this volume
the fundamental elements in the thoughts of opponents of advertising in
Central Europe with a special emphasis on Lassalle and Sombart: 'Two
of them are explicit: that advertising is a foreign implant, "unnatural"
in the German context, and that the inspiration for it is simultaneously
American and Jewish. A third argument, which is implicit in the language all three critics use, is a very thinly disguised rejection of advertising
as a manipulative and indulgent practice.'[21] A rather different development, which Aaron Segal describes in this volume, occurred in France
where, during the tenure of the famous Jules Chéret, one particular
poster became a part of the national memory:

> French officials in a number of cities sought to regulate and quar-
> antine public advertising as part of a broader campaign of republican
> social and political landscaping ... By the First World War, posters
> had been incorporated into the national cultural patrimony...The

national tapestry manufacture at Gobelins converted a Chéret poster into a tapestry ... Those policies coincided with a movement to preserve landmarks, monuments and cityscapes as artistic treasures, embodiments of a national heritage and models of taste and culture.[22]

Despite a distinct hostility to cities in Germany, those opponents of advertising who were also cultural critics were to be found throughout Europe. Whether we consider Esther Cleven's article on the Netherlands,[23] or the ongoing French intellectual debate about the advantages and disadvantages of advertising and its links to civilization,[24] or the fluidity of the boundaries between art and advertising in the United States,[25] differences in perceptions of culture are always at the heart of the matter. The classic nineteenth-century conception of culture turned on the freedom with which it was able to pursue its own ends. Lysinski, a leading theorist of advertising of the 1920s, extended this to the criterion of differentiation: the most basic contrast between advertising and art is simply one of aim and purpose. In his opinion, commercial ends are integral to advertising. Advertisement is for use in the market. Art, by contrast, is an end in itself.[26] This distinction precisely articulates the general understanding of advertising in the twentieth century.

A clear establishment of the relationships among advertising, social structure and the concept of culture is therefore necessary. Pierre Bourdieu theorizes a distinction between 'official' culture (*culture légitime*) and mass culture (*culture populaire*),[27] which I would like to attempt to historicize. According to Bourdieu, 'official' culture usually develops against the background of the educated classes (*Bildungsbürgertum*). It is a culture which is recognized and given weight to by experts and supported by academics and professional aesthetes. It presupposes a long learning process, which is ideally rooted in socialization, developed against a familial background of material affluence and tends towards cultural aestheticism in the second generation. Its central ideas are art for art's sake and the purity of form. This 'official' culture often corresponded with the concept of culture predominant in the nineteenth century,[28] which continued to be a popular measure of 'good taste' well into the twentieth century.[29]

Bourdieu distinguishes this from mass culture. Pre-industrial mass culture was a mixture of regional traditions and the characteristic features of class difference. From the last third of the nineteenth century, however, this mass culture changed to fit the new economic and commercial patterns of life brought on by industrialization and mass production. In the wake of these developments, the aesthetics of advertising spread further and further. This new mentality first gained a firm hold – and became ever-increasingly entrenched – in the consciousness

1.7 'Cheap Substitution': Mr Wamperl is sly! When his relatives came from the country to the city to see the art exhibit, he directed them to the closest wall of advertisements – in order to avoid spending money on admission tickets!

Source: Fliegende Blätter 98 (1893), 79

of the newly established and consumption-oriented middle class. After several interruptions due to wars and economic crises, it finally established itself in all but the very poorest levels of society.

This new mass culture was consistently rejected by the cultural élite. A framework for this position had already been established in the intellectual critique of culture, which was common in these circles and which had always criticized mass culture. The condemnation of the 'industry of entertainment and consciousness' also indicted advertising. Critics could not discover elements of their own 'official' culture in it, and thus 'mass culture' came to be equated with 'bad taste'.

According to Bourdieu, the 'official' critics began with their own cultural backgrounds and assumptions and, as these had never been questioned, misjudged mass culture, which had its own social patterns and rules. Relating Bourdieu's theses to the socio-historical and historical-economic background of the twentieth century, it becomes obvious that the mass culture of the new consumer society was still a culture dominated by scarcity. The primary concerns of consumer society – and of those who study it – are standards of living and patterns of consumption. Most people only sacrificed aesthetics of content for aesthetics of form if conformity and social proximity to the existing standards of everyday life were preserved. Not diverse styles, but similarity was desired. In the twentieth century, advertising and the world of goods managed to fulfil these demands over a long period of time, creating a true culture of the masses.

Social science and advertising: one hundred years of consumer manipulation

The debate over advertising has always been both a social and a scholarly phenomenon. And the social aspects of the debate depend not least on which scholarly paradigm is currently in favour. The basis of an academic explanation of advertising that was put forward in the years around the First World War reflected the change from 'product orientation' to 'market orientation' in the advertisement of consumer goods. This became more apparent as behaviourism penetrated from the United States to Europe. Advertising has often been defined as applied psychology, which means that

> early advertising psychology was mainly interested in empirical, experimental and simple behaviouristic notions ... The basic behaviouristic conception of a flexible human nature was a very broad idea indeed. But because there was no way to look inside the heads of consumers, so to speak, it must have seemed better to cling to visible human behaviour ... The advertising practitioners themselves had come up with what can be called a technical solution to getting closer to the consumer.[30]

Market surveys were helpful to the 'advertising artists'. Advertising campaigns developed by early advertising agencies were replaced by the development of professional advertising departments in the businesses which had fixed advertising budgets and their own notions of how to spend them. It was the heyday of scientific theories of advertising, all of which paid close attention to the actions and reactions of the consumers and which were heavily influenced by the vogue of behaviourism and its interest in the notion of 'stimulus–response'. Advertising tried to use behavioural theories to justify not only current practice but also the historical development of the field. In what follows, I would like to outline the most important concepts of the social and academic debate on advertising.

'Hidden persuaders'

Vance Packard gave an entire area of motivation research a head start with his 1957 book *The Hidden Persuaders*.[31] The premise of the book is the idea that human beings must obey the inexplicable demands of their subconscious. Therefore, if structures and mechanisms of the unconscious were completely understood, it would be possible to control human beings entirely. Perhaps the most famous examples of an application of this 'brainwashing' hypothesis were the short, imperceptible advertising sequences inserted into films, which were designed to condition the observer to exhibit a desired behaviour with increasing frequency. The public latched onto the idea that in the future greater psychological manipulation would be possible and refused to relinquish the notion for some time, despite an increasing body of data which refuted the theory. As a matter of fact, the assumptions made by motivation researchers in these years could never be confirmed and were fundamentally psychologically incorrect. However, because they were popular they gave advertising a bad image, which bordered on comparisons with totalitarian political propaganda, and which stuck for a long time.

In the United States the 1950s saw the birth of various theories of manipulation. The theses developed by David Riesman, Renel Denney and Nathan Glazer in their famous study, *The Lonely Crowd*,[32] had great influence. Although the subtitle of the work was *A Study of the Changing American Character*, the models of political behaviour these researchers developed were soon applied to all modernizing societies. Riesman et al. distinguished between three ideal types of society, each of which was characterized by a different style of behaviour, which they believed to have succeeded each other historically.

> The society of high growth potential develops in its typical members a social character whose conformity is ensured by their tendency to follow tradition ... [these are] *tradition-directed* people and the society in which they live *a society dependent on tradition-direction*.
>   The society of transitional population growth develops in its typical members a social character whose conformity is insured by their tendency to acquire early in life an internalized set of goals ... [these are] *inner-directed* people and the society in which they live *a society dependent on inner-direction*.
>   Finally, the society of incipient population decline develops in its typical members a social character whose conformity is insured by their tendency to be sensitized to the expectations and preferences of others ... [these are] *other-directed* people and the society in which they live one *dependent on other-direction*.[33]

The first of these models is typical, according to these researchers, of a pre-industrial society. It was followed by the 'inner-directed' model, which was based on the internalization of abstract ideas and developed fully during industrialization. Riesman et al. saw in the 1920s the societal advance of a new approach, the 'other-directed' people, which elevated public opinion to the highest authority governing individual action.

The idea that the subconscious guided human orientation peaked in the 1960s and early 1970s. This thesis is mainly associated with the names Max Horkheimer and Theodor W. Adorno,[34] whose ideas were celebrated in these years as they never had been before and never would be again. Their critique claimed, in few words and without regard for the finer distinctions among types of advertising,[35] that advertising's manipulative capacity is great, if not unlimited. Advertising was thought to contribute to the alienation of people from social reality and particularly to diminish awareness of 'real' in favour of 'false' needs. Advertising was considered to have an anti-progressive and myth-making effect. Later scholarly criticism of these positions emphasizes that it is impossible to determine 'real' and 'false' needs without investing some outside authority with the power to define what is real and what is not. Consequently, the cultural imperatives of mass society quickly became associated with the phenomenon of robbing the individual of his individuality.

The philosophical critics of advertising attracted the interest of and swayed public opinion with this message until the mid-1970s. The critique also deeply influenced most modern historians through one of its basic assumptions, that 'advertising always lies', that is, that advertising always presents a distorted image of social reality and social necessities. What self-respecting scholar would be willing to work with sources which 'tell lies' from the outset, considering also that semiological and visual analyses had hardly been a part of the tool-chest of historians? Therefore it is not surprising that the world of advertising had to remain a largely theoretical realm rather than one informed by a historical understanding of reality. In the 1980s and 1990s the history of advertising has been re-examined from a new angle, primarily by English and American historians, who were the first to accept the usefulness of the newer theoretical models from the field of communication.[36]

Communications models

The surprisingly sudden fall from prominence of the intellectual criticism of advertising was brought about mainly by the efforts of communication theorists and behavioural scientists to reformulate their refutation of the theory of manipulation, which had until then been dominant. For a long time the dominant communications model was that of stimulus–response. In the simple, well-known, traditional model of communication (transmitter, message, channel, receiver) the transmitter was considered the most important single element. The primary interest, then, was vested in the syntax and the intensity of the impulse, because it was that impulse which would determine the behaviour of the recipient. Such ideas in communication shaped not only how advertising was conceived of and used, but also the distinctive criticism of advertising in the 1950s and 1960s. However much individual advertisers or advertising firms might disagree, they agreed that there were no limits to advertising's ability to manipulate its defenceless recipients and that they abused this power by creating artificial needs instead of satisfying true ones.

In the 1970s the orientation of behavioural research, which had been based on communication theories, changed entirely and with it advertising changed as well. The reason for the shift was the growing popularity of testing the idea of the power of the 'hidden persuaders' with experimental social scientific studies. These works emphasized the interaction between message and the construction and perception of needs inherent in a process of communication and accorded a lesser importance to the influence of this interaction on the reinforcement of existing behavioural tendencies.[37] In a socio-psychological assessment of previous experiments, Horst Brand drew the following conclusion, noting that it particularly pertained to the well-known effects of subliminal advertising discussed by Packard: 'On balance our result is as sobering as it is simple: subliminal advertising is ineffective advertising, which does not lead to commercial success, wherever it is practised. The assumption ... that Vance Packard is the only person who has nevertheless gained commercial benefits from the possibilities of subliminal advertising is definitely consistent with our findings.'[38] Such studies did not denote an acceptance of advertising by the social sciences, but they freed advertising from the odium of the assumption of its nearly unlimited ability to manipulate. This new freedom, however, also paved the way for the social sciences to re-examine advertising. For advertising it meant that even beyond the social rehabilitation which was now possible, the dispositions and behaviours of the consumers were set at the centre of attention and the question became how an advertising message was received and interpreted by the consumer.

Communication-centred models thus replaced manipulation theories in the late 1970s. The 'big manipulator' with his tricks, endless repetitions and refinements has been almost completely discredited[39] as researchers have acknowledged the ability and willingness of the recipients of messages to interpret transmissions selectively. The possibility of influencing behaviour has now been reduced to a mere reinforcement of existing tendencies. The consequence of these findings for communications theory was the abandonment of an exclusive focus on the transmitter as a part of the stimulus–response model in favour of new models of communication which were based on an interaction of message and recipient in the construction of needs. Such communicative acts also played a role in advertising, where the recipient or consumer now occupied a central position and is generally considered to have a wide range of choices, given the number of different and competing advertising messages. The view of the communication process changed as advertising was incorporated into the known 'cognitive paradigm'. In his seminal work *Konsumentenverhalten*, Werner Kroeber-Riel, an expert on German advertising, defined this term as follows: psychological tendencies – like perception, attitude and behaviour – were seen as a result of the cognitive assimilation of information. In this case the cognitive assimilation of information can be seen as an individually directed process, but one which is susceptible to a number of external influences. Kroeber-Riel sees an active process which prevented behaviour from being reduced to a mere matter of cause and effect.[40]

Late twentieth-century marketing concepts and textbooks work with a comparable communication-based theory. Direct manipulation by the advertising industry is no longer conceivable; an understanding of advertising based on the theory of communication underlies all contemporary concepts of marketing. This ideological shift relieved advertising as a whole of so much social responsibility that some scholars talk about 'advertising apologia'.[41] Schmidt, Sinofzik and Spieß explain that until the middle of the 1970s the model of adjustment dominated the economy: theories of marketing advanced in order to keep abreast of trends in the market. Today businesses practise an increasingly active and deliberate communication policy. It is a combination of a sensitive understanding of the transformation of modern society, a marketing concept which is grounded in this understanding, and a strategy of non-product-oriented initiatives for each individual enterprise. The enterprises play an active and growing role in socio-cultural developments – they try to change the environment itself to position the product or the industry better.[42]

What then makes advertising an effective means of communication between seller and buyer? The classic response is that advertising imparts information. With the abolition of older economic institutions and the development of an anonymous and growing market, advertising became necessary to disseminate information about the offers to the consumers. Advertising made the market comprehensible. If one accepts this notion, then advertising expenses cannot be seen as *faux frais*, as false, artificial, or superfluous costs to the national economy. Economic theory at the turn of the century frequently cited advertising for needless consumption of a nation's economic resources: advertising was considered as an unrecoverable expense. Only gradually was the central economic task of advertising recognized as providing information on the market, which had by then lost its clear structure. The New Institutional Economics of the late twentieth century is regarded as both an impetus for examining the economic role of advertising from a historical point of view as well as a theoretical extension of that role.[43] The new theory assumes that the mechanisms of markets and prices are not free but that transaction costs result from their use. These consist primarily of the expenses for information, and secondarily for contracts. A historical examination of advertising from an institutional point of view is therefore eminently desirable and urgently needed.

'Hidden myths'

Although this theory also concerned itself with the secret powers of advertising, it is unlike Packard's model in that it is not concerned with techniques of subtle or subconscious influence but with reinforcing the underlying organizations and structures of human life. These basic organizations and structures characterize the orientation of life and are interpreted and used by advertising as an act of self-expression. The success of this method is contingent upon the secret wishes of the customer. The French philosopher Baudrillard expresses this fundamental idea:

> Neither [advertising's] rhetoric nor even the informational aspect of its discourse has a decisive effect on the buyer. What the individual does respond to, on the other hand, is advertising's underlying leitmotiv of protection and gratification, the intimation that its solicitations and attempts to persuade are the sign, indecipherable at the conscious level, that somewhere there is an agency (a social agency in the event, but one that refers directly to the image of the mother) which has taken it upon itself to inform him of his own desires, and to foresee and rationalize these desires to his own satisfaction. He thus no more 'believes' in advertising than the child believes in Father Christmas, but this in no way impedes his capacity to embrace an internalized infantile situation, and to act accordingly. Herein lies the very real effectiveness of advertising, founded on its obedience to a logic which, though not that of the conditioned reflex, is nonetheless very rigorous: a logic of belief and regression.[44]

Varda Langholz-Leymore has methodically transposed Baudrillard's theory, with specific application to French structuralism. Her study refers primarily to Lévi-Strauss, but also treats Jacques Lacan. She borrows from them the structuralist theory that there exists an inborn universal subconscious of mankind, the content of which is not defined or predetermined, but which is thought to be a form following inherent psychological structures which are – according to Lacan – reflected in the language. Langholz-Leymore considers her analysis of advertising, which she summarizes as follows, a contribution to the discovery of these inherent structures:

> The analysed product and not-product categories are signified by the following binary pairs: war/peace, new/old, life/death, in/out (or endogenous/exogenous), body/soul, good/evil, normal/abnormal, sacred time/profane time, happiness/misery, knowledge/ignorance, culture/nature, and hot/cold. Already in this list a certain repetition is apparent.[45]

In Langholz-Leymore's view, advertising continually falls back upon the same unchanging elements of human nature:

> I have striven to show that symbolic elements of a certain type are bound together in a specified network. This endeavour would have been utterly impossible if it was not for the supposition that a certain classificatory predisposition of the mind has existed *a priori*. What I did is simply to unveil, in a specific system of appearances, a general tendency which has always been there.[46]

Advertising is not an innovative force, but one which renews and reinforces 'hidden myths':

> As such, myth is precisely like advertising, a conservative force. It is not concerned with revolutionising the existing order of things but with preserving it. Advertising advocates consumption of new products, or reinforces consumption of old products, but both are done using accepted themes and well-established symbols of happiness, health and success. Far from changing values, it very much adheres to and upholds existing ones. Above and beyond this, advertising (like myth) acts as an anxiety-reducing mechanism. This is done first by re-stating, on the deep level, the basic dilemmas of the human condition; and second by offering a solution to them. It reiterates the essential dichotomies of life – good and evil, life and death, happiness and misery, etc. – and simultaneously solves them. To the constant anxieties of life, advertising gives a simple answer. In consuming certain products, one buys not only a 'thing' but also an image, one which invokes – and evokes – belief in and hope of having the good rather than the bad, happiness rather than misery, success rather than failure, life rather than death.[47]

Langholz-Leymore develops a new perspective on advertising, placing the interaction of advertising with basic life questions at the centre of our attention. This interaction is not intended to enlighten anyone or to spur critical thinking, but it reinforces fundamental innate structures.

On this point, the notion of the 'hidden myths' differs significantly from the competing 'signification theory' of advertising. This latter theory postulates that advertising responds very quickly to social shifts. Advertising is not only not an expression of the unchanging; it is rather a seismograph for social changes.

The signifying power of advertising

This theory maintains that advertising does not exist only to reinforce or promote common factors of economic, social, or natural developments, but that it is an independent power in modern society: advertising, since the second half of the nineteenth century, has not been some tangible expression of a long-existing phenomenon, but represents something entirely new. Advertising is regarded as having its own epistemology, as an 'order of the things' of the modern age. To use a term which originated in France and has become increasingly popular in English and German research, advertising stands for a new age of 'representation'. It is seen as a previously unknown way of arranging our perception and understanding of the world and of attaching a specific sense to certain words and things. This theory considers advertising to have created a new principle of signification. Advertising as a new form of 'representation' is described by terms like 'commodity culture', that is, a culture based on material products and/or the exchange of these by sale or barter.

An explicit formulation and application of this theory can be found in the recent work of Thomas Richards, who regards 'commodity culture' as a phenomenon specific to capitalism. Its establishment was connected to the construction of a representational system in the world of commerce, which subsequently occupied the world in a semiotic way as well. The wares themselves, which Adam Smith had considered lifeless, were now – according to Richards – provided with life by means of advertising. The things are therefore considered to speak for themselves and in a language of their own, one which has invented and continues to invent many new terms and names.[48] Let us return to Zola and his description of the first Parisian department stores in *The Ladies' Paradise*:

> Groups of women were crushing each other in front of [the display windows], a real mob, made brutal by covetousness. And these passions in the street were giving life to the materials: the laces shivered, then drooped again, concealing the depths of the shop with an exciting air of mystery; even the lengths of cloth, thick and square, were breathing, exuding a tempting odour, while the overcoats were throwing back their shoulders still more on the dummies,

1.8 Photograph, taken in 1851, of the west end of building for the Great Exhibition of the Works of Industry of all Nations, 1851. The term 'Crystal Palace' was first applied by *Punch* in 1850 and it immediately became the popular name of the building

Source: C. H. Gibbs-Smith, *The Great Exhibition of 1851* (London, 1950, reprint 1964), 51

which were acquiring souls, and the huge velvet coat was billowing out, supple and warm, as if on shoulders of flesh and blood, with a heaving breast and quivering hips.[49]

'Advertising as signification' was born between approximately 1850 and 1890. For England, the beginning of this new era in advertising thought was symbolized by the famous 1851 London World's Fair[50] and most of all, by the Crystal Palace, the industrial glass of which looked 'like crystal' (Figures 1.8 and 1.9). Richards regards the appearance of the 'industrial world', which was concentrated there for the first time, as the beginning of the commercial world's general process of becoming independent. The next four decades saw the development of a specific representational order of advertising, which was completed by about 1890. Advertising's primary focus had shifted from the representation of goods and products to the representation of the modern world and culture. The new aesthetics of the consumer society was in place even before there was a consumer society to speak of. Only slowly did economic development begin to catch up with this new aesthetic.[51]

Advertising appears as an expression of a fundamentally new representation of society, designated by the term 'visual culture', a culture in which images have become the primary means of communication. According to Stefan Haas, advertising, as a new development of the visual culture of the modern age, aims at the cultural environment, unlike

1.9   The transept of the Crystal Palace, looking North with the Fountain of Glass in the middle

Source: As for Figure 1.8

This fountain inspired a poem, excerpted below from a children's toy book.

> This is the Fountain, whose beautiful rays,
> Reflected by crystal and water, amaze;
> I'm sure you'll admit that they sparkle as fair
> As the great Koh-i-nor, the Mountain of Light,
> Which some people say does not look half so bright
> As a piece of cut glass, etc.*

*   *The Fine Crystal Palace the Prince Built* (London, 1851/52, reprint Oxford 1975), 3

early advertisements which tried to draw attention directly to the product. Modern advertising plays with all of the loose associations of meaning that we make in the world of things. Advertising, itself immaterial, can thus turn into pure meaning, pure connotation. And it is the visualizing power of the structure of human consciousness that has enabled advertising to establish for itself an emotional meaning beyond the mere transmission of information about a product or a service.[52] From the signifying power of advertising, Haas draws sweeping conclusions concerning the relation between advertising and the modern city:

The modern city works like a system of signs; its individual elements are symbols that refer to meanings. The modern person is
accustomed to reading and interpreting these signs without difficulty, and easily finds a way through the world ... The first
generation of advertisers, who still regarded themselves as artists,
converted the city into one big art exhibition. They brought art
into the streets and freed it from the chains of the nineteenth-
century tendency to immure art in a museum. Thus, they expanded
the role of art in everyday life, a change which was to become
significant in the twentieth century.
    The next generation, who regarded themselves as psychologists,
continued to build on this base. To them, the world appeared as a
jungle of images, through which each individual had to find a way,
and their aim was to erect guideposts through this jungle. They
altered the city, the true field of orientation of a modern person, so
that it became a signifier, loaded with symbolic meaning.[53]

The thesis put forward here posits that the style and culture of a
consumer society had been developed and represented in advertising
even before the beginning of the transformation of the economy into a
consumer society based on popular culture. Richards, citing England as
an example, emphasizes that the range of expressions used in advertising was fully developed by approximately 1890.[54] The new aesthetics of
the consumer society were complete by the time consumer society began
to establish itself. It continues to develop along with the economic
prosperity it fosters.

The view from the twenty-first century

In the 1950s, European advertising entered a phase of 'Americanization' – defined as the 'substitution of local values, behaviours, procedures,
symbols, standards and institutions by those common in the USA'.[55] It is
true that in the 1920s a first craze of Americanization arose; at that
time, American advertising agencies were establishing branches in European cities and European advertising, in consequence, adopted many
concepts of 'scientific' advertising. But beginning in the 1950s, American influence increased and led to a change in perceptions of the market,
and in the 1970s 'marketing' came into its own, resulting in a 'continuous increase' in the level and intensity of advertising in Europe and the
American influence on it.[56] This shift can be illustrated by the 1971
repositioning of the Marlboro advertisement. The famous cowboy with
the slogan 'Marlboro – the taste of freedom and adventure' replaced the
previous 'Modern people – modern life. Marlboro belongs to it' image
of people smoking this brand in a 'typical' German living-room of the
1950s or 1960s. The cowboy image had become synonymous with this

brand of cigarettes much earlier in the USA. Its transfer – in this case to Germany – brought about a profound change in the message conveyed by Marlboro advertisements showing a confidence in, at least in the view of people involved in advertising, 'representation' whose associations were to be recombined with whatever it was that the American West might mean to the more recently affluent smokers of West Germany.[57]

The latest phase of Americanization began with this transition which, in economically advanced European countries, took place around 1970, by which time, according to a widely accepted periodization, the 'postwar hunger' of the population had long been relieved and could belatedly be properly addressed and satisfied. The indicators of prosperity exceeded all the previous levels and the younger generation now initiated rapid social change. Questions of material needs faded in favour of concepts of lifestyle. For the most part, advertising turned to strategies of emotional positioning and sold experiences along with goods. The consumer's basic needs were considered satisfied, and therefore his or her decisions were no longer expected to be motivated by scarcity or necessity. Those who live in abundance need to be persuaded to buy, and this is accomplished less by means of information than by emotional positioning.[58] The theoretical attributes of a number of products and services are more attractive than their functional properties. Such characteristics include the ability to mediate emotional experiences and to make a contribution to the non-material quality of life.[59] The 'age of advertising', which began in the big cities, had entered a new stage. The conflict between mass culture and official culture, between aesthetics of content and aesthetics of form, had reached a new level. It was not simply based on the victory of the official taste over that of the masses or vice versa, or on the abandonment of an élitist middle-class view of art in favour of a mass commercial culture. The conflict between an aesthetics of content versus an aesthetics of form dissolved into an aesthetic of the experience of a new mass culture. Sociologists were probably the first to label this change, which Gerhard Schulze described in his book *Die Erlebnisgesellschaft* (*The 'Experience' Society*): 'Every aspect of life has become a project of experience (*Das Leben schlechthin ist zum Erlebnisprojekt geworden*).'[60] In the age of visually dominated electronic media, advertising functions as a central coordinating point. What is really advertised is more and more often recognizable only by the insider and is placed within an associative world of images which help the consumer to place the product.

Images used for advertising, in film and especially on television, become part of a universal code accompanying the entry into the modern 'visual culture'. It is obvious that advertising theorists continually ask themselves what demands intercultural advertising must meet.[61] Even if there is only a faint possibility that worldwide standardization and homogenization will become a reality, advertising today reaches an ever-widening circle and is 'not doubted' throughout most of Europe. The city of the nineteenth century has expanded to fill the entire globe, both physically and metaphysically, with advertising making a fundamental contribution to the development of the mental model of the modern city in which we have almost all come to live, that is, the city is a text, 'a world that is created by the combination of elements of the different possible meanings of the visual discourse. To orient ourselves in a constantly changing world we must perpetually combine these anew. The passive *flâneur* of the nineteenth century has become an active patchworker.'[62]

Notes

1. Cf. for example Hanns Buchli, *6000 Jahre Werbung: Geschichte der Wirtschaftswerbung und der Propaganda*, 3 vols (Berlin: 1962–66).
2. Cf. Werner Sombart, *Der Bourgeois: Zur Geistesgeschichte des modernen Wirtschaftsmenschen* (Munich and Leipzig: 1920), 203–5.
3. Cf. Dirk Reinhardt, *Von der Reklame zum Marketing: Geschichte der Wirtschaftswerbung in Deutschland* (Berlin: Akademie Verlag, 1993), 176.
4. Heidrun Homburg, 'Werbung – "eine Kunst, die gelernt sein will". Aufbrüche in eine neue Warenwelt 1750–1850', *Jahrbuch für Wirtschaftsgeschichte* 1 (1997), 11.
5. Claire Walsh, 'The Advertising and Marketing of Consumer Goods in Eighteenth Century London', Chapter 4 in this volume.
6. Natacha Coquery, 'French Court Society and Advertising Art: The Reputation of Parisian Merchants at the End of the Eighteenth Century', Chapter 5 in this volume.
7. Émile Zola, *The Ladies' Paradise*, translated by Brian Nelson (Oxford: Oxford University Press, 1995), 4–5. Concerning advertising in literature, cf. Jennifer Wicke, *Advertising Fictions: Literature, Advertisement and Social Reading* (New York: Columbia University Press, 1988); the best-known example is James Joyce's *Ulysses*, with his hero, Leopold Bloom, the advertising salesman.
8. Michael B. Miller, *The Bon Marché: Bourgeois Culture and the Department Store, 1869–1920* (Princeton: Princeton University Press, 1981).
9. Walsh, Chapter 4 in this volume.
10. Reinhardt, *Von der Reklame zum Marketing*, 434f.
11. Silke Brune, '"Lichter der Großstadt": Werbung als Signum einer urbanen Welt', in *Bilderwelt des Alltags: Werbung in der Konsumgesellschaft des 19. und 20. Jahrhunderts*, edited by Peter Borscheid and Clemens Wischermann (Stuttgart: Steiner, 1995), 90–115.
12. Uwe Spiekermann, 'Display Windows and Window Displays in German Cities of the Nineteenth Century: Towards the History of a Commercial Breakthrough', Chapter 7 in this volume.

13. Ibid.
14. Stefan Haas, 'Visual Discourse and the Metropolis: the Importance of Mental Models of Cities for the Emergence of Commercial Advertising', Chapter 3 in this volume.
15. Rosalind H. Williams, *Dream Worlds: Mass Consumption in Late Nineteenth-Century France* (Berkeley and Los Angeles: University of California Press, 1982), 11–12.
16. Stuart Ewen, *Captains of Consciousness: Advertising and the Social Roots of the Consumer Culture* (New York: McGraw-Hill, 1976).
17. Williams, *Dream Worlds*, 9.
18. Uwe Spiekermann, 'Elitenkampf um die Werbung: Staat, Heimatschutz und Reklameindustrie im frühen 20. Jahrhundert', in *Bilderwelt des Alltags: Werbung in der Konsumgesellschaft des 19. und 20. Jahrhunderts*, 126–49.
19. Elliott Shore, 'Advertising as *Kulturkampf* in Berlin and Vienna', Chapter 2 in this volume.
20. Werner Sombart, 'Die Reklame', *Morgen: Wochenschrift für deutsche Kultur* 6 (March, 1908), 284.
21. Shore, Chapter 2 in this volume.
22. Aaron J. Segal, 'Commercial Immanence: the Poster and Urban Territory in Nineteenth-Century France', Chapter 6 in this volume.
23. Esther Cleven, 'Surrounding the Consumer: Persuasive Campaigns and Dutch Advertising Theory of the 1920s and 1930s', Chapter 8 in this volume.
24. Williams, *Dream Worlds*, 213ff.
25. Michele H. Bogart, *Advertising, Artists and the Borders of Art* (Chicago and London: University of Chicago Press, 1995).
26. E. Lysinski, *Psychologie des Betriebes* (1923), 10f.
27. Pierre Bourdieu, *Distinction: a social critique of the judgement of taste* (Cambridge: Harvard University Press, 1984).
28. For the historical establishment of a 'pure' autonomy of aesthetics in Germany in the nineteenth century see Aleida Assmann, *Arbeit am nationalen Gedächtnis: Eine kurze Geschichte der deutschen Bildungsidee* (Frankfurt a.M., New York and Paris: Campus, 1993), 57ff.
29. Attempts to combine economy and the arts in a synthesis in order to improve the tastes of the masses were made in several countries. In Germany the arts and crafts movement was the leading force: 'Since 1907 members of the arts and crafts movement had been striving for its reform by making advertising a means of elevating taste (*Geschmacksbildung*). Artistically designed advertising was meant to educate the aesthetic perception of the masses while simultaneously providing new consumption patterns for them. The discussion had been triggered by the '*Deutscher Werkbund*'. Thus a variety of groups pursued the idea of *Geschmacksbildung* via exhibitions, public lectures, and by founding a technical college.' Christiane Lamberty, '"Die Kunst im Leben des Buttergeschäfts": Geschmacksbildung und Reklame in Deutschland vor 1914', *Jahrbuch für Wirtschaftsgeschichte* 1 (1997), 53. In France, we find similar tendencies in the form of an '*art social*' designed to uplift class tastes. See Segal, Chapter 6 in this volume.
30. Cleven, 'Surrounding the Consumer', Chapter 8 in this volume.
31. Vance Packard, *The Hidden Persuaders* (New York: Pocket Books, 1957).

32. David Riesman, Renel Denney and Nathan Glazer, *The Lonely Crowd: A Study of the Changing American Character* (New Haven: Yale University Press, 1950).
33. Ibid., 9.
34. Max Horkheimer and Theodor Adorno, *Dialektik der Aufklärung: Philosophische Fragmente* (Amsterdam: Querido, 1947), cit. following the edition Frankfurt a.M., 1986, esp. *Kulturindustrie, Aufklärung als Massenindustrie*, 128–76.
35. A somewhat different view is expressed in Walter Benjamin, 'Das Kunstwerk im Zeitalter seiner technischen Reproduzierbarkeit', *Gesammelte Schriften* 7, no.1 (1989), 350–84; Herbert Marcuse, *One-dimensional Man: Studies in the Ideology of Advanced Industrial Society* (Boston: Beacon Press, 1964).
36. Michael Schudson, *Advertising, the Uneasy Persuasion: Its Dubious Impacts on American Society* (New York: Basic Books, 1984); Roland Marchand, *Advertising the American Dream: Making Way for Modernity 1920–1940* (Berkeley and Los Angeles: University of California Press, 1985); Philip Gold, *Advertising, Politics and American Culture: From Salesmanship to Therapy* (New York: Paragon House, 1987); William Leiss, Steven Kline and Sut Jhally, *Social Communication in Advertising: Persons, Products and Images of Well-Being* (Toronto and New York: Methuen, 1986); James D. Norris, *Advertising and the Transformation of American Society, 1865–1920* (New York and London: Greenwood Press, 1990).
37. Horst W. Brand, *Die Legende von den 'geheimen Verführern': Kritische Analysen zur unterschwelligen Wahrnehmung und Beeinflussung* (Weinheim and Basel: Bletz, 1978).
38. Horst W. Brand, 'Unterschwellige Werbung: Nicht sehen, doch glauben?' *Jahrbuch der Absatz- und Verbrauchsforschung* 26 (1980), 387. For a more detailed account, see Brand, *Die Legende von den 'geheimen Verführern'*.
39. Neil Postman's views, however, which clung to and prolonged the older assumptions and anxieties about manipulation, were still decidedly present in the media even in the late twentieth century. In *Amusing Ourselves to Death*, he combines George Orwell's and Aldous Huxley's visions of the future to illustrate his own. According to Postman, society is controlled by means similar to those used in Orwell's *1984*, in which pictures and independent thought are forbidden, but towards an end more similar to that of Huxley's *Brave New World*, in which control of society was achieved by creating a world of diversion. In this latter work, it is books, rather than pictures, that are prohibited, but here again independent thought is taboo. And this, according to Postman, is exactly our fate. Postman's arguments against the 'conversion of a culture determined by words into a culture determined by images' are characterized by a surprisingly rigid insistence on *a working society of written culture* (*schriftkulturelle Arbeitsgesellschaft*). His explicit hostility to images, which he himself bases on a reference to the Ten Commandments, reveals his constant fear of 'secret seducers'. However, it is worth noting that Postman's reference to Huxley omits something critical: in Huxley's work manipulation is ultimately successful not simply via amusement but only with the help of 'pills of happiness'. Neil Postman, *Amusing Ourselves to*

Death: Public Discourse in the Age of Show Business (New York: Viking Press, 1985).

40. Werner Kroeber-Riel, *Konsumentenverhalten*, 4th edition (Munich: Vahlen, 1990), 19.
41. Reinhardt, *Von der Reklame zum Marketing*, 11.
42. Siegfried J. Schmidt, Detlef Sinofzik and Brigitte Spieß, 'Wo lassen Sie leben? Kulturfaktor Werbung – Entwicklungen und Trends der 80er Jahre', in *Aufbruch in die Neunziger*, edited by Christian W. Thomsen (Cologne: DuMont, 1991), 150.
43. Eirik G. Furubotn and Rudolf Richter, *Institutions and Economic Theory: An Introduction to and Assessment of the New Institutional Economics* (Ann Arbor: University of Michigan Press, 1997).
44. Jean Baudrillard, *The System of Objects*, translated by James Benedict (New York: Verso, 1996), 167. Originally published as *Le système des objets* in 1968.
45. Varda Langholz-Leymore, *Hidden Myth: Structure and Symbolism in Advertising* (London: Heinemann Educational, 1975), 141.
46. Ibid., 149.
47. Ibid., ixf.
48. 'In the first half of the nineteenth century the commodity was a trivial thing, like one of Adam Smith's pins. In the second half it had a world-historical role to play in a global industrial economy.' Thomas Richards, *The Commodity Culture of Victorian England: Advertising as Spectacle, 1851–1914* (Stanford: Stanford University, 1990), 1.
49. Zola, *The Ladies' Paradise*, 16.
50. Utz Haltern, Die Londoner Weltausstellung von 1851 (Münster, Aschendorff, 1971). The author would like to thank Utz Haltern for his help.
51. Stefan Haas, 'Die neue Welt der Bilder: Werbung und visuelle Kultur der Moderne', in *Bilderwelt des Alltags: Werbung in der Konsumgesellschaft des 19. und 20. Jahrhunderts*, 64–77.
52. Ibid., 70.
53. Haas, 'Visual Discourse and the Metropolis: The Importance of Mental Models of Cities for the Emergence of Commercial Advertising', Chapter 3 in this volume.
54. Richards, *The Commodity Culture of Victorian England*, 8.
55. Harm G. Schröter, 'Die Amerikanisierung der Werbung in der Bundesrepublik Deutschland', *Jahrbuch für Wirtschaftsgeschichte* (1997), 93–115.
56. Ingo Böbel, 'Advertising and Economic Development: The West German Experience during the 1970s', *Journal of Advertising* (1982), 237–52.
57. This example also illustrates the complexities of transnational advertising campaigns. The advertisements running for a generation in German cinemas, which had for the German viewer a 'typical' American feel, had been banned from television in the USA, and the USA itself has no tradition of showing advertising films at the movies. Thus, this 'American' cultural icon was alive and present in this form only outside the USA. Inside the mother country of the image, the death of the 'real' Marlboro man from lung cancer was the image that the cowboy projected, as he became a poster boy for an intensified anti-smoking campaign.
58. Dieter Ronte and Holger Bonus, *Werbung* (Münster: 1993), 6.

59. Kroeber-Riel, *Konsumentenverhalten*, 68.
60. Gerhard Schulze, *Die Erlebnisgesellschaft: Kultursoziologie der Gegenwart* (Frankfurt a.M. and New York: Campus, 1993), 13.
61. Wendelin G. Müller, *Interkulturelle Werbung* (Heidelberg: Physica-Verlag Rudolf Liebing, 1997).
62. Haas, 'Visual Discourse', Chapter 3 in this volume.

CHAPTER TWO

Advertising as *Kulturkampf* in Berlin and Vienna

Elliott Shore

From the middle of the nineteenth century into the period of the First World War and beyond, the question of advertising, especially in newspapers, disturbed élite cultural critics and academics from the political left and right. As the pace of industrialization and urbanization quickened, as medieval walls fell and brand names developed, the argumentation by a group of élite German-speaking thinkers over half a century developed into a monolithic cultural construct, into a way of looking at advertising that (though echoed in other Western cultures of the period) took on a simple-minded and dangerous uniformity that thinly disguised a fear of change in a specious argument about a golden age before advertising. At the same time as the cultural élite was decrying what they saw as a perilous state of affairs, another group of theorists/practitioners, at a lower cultural register but in a more intellectually rigorous and more practical way, was describing and promoting newspaper advertising in a manner much more cognizant of the actual state of affairs in places like Berlin and Vienna. Although the élite seemed, in its disdain, to overlook both the potential and the complexity of advertising, the theorists/practitioners all made some gesture toward their subject which reflected their sense of the important cultural implications of advertising and their understanding of how complex this whole area of human activity had become. A richer analysis of advertising in the European city in the late nineteenth and early twentieth centuries would have to weave together these and other insights and omissions.

Previous studies of advertising have been thin because they have focused only on single threads of the élite argument. And although the practitioners did take cognizance of the arguments of the cultural élitists, the contrary was not the case, so that the theory of advertising as a danger to good citizens developed in an absence of any understanding of the practice that it criticized. The document upon which this cultural construct is based comes from Ferdinand Lassalle, a spiritual father of German socialism, who was vehement in his attack on the whole notion of advertising, yet his party, honouring him but not his ideas, decided, in a pragmatic move, to support its huge publications apparatus through advertising. The thin studies of the Lassallean critique of advertising by later German scholars[1] have ignored three important arguments that inspire the comments of both Heinrich Treitschke and of Werner Sombart, both of whom, from different poles of the political spectrum, refined and extended the élite position. Two of them are explicit: that advertising is a foreign implant, 'unnatural' in the German context, and that the inspiration for it is simultaneously American and Jewish. A third argument, which is implicit in the language all three critics use, is a very thinly disguised rejection of advertising as a manipulative and indulgent practice. Sombart, for example, as we will see below, was disturbed by the offence to his aesthetic sense that the preponderance of advertising in Berlin caused him. His sense of the uselessness of advertising partially revolved around an implicit rejection of the new, and precisely of the objects and merchandise that he would never himself, as a member of the male professorial élite, acknowledge as having any cultural value. In rejecting this world of objects, these élite critics were rejecting social relations that were emblematic of the new city.

I started this study by trying to find the first link in the chain of argument that lays the blame for the development of advertising in Germany at America's feet. I think I may have found that link in a visit that P. T. Barnum made to Germany in the spring and summer of 1858, as he toured residential cities in the Rhineland exhibiting his chief money-maker, General Tom Thumb.[2] Thumb and Barnum reaped great benefits from their tour, drawing large crowds throughout the region, and Barnum's lavish advertising, including placing promotional articles in newspapers, may have been responsible. However, when I compared what Barnum did with the contemporaneous practices in the German press, I found that the difference was only in degree, rather than specific devices used. He did not do anything that was new to Germany, but what he may have done was more of what was already being done in the press: advertisements with illustrations and grandiose claims were to be found all over the region, if not in the abundance that Barnum lavished on his amused public. Barnum, the purveyor of humbug, would become the bogeyman for the élite and the ideal advertising man for the practitioner; his works were relentlessly translated and republished in Germany throughout the period of my study. He has even seen a modest rebirth by republication in 1991 in East Germany shortly after the wall came down between capitalist and socialist Germany, as a guide to the benighted.[3]

Five years after P. T. Barnum left Germany, Ferdinand Lassalle, president of the Allgemeine Deutsche Arbeiterverein (General German Workers' Association, ADAV) did a little barnstorming of his own through the lower Rhineland. Drawing huge crowds and keen attention from the police, Lassalle, the fiery 38-year-old orator, writer and lawyer, was hoping to draw thousands of members to the organization that had been founded in Leipzig in May, modelled on his own notions of socialism. For his tour of cities in the Rhineland, Lassalle wrote a bitter and lengthy attack on the liberals that singled out the press as the greatest foe of the working class and advertisements as the greatest single cause of the degeneration of the press. This highly charged attack, delivered before thousands in Barmen (now Wuppertal), Solingen and Düsseldorf, quickly printed and distributed to the local chapters of the ADAV, where it was read in special meetings, became and remained a central text for the workers' movement in Germany and later for practitioners and scholars of the soon-to-be-developed field of *Journalistik* (the study of journalism). In its argumentation, it reveals much about Lassalle and about the movement; for its later adherents and foes, it became a text that stood for one idea: the dangerous combination of journalism and advertising. Its other messages have been ignored.[4]

What did he have to say about the press that made such a lasting impression? The language is hyperbolic: the press is 'our chief enemy'. It is the 'most dangerous, the real enemy of the people' because of its 'mendacity, depravity, immorality', and chiefly, its 'ignorance'. Lassalle considered the Prussian press cowardly in its virtually uniform knuckling under to the threat of censorship from Bismarck; worse still, it let the world know why it had not tried to speak out. He attributes this quote to the *Rheinische Zeitung*: 'How can one,' it cried out, when noticeable grumbling broke out in the mass of the Liberal Party itself over the cowardice of the papers, 'how can one demand of the publishers, that they risk the capital that they have invested in their paper?' Lassalle proposes, in one of the rhetorical highlights of the speech, that all newspaper publishers in concert print the article that was forbidden by Bismarck, and thereby force the Chancellor to carry out his threat to shut them all down. He muses about the reaction of the 'Philistine' who no longer finds his usual paper at coffee time, and his growing rage. But the liberal papers are too timid to pull it off.

The repeated theme is cowardliness, and its antithesis, manliness: risk-averse publishers are cowardly, a political party that doesn't fight is cowardly; in fact, it is the greatest glory for a party to 'die with honour' (*mit Ehren zu sterben!*). Warlike metaphors abound in the text. Dripping with venomous irony, Lassalle explodes:

> What is more holy than publishing capital? Yes, with the most shameless distortion of all ideas, that for a long time has been typical of our newspapers, one construes the duty of the newspapers not,

for God's sake, to endanger publishing capital through a single manly word! It is as if a soldier (and soldiers, freedom's pioneers, are what the papers should want to be) saw as his first duty to station himself where there was no chance of being hit by a bullet!

Newspapers, instead of being 'soldiers and pioneers for freedom, are nothing more than an industrial capital investment and money speculation!'

How did it come to this? It wasn't always that way. There had been a golden age of the press, set, as all golden ages everywhere are, sometime in the distant enough past to be remembered by the speaker, but not necessarily by the listeners. What Lassalle may have had in mind was the time around 1848, although he is unspecific: 'once, it [the European press] was really the pioneer for the spiritual interest in politics, art and scholarship, the shaper, teacher and spiritual educator of the larger public. It struggled for ideas and sought to raise up the great multitudes to them.' What happened to occasion this change? Here I must quote at length:

> Gradually, however, the custom of paid notices [Anzeige] began, the so-called advertisements [Annoncen] or insertions [Inserate], which for a long time found no space in the newspapers, then only a very limited amount on the last page. This habit produced a fundamental transformation in the essence of the newspaper. It turned out to be that these advertisements were a very lucrative means of making a fortune, and gaining immense yearly revenues out of the newspapers. From that very moment, the newspaper became an extremely lucrative speculation for a publisher with plenty of capital or one hungry for capital. But in order to get a lot of advertisements, it was of uppermost importance to gather as many subscribers as possible, for the advertisements flow readily only to those papers which enjoy the largest readership. From that moment on, it was not about fighting any longer for great ideas, to slowly and gradually lift the great public up to their level, but rather the other way around, to pay homage to those opinions which, however you may come to them, are agreeable to the greatest number of newspaper purchasers (subscribers). From that very moment, therefore, the newspapers changed from being the shapers and teachers of the people, the appearance of being pioneers for spiritual interests notwithstanding, into detestable eye-servants of the wealthy and therefore subscribing bourgeoisie and its tastes, that tied one newspaper to the circle of subscribers which it already has and the other to that which it hopes to obtain, both always having in mind the real, golden basis of the business: the advertisement.

This is the basic argument, although slightly adjusted later in the nineteenth century to the effect that the tastes of the lower middle class rather than the bourgeoisie were anticipated, that continued to dominate as late as the 1920s when the dean of German journalism studies,

Karl Bücher, put it rather bluntly: 'The newspaper is an enterprise whose product is the advertising section which is marketable only because of the editorial section.'[5]

But Lassalle doesn't stop there. His simple cause-and-effect argument, his positing of a golden age that was ruined by the intrusion of money – quite an interesting observation for a lawyer and economist – his simple formulations perhaps made more simple given the nature of the occasion, the clear marking of good and evil, need, for the full effect of the argument, a perpetrator. Money itself is not enough. And the evil-doer has to have a victim. He finds victimizer and victim in the largest circulation newspaper of the day, the *Berliner Volkszeitung* and its editor:

> Mr. Bernstein: an ex-head of a rental library [where books were lent for a fee], who profited from the reading-matter available in the rental library, and then believed himself to have gained the education which is necessary to lead a great people. A man, who writes daily about God and the world and many other lead articles, which he can only do because, in his happy ignorance, he has no notion of the fact that he completely lacks every qualification for the job. A man who doesn't even have the capacity to write German, but rather, destroys, slowly and surely, the language of the people and its very genius, by delivering a strange gibberish to his readers, the so-called Jewish-German (not one sentence without grammatical mistakes)!

The perpetrator: a semi-literate Jewish rental librarian (to whom did he lend his books?). The victim: 'the people, [who] reach believing and trusting for this poison', because they think it will provide them with 'spiritual strength'.

Not to leave his listeners without hope, Lassalle suggests the way out of the dilemma, 'the idea social-democracy also carries within it [as] the remedy' for this sickness: a four point programme: (1) complete freedom of the press; (2) lifting the requirement of a security deposit for newspaper publishing; (3) abolition of the newspaper stamp tax; and (4) the absolute prohibition of all advertising in newspapers – the advertising function to be carried out by national or local government-controlled official papers.

None of the four points was new. It was the practice in Prussia until 1850 to monopolize advertisements in its *Intelligenz-Blätter*; freedom of the press was one of the demands of the 48ers and the 5000 thaler security deposit was a halfway measure of the regime to give a semblance of freedom under the constant threat of confiscation. But the history lesson is wrong: the role of the press is idealized, the changes in the economy, in printing, in the nature of the reading public – indeed, in the nature of advertising itself – are ignored to make the argument that there is a clear distinction between good and evil, between idealism and money, between manliness and cowardice, between the people and the philistine, and its subset the learned fighter for justice (Lassalle) and the semi-literate destroyer of the spirit of the people (Bernstein).

The solution was not only not new; it was dangerous. It reveals in its simplicity a longing for purity, for clarity that does damage to the complexity of the human condition. The spirit behind the ideas and the programme itself wandered across the political spectrum, perhaps because of the strings it touched in the hearts of fellow cultural élitists. A clean separation between the holy cause of the people and the profanity of the 'humbug', to which Lassalle himself refers in one of his many rhetorical flourishes – 'the frivolous contempt ... for all ideal aims, against reader and people, that patiently falls for every humbug'– bound together several strands of German thought up to the First World War and beyond.

Heinrich Treitschke, the German nationalist *par excellence*, was at the opposite political pole from Lassalle, but they shared the same ideas about the press. His popular lectures, given possibly as early as 1863, and then repeated over and over again, and every winter semester from 1874 into the 1890s at the University in Berlin, were first published shortly after his death in 1896. He had much to say about the press, and in this excerpt, about its relationship to advertising:

> The modern Press is, indeed, Janus-headed. Next to anonymity, its second deeply-rooted abuse is the totally unnatural connection between its political function, which is the treatment and dissemination of the views of a particular party, and the business of advertisement. It is perfectly obvious that there is no inherent bond between politics and the trade notices of this or that tailor or bootmaker. Nay more. The monopoly of advertisements was once the property of the State, but in Prussia it was allowed to lapse, and the business of advertisement has now become so closely united with the political party journals that it appears to be impossible to alter it. Advertisements have become the very foundation of our newspapers, for none of them can even approximately cover the cost of production through the profits of sale alone; while in the matter of advertisement it is precisely those newspapers that are the most despicable and morally depraved which obtain the most success. They employ any means of obtaining them, and make it a rule to pander to the lowest tastes and the meanest instincts of the public.[6]

Treitschke hated every innovation of the nineteenth century – 'an age of money-grubbing ... it will take a low place in history' – especially socialism, for which he showed his contempt in other lectures in this famous series.[7] Werner Sombart,[8] born in the year Lassalle toured the Rhineland, an economist and sociologist of some renown, and one of the leaders of the Verein für Socialpolitik (a group of left-leaning *Katheder Sozialisten*, who urged a more socially responsible social security system on imperial Germany) stood much closer to Lassalle. This group had been co-founded by Sombart's father, a wealthy landowner, member of the parliament present in Versailles in 1871 when the new German Kaiser was crowned. The younger Sombart unleashed a battle in the press in the spring and summer of 1908 over precisely the same issue, drawing upon the same code words as Lassalle had used, with added emphasis on the American origins of the advertisement:

> The advertisement is therefore a necessary component of all American, that is, all purely capitalist economies. And only this kind of economy. The more developed the Americanization, the more developed the advertising. And it becomes the measure of economic, that is to say, capitalist progress. Therefore, for example, advertising doesn't really flourish in Vienna … [Advertising] is a vexation, and a truly big one. The advertisement is that phenomenon of modern 'culture' which even with the best of intentions one can only find odious. For a person with taste, it is in its whole as well as in all of its parts and all of its forms completely revolting.[9]

The Lassallean argument, concentrated now exclusively on the advertisement, is intact: there was a golden age, before capitalism, when folks just sat around in their shops waiting for the customers to come by. Good people, as Sombart quotes an unnamed Viennese, don't advertise, do they? Not any longer. '*Ärmelausreißgeschäfte*' – doing business by ripping the sleeves out of your customers' coats–dragging the customers in off the street – started in places like Breslau, where cheap men's stores fill up whole city blocks, 'where on one coatsleeve of our Michel[10] Mr. Cohen pulls and on the other Mr. Levy'. Advertisements, though, do nothing for the economy: they only make products more expensive. One could work one hour less each day, if it weren't for the added cost of advertising. They are totally unnecessary, and, although he realizes that they can't be abolished, he wishes they could be. They are plain bad. Where Treitschke found the newspaper Janus-headed, Sombart extends the metaphor to the advertisement itself: 'The advertisement is Janus-headed: with one head, it looks into the shop, with the other, into the street.' Better a single face-to-face economy, in which Michel would have fewer choices.

In contrast to Lassalle's, Sombart's golden age is slightly better defined: 1829 is the date that he affixes to the beginning of the end, to the appearance of the first real advertisement, the first announcement which promoted the wares of one purveyor. But in most respects, the arguments of the 45-year-old professor who had come to the Handelshochschule in Berlin just two years before from Breslau preserve the contours of the originator of the form, Lassalle. Sombart finds his Jewish bogeyman, not in the Berlin press, but in the shops of Breslau, where he himself had been given the title of professor as a 26-year-old, even though he did not fulfil the standard requirement (was the pain of purchasing a suit for that day still with him twenty years later as he penned these words?). Where Breslau, in the Prussian part of Silesia, provided Sombart with his worst example of the excesses of advertising, Vienna, the birthplace of his lover of the time, Mitzi Dernburg, who presided over a literary salon in Berlin, provided the civilized balance. Lassalle himself, although he is not quoted directly in this article, was at the centre of Sombart's affective life: until the end of his life, he preserved as his greatest treasure the death mask of his hero (one of only two that existed), and regaled his own son, Nicolaus Sombart, with the conviction that if Lassalle hadn't been killed in a stupid duel, German history would have been very different.[11]

What kind of history do these three learned men and committed men of politics – Lassalle was a political leader, but Treitschke spoke numerous times before the Reichstag and Sombart became a star attraction as an essayist and lecturer after his move to Berlin – present us with? What are the assumptions about the nature of the economy and the German people? What is the history of advertising in Germany? Is the American influence so great? Is it so powerful and so culturally dangerous? Was there a definable golden age before the newspaper and the advertiser came together in their unholy alliance? Is advertising identifiably Jewish? Was there any perceptible shift in thinking about advertising in the forty-five years that spanned Lassalle and Sombart?

Let us start with the last question. What did change was the response. Although there were isolated voices that defended advertising as early as 1857, which we will treat in detail below, most opinion-makers agreed with the judgements of the cultural despairers. But by 1908, a sizeable community, built around the actual advertising industry and allied academics, was ready to reply, and had a scholarly apparatus to back it up. And, unfortunately for Sombart's argument, right at the time he was writing, Victor Mataja was putting the finishing touches to the first real scholarly investigation of the topic, which would help put Vienna at the centre of the advertising question. And, unlike Lassalle's attack on the *Berliner Volkszeitung*, which was met with a stoical silence, the *Berliner Tageblatt*, the fortune of whose owner, advertising magnate Rudolf Mosse, was completely tied to the cultural acceptance of the advertisement, launched a sustained and full-scale counter-attack, which attempted to undermine the position of the Professor of National Economy at the Berliner Handelshochschule. From the first paragraph on the front page of the *Berliner Tageblatt*:

> Earlier Sombart also had a strongly political vein, he appealed to
> the masses and made a great impression upon them. That has
> changed in the meantime. Everyday politics disgusts him ... Sombart
> had shown a certain aesthetic tendency, always representing him-
> self as a master of style. This has carried more weight of late and
> he has even clothed removing himself from political affairs with
> the call: 'Back to Goethe!'[12]

The reaction to Sombart's blast was swift and many-sided, ranging
from professional colleagues to businessmen, cultural critics to newspapers from right to left. And it was overwhelmingly negative. It led to a
break between Sombart and the periodical that he had ostensibly helped
to found. The publication in which his original attack appeared, *Morgen:
Wochenschrift für deutsche Kultur*, had carried Sombart's name on the
masthead as a co-founder and publisher, responsible for
Kulturphilosophie. He had already received several thousand marks in
compensation from the fledgling journal and had just signed a contract
that meant he would additionally receive ten per cent of its net profit
for two years after his last essay appeared.[13] This had led readers to
assume that the publication itself stood for the issues raised by Sombart,
a position from which it retreated quite quickly by publishing numerous
letters from irate readers. The business manager gleefully sided with the
most negative of Sombart's critics, perhaps fearing the loss of potential
subscribers and hoped-for advertising revenue if *Morgen* appeared to be
supporting Sombart's attack. Sombart would claim that he was not an
editor of *Morgen*, was denied space to defend himself and so had to
seek it elsewhere. He fumed against the attacks on him published by
Morgen; the one that especially hurt (part of which was cited above)
was that of a fellow academic, Magnus Biermer, at the University in
Giessen, who claimed that he had heard Sombart give the main talk at
the 1899 conference, in Breslau, of the *Verein für Sozialpolitik*, on 'The
Developmental Strategies of Modern Small Business', where he stated
that the advertisements that bring people into the shops and the business practices that get them to buy 'are the keystones of modern business'.

This quote was front-page news in the *Berliner Tageblatt,* as was the
first report of Sombart's musings. Rudolf Mosse, founder and owner of
one of the largest advertising agencies in the world, publisher of this
and other Berlin newspapers and pillar of the Berlin Jewish community,
was outraged on many levels, and devoted a week in the life of his
paper to slamming Sombart in several different ways: with a reasoned
front-page report that picked Sombart apart, including long quotes
from the *Morgen* article, together with the anti-semitic one; a lampoon
that suggested that the learned man was not really serious, that the
article he wrote was merely an April Fool's joke; and attacks such as
Biermer's on his scholarly credibility.

If any one theme runs through all the responses to Sombart, it is the perceived incompatibility between his position as a professor who gives talks on small business practices, who writes big volumes on the history of economics, and his vehement anti-advertising tirade. Professor Biermer and others attributed his anti-advertising mentality to an overdeveloped aesthetic sense, to put it charitably. One went so far as to say that without advertising, Professor Sombart himself would not have had a job. Sombart did not deny the contradictions, but rather asserted that there were two persons that he inhabited, a private and a public one, and as a private man he had the right to hold opinions that were contradictory to those that he held as a professional academic.

But those kinds of artificial distinctions start to dissolve when one considers that one of the professional magazines that had sprung up in Germany in the 1890s, *Organisation*, had, about six months before Sombart's outburst, published an article celebrating the advertising campaign that had accompanied the launching of Sombart's own journal, *Morgen*, the previous year! And not only did it celebrate the manner in which the journal had gone about its work, but linked it favourably to an American-inspired advertising campaign that was being run in Germany at the time for Edison phonographs. And the praise for the Edison campaign was modulated with culturally sensitive statements to the effect that Germany had something to learn from American examples, but it shouldn't slavishly copy them. *Morgen* was praised for its campaign which had set up a series of lectures in major cities throughout Germany and tied attendance to subscriptions. In order to get the attention of possible advertisers, the German cultural weekly had sent out a very fancy leather portfolio with two postage-paid postcards included: one for a free, one-year subscription and the other for a new pad of paper for the portfolio.[14] *Organisation* had the last laugh as well: summing up the whole Sombartian debate in the summer of 1908, it commented that had Sombart wanted to make advertisements for advertising, he couldn't have gone about it any better than he did.[15]

This other level of academic discourse in Germany and Austria at the time, represented here by Professor Biermer, as well as a professional and practical one in such journals as *Organisation*, was beneath the notice of people like Lassalle, Treitschke and Sombart, but bore much more of a resemblance to the ideal of objective scholarship than the leading lights could. One is struck how often they made *ex cathedra* statements – especially Sombart, the greatest offender in this group – without the slightest shred of evidence. That this did not go completely unnoticed, at least in Sombart's case, is evidenced in the devastating criticism by Lujo Brentano[16] of Sombart's scholarship a few years later and by the riot of criticism that the Berliner's attack on advertising received in the press. Brentano characterized Sombart as 'frivolous, arrogant, irresponsible, ruthless and arbitrary'.[17] But both of these criticisms stem from the decades-long development of a professional and academic interest in advertising that paralleled the development of the advertisement itself. What one is struck by in the 'bah humbug' mode of thought – its almost total disengagement from the development of society – is not so sharply evidenced in the other literature. That those who were involved in the economy would see the world differently from professors with prestigious chairs whose shopping exploits were limited to ordering wine and getting another suit from the same tailor who had delivered the last one or from political leaders who lived off interest income should not come as such a great surprise, although Sombart's blindness to his surroundings when it came to the question of advertising seems to have been almost complete: one critic rebutted his notion that Vienna was relatively free of advertising in relation to Berlin (because it was less Americanized) by rattling off the following:

> Completely contrary to these views [of Vienna] is the picture of Viennese newspapers. Below I give a tabulation of the state of advertising in the major Viennese papers of March 8, 1908 [i.e., the date of the publication of Sombart's screed]:
> *Neue Freie Presse*, 70 pages long, about 39 pages of advertisements, of which about 21 pages are display advertisements; *Neues Wiener Tageblatt*, 108 pages long, about 80 pages of advertisements of which 30 pages are display advertisements; *Fremdenblatt*, 70 pages long, about 31 pages of advertisements of which about 25 are display advertisements ... [18]

What this last critic describes had been developing since at least the time when Barnum took Tom Thumb on his European tour, and did not go unnoticed by all German scholars. In fact, what was perhaps the shrewdest contribution to the debate over the place of the advertisement and the newspaper was one of the first, made the year before Barnum arrived in Germany and fifty years before this controversy. Karl Knies, a professor of National Economy at the University of Freiburg im Breisgau, saw the newspaper advertisement as part of the development of society's general need for news. As people moved about more and more, especially on trains, as people immigrated overseas, to other European countries or from the village to the city, the private letter was no longer sufficient as the sole means of newsgathering. The advertisement, he saw, then, not as separate from the development of the newspaper, as did the more famous contributors to the debate, but as an integral part of the news. That is, the newspaper included from the beginning the function that only advertisements could serve. To Knies, it was obvious that an industrial society needed something like a newspaper and its announcements in order to function. The simple-minded and dangerous notion that both Lassalle and Treitschke shared, that of a strict separation of political and economic functions of the news, is nowhere to be seen in this more sophisticated approach to the problem. Knies fought against the 'absolutism of theory' of the kind championed by the élite argument against advertising. Throughout his career, Knies advocated the integration of theory and practice when looking at questions like advertising, which could only be understood in context.[19]

But Knies went even further, to the point of saying that the newspaper advertisement was a way into a society's 'economic and cultural-historical present and future'.[20] He prophesied the use of the advertisement by cultural historians of the future, because it was really only in the advertising section that one could get a sense of what might be going on in society, at all levels, in a way that was totally unconscious, unlike all other forms of written communication. It was 'precisely because advertisements weren't confined to the communication of the obvious' that they were a barometer of what was happening in society. Instead of railing against patent medicine advertisements, for example, Knies realized that it was 'only out of the advertisements in the local paper' that one could study such things as folk medicine or the ministrations of quacks.[21]

Knies was well known in his chosen fields of expertise – statistics and the railways – but the matter-of-fact tone and casual, almost off-hand insights in this early work of his have never in any serious way become part of the public debate over advertising in Germany and only quite recently elsewhere. This may have been due in part to the fact that he spent the last thirty years of his career in Heidelberg, not in Berlin. Those who wrote about advertising directly afterwards, in the 1870s and 1880s, seemed to be concerned with other issues, such as practical ones about how one actually went about producing advertisements, or reacting against the Lassallean notion of the corrupt press with practical solutions like professional education for journalists.[22] There were always, of course, the more coarse contributions about newspapers in the ongoing anti-semitic debate, which, if not quoting directly from the leading lights, matched the spirit of their remarks in a language that had the advantage of at least being much more straightforward.[23]

Straightforward also was the language of those for whom business was not only not an evil, but a positive good. Before such audiences as that of the Verein für Handelsgeographie, whose purpose was to learn about the world in order to take advantage of trade possibilities, speakers could combine the academic interest in the advertisement with its practical effects. In an address on 'The Press in Service of the Businessman'[24] Christian Heinrich von Dillmann took off from Knies's work to describe how he thought appropriate advertising in Germany should look. He asserted that advertisements worked differently on men and on women, appealed to the eye and to the ear; in short, that the advertisement itself was a complex phenomenon. He admitted that in lands where freedom of the press was a longstanding fact, such as in England and the United States, the advertisement had developed beyond the scope imaginable in Germany, not to speak of the other authoritarian lands that surrounded the newly created national state.

But these complex advertisements would not follow the development that they had in England and in the United States, because advertising can't go too much against the national grain, and because business and trade, like a free press, were relatively late in getting started in Germany. On top of the newness of the phenomenon, the Germans, he asserted, disdain self-praise and are extremely diffident about revealing much of their inner selves. However, business, industry and trade had become the lifeblood of the modern nation state and the circulation of the blood was crucial to the life of the body: 'As wine is to the body, so is the advertisement for business.' And like wine, which stimulates but can also numb, the advertisement must be drunk in moderation. (Were the Americans and the English drunk on advertisements?) What will save the German economy from getting drunk will be the German distaste for ballyhoo, so the advertisement must clothe itself in an artistic fashion, appealing to the higher tastes in people.

Now that the businessman knows that he must advertise, but must do it in moderation and in an artistic manner, the question of where to advertise becomes crucial. Of course it has to be in a newspaper, but which one? Here von Dillmann makes his most interesting contribution to the debate:

> Unfortunately, our newspapers are almost all party papers. Whoever places his advertisements in an outspoken party paper, appears to be supporting the direction and purpose of the paper. How easily could this lead to confusion, doubt and unrest? A rigidly conservative man can't allow the imputation, one would argue, of using a liberal or even a radical paper for his purposes and therefore directly furthering its effectiveness. And vice versa, the way party onlookers are here, a radical party man could hardly forgive his comrade if he were to use a reactionary paper for his business purposes.[25]

Von Dillmann doesn't proscribe the use of these papers; on the contrary, he says that a small businessman, who is fighting for his life, 'can hardly avoid becoming a partisan'. But the big businessman, now that Germany has become a world power, must overcome the tendency to become involved in party squabbles, must rise above the 'petty mercenary spirit' of the previous century. He must use such 'politically neutral' periodicals as the *Gartenlaube* for his advertising purposes. Von Dillmann's fondest hope is that the businessman will some day, as a result of his newly found place in German life and his understanding of how the advertisement should be used, replace the stereotyped image of him in previous German literature with one that now accords with his new standing. This is not so different from what, at least in England, the leading novelists had already admitted.[26] The literature on the ad-man was on the minds of the great European writers of the period, and none other than Dickens and Joyce, the most celebrated authors who bracket the period at which we are looking, made the advertisement and its language crucial to their work, if not quite in the way that business booster von Dillmann would have liked. The greatest work of English literature in the twentieth century, *Ulysses*, centres on a day in the life of Leopold Bloom, practising a trade that was being phased out in his lifetime by a variety of professional organizations and new insti-tutions, that made the advertising salesman an endangered species early in the new century. The development of this new branch of the economy had been proceeding apace in England and America, and in Germany as well, although German professional writers bemoaned their position in third place in this race. The late start in the industrial race, to which von Dillmann alluded, was being rapidly overcome in Germany, with the creation of advertising agencies, a professional press, professional organizations and a scholarly literature.

Victor Mataja, born the year before Barnum came to Germany, was the first to write a comprehensive work on advertising in the German language. From a Catholic Croatian–Italian background, born in Fiume, he studied law and political economy, became a professor at Innsbruck and later in Vienna, where he lived and worked for most of his life. After 1892, he worked for a series of economic organizations that were connected to the state, dealing with trade statistics, employment statis-tics and then moving to a leading role in the trade ministry. He practised a complicated brand of politics that coupled support for the German-speaking elements in the Austro-Hungarian Empire with activities that fostered working-class wage demands and social security.[27]

Mataja simply demolished the arguments that Lassalle and Treitschke had made, feeling apparently no need to contend directly with Sombart, although mentioning him and the response to him in the bibliography of his major work of 1910.[28] Mataja set out the programme for his larger work on the advertisement as early as 1903 in the *International Quarterly*.[29] Aware, as few of his German contemporaries, of the wider world literature on the subject, Mataja made reference to the then current debate on how advertising was instrumental in the reform of hygiene by championing the discarding of outmoded practices, but balanced these remarks with the warning that the super-abundance of newspaper advertising could help to cause wasteful purchasing on the part of the consumer. And, much newspaper advertising was not really intended to foster hygiene or open up new markets, but rather intended to split the market between competing brands with the added cost passed on to the consumer.

But advertising was here to stay. It had become a big business in and of itself, and had diversified into many smaller branches, just like industry itself had. It was the major source of income for magazines and newspapers, which was the most important and effective form of advertising, on top of massive campaigns. Why the huge increase in advertising? Growing wealth and technical development working hand in hand to produce more luxury items and the demand for them. The change in retailing, where the consumer no longer relies on the shopkeeper to be informed about what he sells, but is made aware of what to purchase by the increasing advertising of brand names. And the change in the store itself, with the development of the huge department store that cannot just rely on the neighbourhood trade, but must bring the customer through the door. Whereas for von Dillmann, the advertisement was wine that stimulated the circulation of the blood of business, Mataja recalls Macaulay as saying 'advertising is to business what steam is to machinery, the grand propelling power'.

But, Mataja contends, not one with overwhelming power. Advertisements themselves start to suffer from laws of diminishing returns, and it is only by their refinement and their increasing artistic sophistication that they continue to have effect. Consumer cooperatives, which have aims partially opposed to those of business interests, provide an important counterweight to the advertisement. The concentration on a huge scale in the business world also has a braking effect on the amount of advertisement, as competition ceases to exist in various fields of trade. And the development of a large state sector in many countries marked out large areas in which advertisements were superfluous. Laws enacted in various countries – in Germany in 1896 – prohibiting false statements in public announcements have also had some effect on curbing the reach of advertising.

But the fact remains, according to Mataja, that in addition to the fact that advertising furnishes the livelihood of many people, it 'is intimately bound up with the intellectual life of nations, having won over to its service to a marked degree art and taste, and having made possible the modern newspaper and magazine'.[30] Not that the modern media are very reliable or even good for the public interest. Remedies such as laws do not get to the heart of the matter: 'the organic shortcomings of advertising ... are themselves a product of and share the weaknesses and faults of the modern economic system, in which production in general becomes subservient to speculative individual interests'. Moreover, since the real advantage to advertising comes in repetition, it is only the largest enterprises that will reap its greatest benefits. The limitation of the amount of advertising, its cost and its effectiveness, might some day perhaps be possible through a general public that is educated about what goes on in business, Mataja asserts, but he ends his essay with the bald comment that he believes that there is no hope in reining advertising in.

Mataja more than backed up these assertions with a work that appeared seven years later. Advertising was an industry that was not only growing in the numbers it employed in 1910, but in the salaries that it paid. It was one of the new professions in which women were not only employed, but also led and owned their own agencies, at least in the United States. There was of course a good reason for this: the consumer advertising that took up much of the advertising budget was either for articles that were directly consumed by women or for the household.[31] More reason for academic disdain. A further cause to grumble was the impetus that advertising gave to photography, as opposed to 'art', as the modern form of visual representation.[32] The St Louis World's Fair of 1904 paid special attention to the advertisement – as it did to the social sciences in general, bringing a large contingent of German scholars, including Werner Sombart to the American midwest – and gave impetus to advertising exhibitions in the next several years in Chicago, New York, Paris, England, Berlin – in 1908! – and one even in Cape Town, South Africa.[33] The St Louis World's Fair was also the place where the idea for the founding of the International Advertising Association was developed.[34]

But it is in the chapter on newspaper advertising that Mataja directly confronts the assertions and arguments of the cultural despairers. 'Since the invention of the art of printing books one has had to reckon with the advertisement.'[35] Citing numerous examples, many of which could have been found easily in other secondary sources, Mataja simply refutes the notion that Lassalle and Sombart and Treitschke all shared, of a golden age in which there was no advertising, and makes a laughing-stock of Sombart's assertion that advertising started on a certain day in 1829. He takes on Lassalle and his disciples directly, including Robert Schmölder, whom we have not discussed, Treitschke and Karl Bücher, the then reigning authority in German universities on this theme, who phrased it in a way that would have pleased Lassalle: 'on the same page, often right up against the place where the most important interests of mankind are represented or should be found, buyers and sellers carry on their lowly search for profit'.[36]

Mataja explains in detail why one could not go back to the system where the 'lowly search for profit' was not coupled with reporting of 'the most important interests of mankind' such as in the *Intelligenzblätter*, the official advertising monopoly prevalent before the revolution of 1848, beloved of Lassalle and his devotees, by quoting another professional writer on the press: 'Advertisements can only flourish in direct connection with news. Only those newspapers, in which all of the functions of the modern newspaper are combined, enjoy the amount of public visibility that is the essential growth medium of the advertisement.'[37] It is not a reform of the press that Lassalle and company want, but the death of advertising that they seek. Treitschke's charge that the connection of advertisements with newspapers is unnatural gets it backwards as well. The development of lead articles that stake out important political ideas, seen historically, was a secondary development, one that came about only gradually, at first merely as an emergency measure when there wasn't enough news to fill the paper. The question, as Mataja would have it, is whether, when one talks of 'unnatural' connections, one shouldn't see the political analysis in the paper as less natural than the advertisement, which is at least an extension of the news.

Mataja's most striking insights, taken together with those of Knies, either foretell future developments or chart the way scholars are starting to understand this elusive subject. Mataja notes, for example, a direction that advertising itself had already begun to take in the political arena, a development which, ninety years later, has become the major way that politics is practised in Western countries. He tossed off another thought which may be a key to understanding the 'success' of the advertisement as a cultural form. 'The advertisement is a place of cheerfulness, of trust; it knows only superior and indispensable things – it cannot speak about any misfortune, without immediately producing a remedy to clear it away.'[38] The only way to be in a position to articulate such notions about cultural artifacts of contemporary life is to be both in the debate and in the practice and not, as Sombart or Lassalle or Treitschke, trying to occupy a position outside and above the rest of society.

This is not to argue that the advertisement is a wholly positive force, nor that the critics who write about it positively are better. But it is to argue that the world-view of scholars like Mataja and Knies, whose interests in theories about advertising come from experience in the world as well as from their academic training and whose inclinations are to find out why rather than to condemn the fact that advertising is accepted and even enjoyed by large numbers of people, is a better way to understand the subject. It leads them to argue that advertising is an integral part of modern societies and as such needs to be understood within its contexts. The yearning for purity that the élite critics desired, the yearning for a golden age, an age when there were either no advertisements in the newspapers or the separation between them and the editorial sections was complete, when the newspapers were edited by stalwarts who wrote and thought well, when there were precious few new products and when all economic activity happened face to face – this kind of yearning is a yearning for simplicity, not an elegant simplicity, but one that is antiquated and lifeless.

And if one yearned to turn the clock back, and to argue that there is a precious simplicity that has been lost and that is not lifeless, then one would have to argue in ways that Lassalle, Treitschke and Sombart seem incapable of doing. For these three main figures evade the responsibility that their positions as powerful public intellectuals give them to acknowledge the deep contradictions in their views. One of the chief implications of the arguments that all three have made, especially the two social democrats, is that the people on whose behalf they claim to work are the very people who seem to enjoy consuming things and being entertained by the representations in the world which Mataja calls 'a place of cheerfulness and trust' and that therefore they must all be somehow deluded or duped or worse. To make sweeping statements about the invidiousness of advertising is to deny the validity of certain kinds of ways of making meaning. Sombart decried advertising, but only after he moved to Berlin in large part to ensure a higher standard of living by having access to literary and cultural markets. He boosted his income by his involvement in a new magazine that tried, ultimately unsuccessfully, to establish itself, with the help of advertising. The deepest contradiction in Lassalle's position is the seeming desire to liberate the working class of Germany whose tastes he abhorred and mocked. Treitschke, who despised the politics of the social democrats along with the course of much else that went on in the nineteenth century, could not begin to fathom how these prejudices would make him the least qualified person to address the German parliament, as he did on innumerable occasions, on burning issues of the day. But neither could the people who invited him to speak.

The desire for purity, for the separation of one aspect of social life from another, characterizes much of what the élite critics wanted. Sombart saw himself as two different people, Lassalle and Treitschke wanted newspapers that had no advertising in them at all. The inability to integrate the world around them with the world they wanted to inhabit made these critics try by force to keep the two apart – and to characterize what they liked as straightforward and pure and what they detested as manipulative and evil. Something as dynamic as the evolving changes in advertising in the period in which they lived, that demanded an integrative approach to begin to understand the complexities of modern societies, and the ability to embrace the new while aware of its complexities and dangers, cannot be understood by powerful men afraid of change, afraid of stepping into the cities of Berlin and Vienna which contained within them in their confusing swirls people who were dazzled and people who were annoyed, people who enjoyed and people who tried to ignore the advertisement.

Notes

1.   The state of affairs in the study of advertising in Germany has recently been completely transformed, under the leadership of Clemens Wischermann, Peter Borscheid and Dirk Reinhardt. Two works are especially important: Dirk Reinhardt, *Von der Reklame zum Marketing: Geschichte der Wirtschaftswerbung in Deutschland* (Berlin: Akademie Verlag, 1993) and Peter Borscheid and Clemens Wischermann (eds), *Bilderwelt des Alltags: Werbung in der Konsumgesellschaft des 19. und 20. Jahrhunderts* (Stuttgart: Franz Steiner Verlag, 1995). These two works and others by the contributors to the Borscheid/Wischermann collection have moved the study of advertising in Germany well beyond the debate that I will be discussing in the following pages, to the study of advertising as part of the modern world. But what has not yet been investigated in any way, as far as I can ascertain, are the sources of the debate on advertising; that is, the investigation of Lassalle and Sombart has relied on a quick reading of the canonical texts, mostly because, I would surmise, this group of scholars has before it the task of filling in large gaps in our knowledge of the actual extent and development of German advertising in the last century. See, in *Bilderwelt des Alltags*, Peter Borscheid, 'Am Anfang war das Wort: Die Wirtschaftswerbung beginnt mit der Zeitungsannonce', 20–43 and Uwe Spiekermann, 'Elitenkampf um die Werbung: Staat, Heimatschutz und Reklameindustrie im frühen 20. Jahrhundert', 126–49.
2.   The following is based on a paper I delivered to the 1995 American Studies Annual Conference in Pittsburgh, Pennsylvania entitled: 'Transatlantic Humbug: P. T. Barnum and General Tom Thumb in Germany in 1858'.
3.   This is the republication of the 1884 German edition, P. T. Barnum, *Die Kunst Geld zu machen: Nützliche-Winke und beherzigenswerte Ratschläge* (Berlin: Eulenspiegel Verlag, 1991), foreword by Karl Emmerich. From the 1884 edition, 'Für das deutsche Publikum umgearbeitet von Leopold Katscher'. Emmerich's introduction suggests that the republication of this work in German, for the first time in more than a hundred years, 'comes just at the right moment, when we "poor children" that Barnum called the "strivers for success," start off in the new Germany' (7). Emmerich makes the telling point that Barnum 'extolled in his little book all of those virtues, that are characteristic of us Germans, that we learned, practised so long and which have of late borne so little fruit' (8–9).
4.   In the following discussion, I am relying on the text printed in the

Arbeiterfreund for its spontaneity and its choice of excerpts. The pamphlet, *Die Feste, die Presse und der Frankfurter Abgeordnetertag: Drei Symptome des öffentlichen Geistes. Eine Rede gehalten in den Versammlungen des Allgemeinen deutschen Arbeiter-Vereins zu Barmen, Solingen und Düsseldorf* (Düsseldorf: Schaub'sche Buchhandlung, 1863) was reviewed as early as 10 October 1863 in the *Nordstern* and excerpted starting on 16 October in the *Volksfreund*. The full text, with a critical introduction by the editor, can be found, among other places, in vol. 3 of the complete works edited by E. Bernstein. The reports of contemporary events surrounding the speech are also followed mostly in the *Arbeiterfreund*, nos. 114–43, 23 September to 29 November, 1863 and the *Nordstern: Organ für das deutsche Volk* (Hamburg), nos 231–8, 26 September to 14 November 1863.

5.   Karl Bücher, *Gesammelte Aufsätze zur Zeitungskunde* (Tübingen, 1926), 377, as cited in Gerd F. Heuer, 'Anzeigewesen', in *Handbuch der Publizistik*, Praktische Publizistik, edited by Emil Dovifat, vol. 3 (Berlin: DeGruyter, 1969), pt 2, p. 263. Heuer is himself a student of advertising who published his dissertation in the 1930s and this handbook, which still has currency in its field, was edited by Bücher's successor, who also participated in the infamous National Socialist journalism handbook.

6.   This translation is from a First World War British publication, with an introduction by Arthur James Balfour, which was designed to instruct the British public in the mentality of their enemy! Heinrich von Treitschke, *Politics*, translated from the German by Blanche Dugdale and Torben de Bille with an introduction by Balfour (London: Constable and Company Ltd, 1916), vol. 1, 171–2. The original can be found in Heinrich von Treitschke, *Politik: Vorlesungen gehalten an der Universität zu Berlin*, edited by Max Cornicelius (Leipzig: S. Hirzel, 1897), vol. 1, 176–7.

7.   Lassalle himself is mentioned several times in the lecture on 'Political Economy', *Politics*, vol. 1, 391–400.

8.   The 'definitive' biography by Friedrich Lenger, *Werner Sombart, 1863– 1941: Eine Biographie* (Munich: Beck, 1994), is not helpful on the issue of advertising in Sombart's thought.

9.   Werner Sombart, 'Die Reklame', *Morgen: Wochenschrift für deutsche Kultur* 2, no. 10 (6 March 1908), 284. This article, on pages 281–6, was the text of Sombart's which was most debated in the press. I have found the following most useful: in *Morgen*: 'Zur Reklame', vol. 2, no. 18 (1 May 1908), 576; Johannes Steindamm, 'Zu Sombarts Reklame', vol. 2, no. 19 (8 May 1908), 599–601; Edmund Edel, 'Kunst, Kultur und Reklame', vol. 2, no. 19 (8 May 1908), 601–5; Arthur Jacoby, 'Amoklauf', vol. 2, no. 19 (8 May 1908), 606–8. Three letters were then published in *Morgen* in the second half of 1908: M. Biermer, 'Sombart: Ein Brief', 887–9; Werner Sombart, 'Offener Brief an den Schriftleiter Herrn Dr. Artur Landsberger', 965–7; and G. Leonhardt, 'Offener Brief an Professor Werner Sombart', 1003–7. In the Berlin weekly review *Plutus: Kritische Wochenschrift für Volkswirtschaft und Finanzwesen*, published by the influential Georg Bernhard: Ernst Growald, 'Sombart über Reklame', vol. 5, no. 14 (4 April 1908), 276–8; H. Dose, 'Sombart der Reklamefeind', vol. 5, no. 17 (25 April 1908), 337–8; Carl Kujath, 'Reklame, Volkswirtschaft und Aesthetik', vol. 5, no. 19 (9 May 1908), 376–8; Leon Zeitlin, 'Götze "Reklame"', vol. 5, no. 22 (30 May 1908), 433–7; Jul. H.

West, 'Die Wirkung der Reklame', vol. 5, no. 26 (27 June 1908), 511–12. The two front-page articles in the *Berliner Tageblatt und Handelszeitung* on Sombart by M. Biermer appeared on 30 April 1908 (vol. 5, no. 218), 'Sombart wider Sombart' and 6 May 1908 (vol. 5, no. 229), 'Reklame und Sensation'. See also the January 1909 pamphlet by [Paul] A[venarius], 'Reklame und Kultur', published by the Dürer Bund as number 46 in the series *Flugschrift zur Ausdruckskultur*.

10. 'Michel' is the name of the German national figure, akin to John Bull in England or Marianne in France or Uncle Sam in the USA, with the important distinction that he is portrayed as a comic and pathetic figure, which makes this a passage that not only sneers at Jewish businessmen in Breslau but also at their customers.

11. Nicolaus Sombart, *Jugend in Berlin. 1933–1943: Ein Bericht* (Frankfurt a.M.: Fischer Taschenbuch Verlag, 1986). See in particular chapter entitled 'Der Herr Geheimrat'. The description of the life of Sombart and son reveals a life that helps one understand how this kind of scholarship was fostered. Alternately moving and unconsciously hilarious – Sombart wanted to complete Marx's work, or, 'my grandfather was alive when Marx and Goethe were also alive' – his memoir proves ammunition for those who think that prejudices and antipathies can be inherited.

12. Biermer, 'Reklame und Sensation', 6 May 1908.

13. Lenger, *Sombart*, 179.

14. 'Eine amerikanische Reklame-Kampagne in Deutschland: Der "Morgen" und der "März"', *Organisation* 9, no. 22 (November 1907), 417–19.

15. Paul Hennig, 'Moderne Reklame', *Organisation* 10, no. 16 (20 August 1908), 384–5.

16. See the essay on Brentano and Sombart by Hartmut Lehmann, 'The Rise of Capitalism: Weber versus Sombart', in *Weber's 'Protestant Ethic': Origins, Evidence, Contexts*, edited by Hartmut Lehmann and Guenther Roth (Washington, DC: German Historical Institute and Cambridge: Cambridge University Press, 1993), 195–208.

17. Lehmann, 207. The words quoted are Lehmann's in describing Brentano's *Die Anfänge des modernen Kapitalismus [1913]* (Munich: 1916), 78–199.

18. H. Dose, 'Sombart der Reklamefeind', *Plutus* 5, no. 17 (25 April 1908), 337.

19. Walter Braeur, 'Karl Knies', in *Neue deutsche Biographie* (Berlin: Duncker & Humblot, 1980), vol. 12, 183.

20. Karl Knies, *Der Telegraph als Verkehrsmittel: Mit Erörterungen über den Nachrichtenverkehr überhaupt* (Tübingen: Verlag der H. Laupp'schen Buchhandlung, 1857), 50.

21. Knies, 50–51.

22. See, for example, Detlev Freiherr von Biedermann, *Das Zeitungswesen sonst und jetzt* (Leipzig: Verlag von Wilhelm Friedrich, 1882), 36–7. France is held up as the example for Germany to follow. J. G. Wehle, *Die Reclame: Ihre Theorie und Praxis. Uebersichtliche Darstellung des gesammten Ankündigungswesens* (Vienna, Pest, Leipzig: A. Hartleben, 1880), admits that the newspaper advertisement has become an integral part of the newspaper itself, but is reluctant to give up the Lassallean notion that it is a bad thing. At any rate, he says that the public itself is used to the newspaper advertisement and 'sees the income that the news-

paper gets from the advertiser as the legal profit of the undertaking' (83). Much more important for Wehle is the strict separation of editorial and advertising space in the paper.

23. Typical of the genre, which accuses the press of being completely in Jewish hands, of attempting to destroy 'our beautiful German Germany', is Paul Maria Baumgarten, 'Zur Naturgeschichte der Presse: Eine kulturhistorische Skizze' in *Frankfurter zeitgemäße Broschüren*, edited by Paul Leonard Haffner, new series, vol. 7 (pamphlet is also separately numbered 1–32) (Frankfurt a.M. and Lucerne: A. Foesser, 1886), 73–104. The quotation is from page 80 (page 8 of the pamphlet).

24. Christian Heinrich von Dillmann, *Die Presse im Dienste des Kaufmanns: Vortrag gehalten am 12 Dezember 1890 im Verein für Handelsgeographie zu Stuttgart* (Stuttgart: G. J. Göschen, 1891).

25. Ibid., 28.

26. The argument that advertising is of central importance to English literary culture is made with extraordinary force by Jennifer Wicke, *Advertising Fictions: Literature, Advertisement and Social Reading* (New York: Columbia University Press, 1988).

27. Lothar Höbelt, 'Mataja', in *Neue Deutsche Biographie*, vol. 30 (Berlin: Duncker und Humblot, 1990), 363–5.

28. Victor Mataja, *Die Reklame: Eine Untersuchung über Ankündigungswesen und Werbetätigkeit im Geschäftsleben* (Leipzig: Duncker & Humblot, 1910).

29. Victor Mataja, 'The Economic Value of Advertising', *International Quarterly* 8 (1903–4), 379–98.

30. Ibid., 397.

31. Mataja, *Die Reklame*, 185–6.

32. Ibid., 190.

33. Ibid., 217–18.

34. Ibid., 220.

35. Ibid., 227.

36. Robert Schmölder, *Das Inseratenwesen: Ein Staatsinstitut* (Leipzig: C. Reissner & Ganz, 1879) and *Wie können die Schäden unserer periodischen Presse dauernd geheilt werden?* (Barmen: 1880); Karl Bücher, *Die Entstehung der Volkswirtschaft* (1893) and *Die allgemeinen Grundlagen der Kultur der Gegenwart* (1906). Mataja, *Die Reklame*, 235–7.

37. Emil Lobl, *Kultur und Presse* (1903), 163 as cited in Mataja, *Die Reklame*, 242.

38. Mataja, *Die Reklame*, iv.

CHAPTER THREE

Visual Discourse and the Metropolis: Mental Models of Cities and the Emergence of Commercial Advertising

Stefan Haas

No place has been as strongly affected by the modern age as the city. It has become the testing ground for new lifestyles and new social connections, the forum for political decisions, and the locus of new social movements. The city has come to embody the best and worst of possibilities for the avant-garde in the arts and sciences, and to be in every way more than the sum of its parts. This becomes particularly clear if one thinks of the archetypal cities of the classic epoch of industrialization: Paris, London, New York, Vienna and Berlin. In the minds of today's thinkers, they are more: symbols of dynamism and superhuman speed, places of poverty and dissipated luxury, of avant-garde culture and estrangement from nature, a maelstrom of the positive and the negative – and it seems to us almost as if they were individuals, with their own characters, minds and goals. Thus the city is not entirely independent of our conceptions, but neither is it only an abstract construction of either our own or society's making. The true site of the city lies in the profound gap between the individual's *Lebenswelt*[1] and objective reality. The city has the inexactness of thought, the fleeting quality of images and the discontinuity of the discourses which characterize our *Lebenswelt* – the world of meanings, emotions and experiences. To describe the city in this context is the task of this chapter.

The thesis of this essay is that this other city wasn't always there, but has its own history and came into being at a historically identifiable place and time. And that it will one day cease to exist again – overtaken by yet another way of building and thinking about population centres. I choose to formulate the subject which I examine here as visual discourse: visual, in that the contents of the 'other city' cannot be expressed solely in language and realize themselves more as feelings or emotionally charged images, and discourse, in that they do not lie in the inaccessible realm of the individual's psyche, but rather are formulated in a specific public form. Furthermore, like the discourses described by Foucault, they lack any intentional subject and result from an almost anarchical interplay of diverse elements, which is created and recreated by every participant.

For an analysis of this discourse a lens is required through which we can examine the development of mental images of the modern city. Within existing historical research there is a widespread belief that advertising represents an essential part of the modern city, whose appearance is fundamentally influenced by it.[2] The development of advertising is therefore seen in connection with the process of urbanization in the late nineteenth century and is considered to be both the result of the growth of complex patterns of communication in modern life and a link between manufacturers and consumers in an increasingly anonymous economic communication process.[3] However, this does not entirely explain why advertising in Germany since the 1890s has been mainly conceived of as visual. For the question then arises: is the order in which this model of explanation arranges its separate elements at all convincing? The model starts out from the assumption that a large structure – 'city' – is subject to a general tendency to change, and further supposes that the individual elements of this development are the consequences of a meta-development which is usually referred to as the process of modernization. I ask how this fundamental supposition would change if cultural rather than social models of the history of advertising were used as a basis of analysis, and what role in the phenomenological genesis of the city might eventually be attributed to advertising if it were no longer seen purely as a phenomenon of structurally oriented city history.

This conception of the city, which is the foundation of my argument, assumes that structural concepts cannot encompass both the mental and the emotional aspects of urban life. For some years the study of the city has been a key component of the social sciences, and with significant research results.[4] More recently, however, the 'new cultural history' has increasingly addressed the topic of urbanization. It regards the city as a paradigm of the transition from the order of the symbols of everyday feudal life, to the early bourgeois world of the sixteenth and seventeenth centuries, and finally to a place of cultural modernization in the nineteenth and twentieth centuries. While the historical approach concentrates primarily on the intramunicipal distribution of power – the rise of the bourgeois and later the proletarian desire for emancipation – the cultural approach focuses on orders of symbols and systems of representation. Although these transitions of urban life – the distribution of power and the orders of symbols and systems of representation – are in fact linked to social change, in the long term they result in a replacement of the traditional conception of estates and classes by new ways of life and of thinking. Therefore it is not surprising that the definition of the word 'city' is subject to change.

One of the most interesting definitions – and one which will allow us to see the history of advertising in a new light – interprets the city as a text, taking into account the linguistic turn of cultural studies. Manfred Smuda summarized this as follows: 'The city is a discourse, a language, a form of writing, and whoever is moving in it is a kind of reader (Roland Barthes); it is a complex fabric of texts (Michel de Certeau), a palimpsest (W. Sharpe and L. Wollock), and like a literary text it has as many interpretations as it has readers.'[5] The modern city works like a system of signs; its individual elements are symbols that refer to meanings. The modern person is accustomed to reading and interpreting these signs without difficulty, and easily finds a way through the world. However, the question remains: how did this world of signs and symbols, this text, emerge, and what role did advertising, an essential and integral part of the cultural sphere of the city, play in this process?

In short, I propose developing a specifically modern definition of the term 'city', using advertising as a key part of a visual urban discourse. To address this question effectively, I must consider how advertising has developed, what interfaces existed between it and the city, what effects advertising had on the city and the city on advertising, and how opening up a new communication space has affected modern life. I have chosen to base the development of this argument on an analysis of the most important German advertising journals.

Sources and methods

Although professional advertising journals remain largely ignored as historical sources, they contain a vast quantity of material relevant to a number of subjects. Conceived of as periodicals of the various professional advertising organizations, they promoted the viewpoint of the advertising managers. Their articles, which were frequently only short statements, offered reports on advertising experiences, commented on innovations or political events or judged state attempts to support or hinder the advertising industry. Innovative advertising strategies which had been introduced and failed were favourite targets of critical articles. These commentaries thus provided a means by which the advertisers could read evaluations of their work. Like newspaper articles, these texts referred almost exclusively to current problems, and, unlike scholarly literature, were not meant for posterity. They communicate in a direct and frank way, offering good insights into the development of the advertising industry in general and the advertising manager in particular.

Die Reklame, the first professional German journal devoted to advertising, was founded and published by advertising manager Robert Exner, one of the most important organizers of the industry during its early period. *Die Reklame* was published only from 1891 to 1900, and new magazines soon developed; every branch of the profession and professional organization produced its own journal. In German, it should be noted, there are several different words for 'advertisement', but only two of these concern us here: *Reklame* and *Werbung*. Although nearly synonymous, they have somewhat different connotations. *Reklame* suggests an announcement or proclamation, while *Werbung* implies an emphasis on a thing or product and suggests something 'solicited' or 'recruited' as well as 'advertised'. One can, for example, solicit (*werben*) goods or recruit (*werben*) a soldier. At the turn of the century, *Werbung* replaced *Reklame* as the professional term for advertising; this change came about because of new advertising strategies which will be discussed below.

From the enormous and, until now, largely ignored official press, I have chosen three journals which represent the national association of advertising professionals to use as a basis for this essay. I have already mentioned *Die Reklame*. The second of these, *Propaganda*, is, after *Die Reklame*, the most important source for the early modern period of advertising history. Produced weekly in its own Berlin publishing house by the Bund der Industriellen (association of industrialists), *Propaganda*, the central organ of advertising before the amalgamation of the various professions related to advertising, appeared between 1898 and 1901 in three volumes and was dedicated to publicity, advertising and posters. Like *Die Reklame*, *Propaganda* had as its managing editor the advertising expert Robert Exner.

Not until a year after the government's 1908 attempt to enact a law which would impose a tax on advertisements did some of the managing editors form a special interest. Founding firms, among them Knorr, Maggi, Sunlight, Oetker and Kathreiner,[6] established their own specialist journal, *Die Mitteilungen des Verbandes der Reklamefachleute* (*Proceedings of the Association of Advertising Professionals*), which became the most important advertising journal in Germany. From January 1909 to February 1919, it was produced at the publishing house of Franck & Lang in Berlin, and from 1922 to 1933 continued to be published under the title *Die Reklame: Zeitschrift des Vereins deutscher Reklamefachleute* (*The Advertisement: Journal of the Association of Advertising Professionals*). Because members of the association received the periodical free of charge, it circulated widely. After the rise to power

3.1   First artifical light, then the illuminated advertisement conquered the city. Friedrichstraße in Berlin, 1909

Source: *Mitteilungen des Verbandes der Reklamefachleute* (July 1914), 253

in 1933 of the National Socialists, the journal was renamed *Die deutsche Werbung* (*German Advertising*) and was printed under that title from December 1933 until 1943. Using these sources, I intend to demonstrate how the terms 'advertising' and 'city' are semantically related and what conclusions we can draw from their relationship.

The development of advertising

In 1897, advertising expert William Roland compared the structure of an advertisement to that of a modern house. He felt that, while architects attached importance to a well-proportioned, aesthetically balanced façade, with flat as well as protruding ornaments, the advertisements of the time were visually unbalanced and composed of elements which did not work together to form a coherent whole.[7] Behind these remarks is hidden not only criticism of a lack of professionalism in advertising, but also of a certain self-conception typical of the publicity specialists of the period.[8] These specialists focused on the advertisement itself and on the logical layout of the specific elements, which were supposed to come

3.2   Advertising tried early on to evoke new possible meanings, playing with the imagination of its recipients. 'What is happening? Half and Half.' Advertising for a liqueur

Source: *Propaganda* (3 May 1900), 253–4

together as a well-rounded, finished work. Their ideas were rooted in the visual arts, which is hardly surprising, since the advertising experts of this decade regarded themselves as artists. Moreover, as specialized categories within advertising had not yet been developed, nor did specific training for them yet exist, visual artists often took over the overall planning and implementation of an advertising campaign.[9]

It is telling that while a number of fully trained artists earned their living as graphic designers,[10] advertising managers who deliberately turned to a career in advertising from as early as the 1890s attribute this choice, in their memoirs, to visual impressions. Max Poculla, for example, credited his choice of career to his childhood memory of the nameplate of his father's firm, while Otto Büsser ascribed his professional interest in advertising to the strong impact which a poster had on him as a child: the poster, printed for the 1896 industrial exhibition in Berlin, portrayed a fist as a hammer.[11] These advertising artists thus support the idea that an aestheticization of advertising took place at the end of the nineteenth century. Aestheticization does not necessarily imply an emphasis on the artistically beautiful, but rather an increasing stress on perception as the most critical link between the perceiver and the surrounding world.

This approach soon changed. In a way that was reflected in other fields, the perceiver, and not the subject of the advertisement, became the centre of attention. Advertising discovered the consumers,[12] and they and their perceptions of advertisements became central elements in the professional discussion of advertising. Several years earlier, a similar development had begun in the field of art: pointillism transferred to the viewer the responsibility for creating a coherent image from the individual elements of the picture. Around the turn of the century parallel developments also occurred in the sciences in the form of increased focus on psychological concepts, which now more and more replaced the pure aestheticism of the *fin de siècle*. The advertising specialists now shifted their attention to the interaction of individual elements in advertising.[13] Advertising was meant to convey a message; the design of the advertisement itself became the means and not the end of this task. However self-evident this notion may appear to us today, little attention was paid to it in the process of aestheticizing advertising.

These two concepts of advertising met at a point where the perception of the advertising comes to the fore. We must not forget that throughout the aestheticization process, the appeal of advertising was of very great importance, although at that time one focused primarily on the design format of the advertisement. The synthesis of these approaches achieved something which was decisive for the development of the modern city. The first generation of advertisers, who still regarded themselves as artists, converted the city into one big art exhibition. They brought art into the streets and freed it from the chains of the nineteenth-century tendency to immure art in a museum. Thus, they expanded the role of art in everyday life, a change which was to become significant in the twentieth century.[14]

The next generation, who regarded themselves as psychologists, continued to build on this base. To them, the world appeared as a jungle of images, through which each individual had to find a way, and their aim was to erect guideposts through this jungle. They altered the city, the true field of orientation of a modern person, so that it became a signifier, loaded with symbolic meaning. Ideally, they had but one target: the universal interpretation of the modern city as a symbol representing the exchange of money and of products. They contributed considerably to the metamorphosis of the city into a text which one had to learn to read in order to be able to move through it. Even in the 1920s, when an economic approach to advertising started to succeed, this development remained fundamentally the same. The advertising expert became an

3.3 The *Litfaßsäule*, or advertising pillar, in Berlin in the early twentieth century

Source: *Mitteilungen des Verbandes der Reklamefachleute* (1915), 212

economist who, increasingly, purchased the creative elements of his occupation. His role now consisted primarily of determining the viability of marketing processes – their value was measured by economic success – and implementing them.[15]

Up to this point, advertising had established itself as a part of modern visual clutter; it attempted to catch the eye, but only for a moment. In this respect, advertising was not only the result of, but also an important factor in, the process of urban moderation. The specific interests of advertising agencies combined with the tendency to aestheticize and psychologize, which was a hallmark of the time, to create a densely packed array of cultural symbols or psychological triggers, which transformed the city into a text. This explains why advertising in Germany since the 1890s turned increasingly to visual forms: such forms corresponded more closely to these two basic intentions and allowed the formulation of short and easily remembered signs. The people living in the cities thus became *flâneurs*, strolling through this new textual world. This and the numerous – and interconnected – potential interpretations of these symbols still distinguish the city today.

Early advertising strategies and anonymity in cities

The city is not the preferred topic of textual discourse in advertising, but it is the place where modern advertising arose. The oversized metropolis made necessary changes in forms of communication, in order to bridge the gaps created by the new anonymity in the exchange of goods. The cities symbolized the end of the corner shops, in which the clerk knew the customer and where familiarity sufficed to guarantee a loan. In response to the demands of the growing market, brand-name articles, which promised a steady quality no matter when or where they were bought, were emerging in the late nineteenth century. Together with department stores, brand-name articles were the first systematically advertised products, competing for the favour of customers. The owners of these companies took over the development of advertising campaigns, which until then had had neither long-term plans nor any systematic campaigns.

An excellent example for the first period of modern advertising in Germany is Karl August Lingner. He acquired a recipe for an antibacterial lotion which could be used as a mouthwash, and marketed the product under the name 'Odol' (the name was created from the Greek word *odontos*, 'teeth', and the Latin *oleum*, 'oil').[16] However, Lingner not only had to cope with establishing a new product on the market, but also with the reluctance of his contemporaries to see that there was a problem requiring daily addressing – mouth care – and that it was worth spending money on.[17] In order to explain the advantages of Odol and to establish the product within the official discourse, a new advertising technique was necessary. Lingner chose elaborate visual campaigns to solve his problem; this approach was so successful that 'Odol' quickly became a synonym for mouthwash in Germany and remains so in the early twenty-first century.

Brand-name articles and department stores became the *raison d'être* of systematic advertising as a new communication form.[18] Systematic advertising reached the inhabitants of the increasingly anonymous cities, and was created by experts who lived and worked in them. Advertising was at first merely a medium, used solely to convey information, which arose in a period of increasing product innovation. New goods, like Odol, required a forum in which their manufacturers could tout their advantages. This was advertising. With the shift from a primarily textual form to one with a more visual focus, something crucial happened to advertising in the 1890s: the advertising managers could now reach consumers faster with pictorial messages. For them, advertisements were a means of manipulating the consumer and for a long time this theory has shaped the arguments of the critics of advertis-

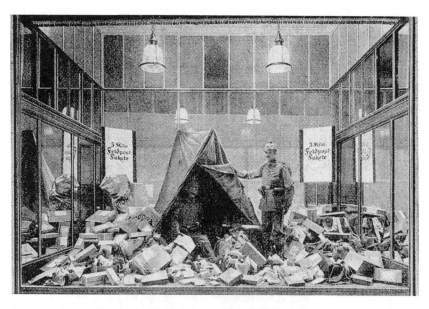

3.4 During the First World War the language of advertising was reworked in order to make it fit contemporary circumstances

Source: *Mitteilungen des Verbandes der Reklamefachleute* (December 1914), 355

ing. If, on the other hand, one insists that perception and reception are creative acts,[19] then it follows that advertising pictures do not create a means of manipulation, but rather propose images which can be attributed to a product and are added to the consumer's conception of the world. In the big cities, advertising deliberately created a gap between the literal message and the idea it carried for the reader, which conveyed an idea even though the language used often lacked clarity. Thus the conception of the city as a text must be refined, taking into account the presence of advertising as one of the most important means of communicating specific elements or themes of that text.

That the cities in particular were the site of the development of this characteristically modern level of meaning is made clearer by the still noticeable differences between city and country in early advertising. Throughout the twentieth century, radio, television and film, not to mention universal school education, have erased, or at least reduced, these psychological, social and cultural differences. At the beginning of the twentieth century, when the period of urbanization in Germany was at its height, but the bulk of the nation remained agrarian in character, the difference between the urban and rural areas was still evident. As

3.5 Advertising becomes architecture. A 12-metre-high advertising tower in Budapest with four stores

Source: *Die Reklame* (1927), 19

late as 1928, E. Saloman wrote, 'What will be needed in the cities is not yet suitable for the countryside.'[20] Advertising had not yet conquered the space completely, so it could not impose itself everywhere. For a long time, advertising was seen as an urban accessory, even though, as many contemporary photographs show, it still had to adapt to the limits of the surrounding space even as it evidenced an inclination to monopolize all that was available.

As the city became more and more clearly the 'natural' place of advertising, it developed into a genuine urban phenomenon, literally as well as figuratively. Advertising itself became a building, a structure. Special advertising buildings were put up at trade fairs and urban exhibitions, but, more importantly, these could also be found in cityscapes. In the 1920s one building twelve metres high stood in the Hungarian capital of Budapest; it offered space for four shops to advertise and each advertisement in turn was brightly lit from behind (Figure 3.6).[21] In the textual discourse as well, advertising was described in terms of the city and its architecture. For example, in a review, the work of advertising graphic designer Willy Willrab was referred to as 'poster architecture', because he painted in a reduced, constricted style.[22] And as we have already seen, as early as 1897 Wilhelm Roland compared a well-designed advertisement to a well-proportioned building.[23]

In summary, brand-name articles were the first products to be systematically advertised in a modern form. These items were designed for a large and anonymous market and required advertising as a means of drawing attention to themselves. The development of department stores proceeded similarly. They began as a response to the consumer culture[24] of cities in the last quarter of the nineteenth century. For them, advertising was a communications tool. Because they were created for an urban audience, it is hardly surprising that the urban lifestyle determined the stores' early character, both in the design of advertisements and in the way it was discussed in the advertising discourse. Not until the First World War did the situation change.

Taking over the city

Modern advertising was developed in the cities, but then advertising took over the cities, spreading over the entire urban space (Figure 3.5). The professional discourse early discovered the impact of advertising on the appearance of cities.[25] At first older methods of promoting goods were transformed to change the city into an advertising surface. As early as 1898 we read in *Propaganda*

> that the content of shop-windows (*Schaufensterauslagen*) establishes the character of a city almost as much as do the streets and the architectural style of the houses. Architects plan for the largest possible display-windows when drawing their floorplans. Shops are willing to reduce their floor space in order to have high and spacious display-windows. Large sums of money are set aside to defray the cost of the window decoration, and a skilful window-dresser is not merely sought after and highly paid, but actually indispensable.[26]

With the display windows, advertising still remained in its own space, the space of consumption. But the transparency of these windows pushed their contents into the urban space outside the commercial realm. During the second decade of the twentieth century, a dispute arose between those advertisers who held to an older, more aestheticized viewpoint and the newer generation, who aggressively tried to conquer urban space. Little by little those voices that had demanded that the placement of the display windows into the façades be visually pleasing faded away.[27] With the new glass architecture of the International Style, the city changed into a single enormous display window of the urban dynamic. The need for a display window now increasingly determined the architecture, whereas before the architecture had determined the presentation of the merchandise. Architecture became subordinate to advertising; the sole criterion by which the advertiser judged architecture was its ability to represent a good background for a striking display. A broad discourse in professional journals about the design of façades established their central place in advertising thought.[28]

The first visible sign of this development was the department store, which became a multi-media advertisement. The architecture, the clerk, the running of the elevator, the presentation of the merchandise – all became elements of this advertisement.[29] In 1918, the Berlin advertising expert Alfred Wiener wrote a long essay on the 'Werbekraft des Geschäftshausbaues' ('Advertising Power of Office Building Architecture').[30] He subordinated all the interior design and architecture of the building to the primacy of advertising. The building represented – and advertised for – the commercial enterprise within. Wiener even held the opinion that this was more important then conventional advertising, because consumers would prefer to patronize a shop that had a striking design. He designed company headquarters as well, but department stores dominated his interest. The arrangement of the lights, the interior design, the technical equipment, the façade – everything was seen as an advertising device and their form regarded from an advertising perspective. Architecture and city planning lost their independence: these ceased to be autonomous arts, and thus buildings became more nearly purely functional, subordinate to the needs of advertising and selling.

Department stores and display windows were only the first step in the process of the takeover of the whole city by advertising. Between 1890 and 1930, an abundance of innovative advertising techniques and ideas flooded German cities. Although much was copied from American cities, before the turn of the century London, and especially Paris, served as models for advertising strategies. France was regarded as an example for artistically inspired advertising and its theatre and coffee-shop posters were much admired. In France, the roofs and the night were conquered much earlier than they were in Germany: large billboards were set up atop buildings and were illuminated as darkness fell.[31] In the period of aestheticized advertising, during the 1890s and early 1900s, as described above, French posters were the undisputed models. This situation changed as advertising became increasingly psychologically and economically focused, and from approximately 1910 onward, the United States became the central source for the discussion of innovations in the advertising industry.

The United States was a distorted image as well as a model – not only on the question of city planning, but also advertising. Germans inter-

3.6   The highest illuminated advertisement in Europe in the late 1920s on top of the White House of Rotterdam

Source: As for Figure 3.5

ested in the field admired the willingness of American society to acknowledge advertising as an integral part of cities, but at the same time emphasized, especially in nationalistic circles, what they believed to be the superior taste and design of the German product.[32] Shortly before the First World War the mood changed. S. Mandelbaum reported on a journey to New York that from all corners and walls 'garish posters and fiery lighted signs' 'roar at' passers-by.[33] Nevertheless the United States led the way, particularly during the 1920s. Those advertising experts who didn't want to miss out on current trends began to adopt the organization and design concepts of American advertising departments in the early days of the Weimar Republic.

One such concept was the increased illumination of advertising spaces (see Figure 3.7). After the display windows and the department stores, lights were the next step in advertising's conquest of the city. Even more powerful than street lighting, advertising lighting promoted a change in the perception of the city.[34] There was nothing more fascinating for many contemporaries than the lighting-up of the night.[35] Advertising designer Fred Hodd, for example, felt as if 'someone is writing flaming letters in the night sky'.[36]

A conflict developed for the control of the night. The advertising industry united in the struggle for the distribution of nightly city illumination. 'Lightfests' were carried out as 'advertising campaigns' in many German cities in the 1920s.[37] 'Display window lighting campaigns' – the military vocabulary is a sign of the prevailing mood – were performed in over seventy cities. The highlight of these campaigns was an event that occurred between 13 and 16 October 1928, in Berlin, sponsored jointly by Berlin businesses, labour and the local authorities.[38]

The aim was 'to place Berlin among the other major cities of the world – Paris, London, New York – all of which owed a large part of their splendour and reputation the world over to their careful attention to illumination'.[39] The nationalistic fighting spirit, which had frequently inspired advertising managers, allowed advertising, which like no other medium sprang from an individualistic principle of competition, to assume a greater role. What was good for advertising was good for the whole of society.

Once the night was conquered, there were no limits to the expansion of advertising over the entire urban space. As early as the end of the nineteenth century vehicles were employed:[40] in Hanover, before the turn of the century, the chocolate company B. Sprengel and Co. was using a horsecart, illuminated at night, to advertise.[41] Columns surmounted by clocks grabbed the attention of those who were checking the time, and so the *flâneurs* had to 'pay' for their use of the public clocks with a glance at the advertisements posted on them. These columns were particularly prevalent in public places during the 1920s, when two Prussian provinces led the rest of Germany: in the Rhineland, thirty such clocks existed, and in Westphalia twenty of them were to be found in busy places.[42]

In addition to these successful innovations, most of which can still be found in cities at the start of the twenty-first century and whose absence we can scarcely imagine, there were other attempts, whose poor taste was readily criticized by contemporaries. A boundary which advertising could not seem to cross was the human body. Admittedly there were many sandwichmen who, wearing a pair of placards, carried a message through the streets. The body itself, however, could never be conquered as an advertising medium. In 1899, a clothing manufacturer in Nuremberg hired a man to visit coffee-shops and restaurants, where he did nothing but sit around and display the message 'G. Symander, Jacobhofstrasse 7', which was written on his shaven scalp. This technique, however, met with immediate condemnation from the advertising association.[43]

Besides the obvious – that is, the visible – devices used to transform the city into an advertising surface, there were subtler methods by which it could spread its influence. Using the example of Odol (another excellent example is Tempo, the dominant brand of facial tissue), I have demonstrated the ways in which an associative relationship between the consumption of goods and everyday life was established. In addition, the significance of the use of language as a symbol fraught with more than semantic content soon became clear to the advertising experts.[44] Together with the above-mentioned visual forms of advertising, language itself became a visual design element of increasing importance. One example is Hermann Schmidt, who shortly before the First World War developed a campaign for Manoli cigarettes, which was designed by such well-known artists as Lucien Bernhard or Etzel. By the end of the campaign, only the letter 'M' in a circle was needed to symbolize the product. One glance, caught in passing, was just enough to convey a message to the city-dweller, always on the move. The reduction of the message to an emblematic doubling dissolved the identity of the product in accordance with the theory of alienation – a theory which also influenced modern art.

The influence of advertising thus extended over the whole city as a physical living space as well as over the psychological city in the individual's consciousness, to mental images dealing with and thinking about urban space. It determined both architecture and city planning. Even the sky became a medium for advertising messages, leaving the city-dweller no space without advertising and its related messages.[45] The city became an advertising surface, on which advertising experts engraved content, design and a goal-oriented aesthetic. Inevitably, this led to conflicts with other social groups, who saw the city as their living space too, as well as the advertising expert's canvas, and wanted to fill it with their own symbols and meanings.

The struggle for the city

The spread of advertising across the city went beyond the covering of increasing amounts of public space with posters, and so conflicts broke out among different factions. The domination of public space mattered so much that each tried to impose its specific view of reality; the conflicts centred on different ways of creating and communicating. In respect of the influence of these conflicts on the development of advertising, the most important were those between the advertising industry and the local government on one hand, and between the advertising industry and the designers of the posters of political parties on the other.

Municipal government appeared in the advertising discourse most frequently as an enemy, portrayed as a limiting force, hindering the free exchange of goods and advertisements. This is particularly apparent during the second decade of the twentieth century, for until the turn of the century visual advertising in Germany had not yet advanced so far as to be a central element in the cityscape. The first years of the new century were shaped by a rapid growth in advertising revenue and the sudden spread of posters. The Heimatschutz, a movement for the protection of the homeland, became increasingly prominent. Adherents of this movement regarded advertising as a disturbing contaminant of the visual environment.[46] The debate escalated before the outbreak of the First World War, after the first Preußisches Verunstaltungsgesetz (Prussian Defacement Law) was enacted in 1907. Caught in the cross-fire, city administrations tried to formulate a separate position which would clearly establish their own claim to power. The local authorities, especially in Prussia, held that public space should be subject to their jurisdiction. Special interest groups would not be allowed to compete without governmental mediation. The imposition of associative symbols in public space was first a political, and later a legal, dispute. House walls, public transportation[47] and pavements became objects of public contention.[48]

The proposed new street regulations, which were announced by the Berlin authorities in the spring of 1914, demonstrate this. The proposal met with the resolute opposition of the advertising experts. On 11 March, lawyer and advertising expert Dr Höniger gave a lecture to the members of the Verein der Reklamefachleute (Association of Advertising Managers), in which, amidst a storm of applause, he critically examined the proposed regulations.[49] In the eyes of the administration, advertising was an obstruction of traffic and its further development ought therefore to be regulated. The state, with legislative authority, insisted on its right to censor anything posted in a public space. National and local administrations were both trying to gain control of the public space. This the advertising manager could not accept. Thus the law which sought to require official approval for all public advertisements met with sharp disapproval. In the end, the conflict led to a verbal confrontation with the national authorities. Höniger wrote, 'Advertising has shown its worth and yet the police try to suppress it.'[50]

Intervention in the activities of the advertising industry was especially heavy during the First World War.[51] The cinema was of particular concern, because as a new medium it used an aggressive, eye-catching strategy. The authorities wanted to use their regulatory power, because the darkened movie theatres were regarded as places of moral excesses. In June of 1917, a regulation was passed which affected all posters advertising a public performance. Cinemas were already legally required to publish their programmes. Posters depicting crime, accidents, violence and other morally objectionable scenes were no longer permitted to be hung where they would be visible from the street. At that early point in cinema history, movies portrayed the sensational rather than the ordinary, and thus the proscription amounted to a ban on visual advertising of films. The high-minded national advertising association, whose members were only infrequently entrusted with movie publicity, took care not to become involved in advising on the suitability of posters, leaving this task to civil servants.[52] Again this shows the conflict over competence in assessing and evaluating advertising. Movie posters were often produced by artists and used expressionist stylistic devices much earlier than did commercial advertising.

The question of expressionist elements in advertising graphics leads us to the debate within the advertising industry over political posters. A sign of both the consolidation of the advertising industry on the one hand and the fragility of its pretension to power on the other was the increase in the number of arguments between advertising managers and the artists who designed political posters after the revolution of November 1918. The chaos caused by the decline of the Hohenzollern monarchy and Wilhelmine Germany was accompanied by the formation of a great number of political splinter groups and newly founded, more or less radical, parties. Modern artists, who devoted themselves to the building of a better, more socially balanced culture, used expressionist stylistic elements to represent their protests against war, violence and social injustice. In comparison to that, advertising posters, even those which covered entire house walls, appeared gentle and harmless. Therefore it is not surprising that the advertising managers, who had asserted themselves throughout a two-decade-long debate in order to be able to impose their own signs and symbols on the city, crusaded against these loud rivals, who attracted more attention in the streets.[53] This debate within the political sphere was foreshadowed during the First World War, when commodity advertising was forced on the defensive because of a lack of sponsors. Commercial advertising then had to compete with government posters soliciting war loans.[54] During the revolution of November 1918, this problem increased to the point where, at highly visible urban locations, sign-posters queued to stick up their posters over those which were freshly hung up. In such a competition, he advertises best who advertises last.[55]

In the conflict over party-political posters two positions can be distinguished. One supported the demands for aesthetics and advertising subtlety and mounted a public attack on party-political posters,[56] while a second integrated the methods of expressionism into their advertise-

ments and tried to be as loud as radical political propaganda. On 7
April 1919, Berlin advertising lawyer (*Werbeanwalt*, one of the contemporary terms for an advertising manager) Karl Jahnke gave a lecture,
later published in *Die Reklame* and bearing the significant title 'Berlin
Poster Terrorism', to the *Verband deutscher Illustratoreen* (Association
of German Illustrators).[57] He explained:

> The freedom of verbal and visual expression caused by the *coup* of
> November 9th has produced for us, who until now have been too
> regulated and censored by the police, a lack of restraint in public
> advertising which cannot be called anything but a rape of good
> taste. This *en masse* rise of bad taste forces us to an energetic
> counterattack. Treating this moral decadence as a minor matter
> and allowing it to go unchallenged confirms and makes permanent
> our reputation abroad as a nation of barbarians. Every person of
> taste, and especially the foreigner, when confronted step after step
> by grimaces of fright and horror, will find it not difficult to believe
> that the German people have no culture. These at times horrifying
> products of graphic arts and crafts are not excusable, even by the
> after-effects of the insanity of war.[58]

These unambiguous words were directed against the political posters,
which used vociferous means to attract attention. In contrast to the
creators of these posters, Jahnke, who belonged to the older generation
of advertising managers, emphasized the significance of good taste and
clear ideas. Aesthetics and sensitivity to advertising psychology were his
criteria. This recalls my earlier analysis of the formative period of visual
advertising, to whose ideals Jahnke felt indebted. To survive after the
war, however, many advertising managers had to use the new methods.
Expressionism gradually became a common means of communication
in posters and in the producing of advertising films, one of the new
media of the 1920s.[59] The advertising industry won the debate by using
the enemy's stylistic devices and grafting its principles onto their own
work. This strategy worked for a long time and the advertising industry
grew as never before during the Weimar Republic. In 1933, however, it
failed as National Socialism forced the entire German economy to
conform to its standards.

The end of unregulated advertising under the National Socialist dictatorship

Advertising was a fundamental component of the visual discourse which
shaped and reshaped the lives of the people of the modern age. It
created a space where associative messages could be communicated. For
a long time, advertising managers made the mistake of believing that

they could determine how advertising messages would be perceived. At the start of the twenty-first century, differences in perception are the main concern of the professional debate, and perception is often described as an act by an individual, who receives the communication offered by the advertisement. The time when the constant repetition of a word or an emblem was used to turn the consumer into a buying machine is largely over. In the new paradigm, which also informs this essay, an advertisement becomes an attempt to offer the individual different types of lifestyles and to construct his own from them.

The conclusiveness of this new paradigm was proven in Germany when the first period of the visual discourse of advertising came to an end. In 1933, another group tried to acquire power over advertising and thus to direct the life of the people. At first, the National Socialists didn't recognise the rivalry of different *Konnotationsysteme* (symbolic codes), and for a long time Nazi emblems and even pictures of Hitler were used for advertising campaigns. On 19 May 1933, a 'law for the protection of national symbols' was enacted which forbade the use of National Socialist brown shirts or other Nazi symbols in advertisements. In 1933, National Socialist officials quickly succeeded in dissolving the German association of advertising managers, abolishing the magazines cited in this essay and replacing them with publications which toed the party line. The law of 19 May is astonishing in that the management of the new association wanted to abolish economic competition and to establish nationalistic advertising. A subordination of advertising symbols to the National Socialist Party symbols would have been sufficient to make this objective clear. By preventing this, the law reflects the contradictions between the two different *Konnotationsysteme*, whose merging seemed to the Nazis to endanger the dominance of their visual political discourse.

The Nationalsozialistische Reichsverband Deutscher Werbefachleute (National Socialist Advertising Association) invented no new advertising strategy. It manipulated the advertising industry and exploited the weaknesses of the advertising discourse, but the Association was dealing with an industry whose growth had been stunted. At the beginning of the 1930s at the latest – rather late in comparison with the United States – rationalization and professionalization had made the advertising industry vulnerable to what followed. In 1933, advertising managers were responsible for losing the debate against the National Socialist Party. They lost not because they had created a place for visual discourse which the Nazis could occupy, but because they persisted in the illusion that they could not only prescribe the discourse but also determine its meaning.

National Socialist propaganda was deluded in this way as well, but its resources were greater. Many of the advertising managers privately admired National Socialism, because it seemed to achieve what they had tried to do for many years: to manipulate an anonymous mass of people through advertising.[60] They succumbed to the temptation of power, but in the end added only to their own discredit complicity with the regime. Their mistake was not to attribute a measure of independence to the recipients of the advertising discourse but to seek to explain the rules of perception, be it by improving advertising psychology or by more rigorously organizing their own work. Now they were involved in a crime which not only tried to restrict freedom of individual perception but whose goal was the destruction of mankind. As they began to realize what they had done, all that remained to them were half-hearted justifications.

From *flâneur* to patchworker

As early as the middle of the nineteenth century advertising activity began to increase, but it was not until the 1890s that visual advertising, whose beginnings can be found in France, became dominant. At the same time professionalization began. Specialist journals were founded, which provided a commentary on and analysis of the methods of advertising. In them one can see the development of advertising from the aesthetic period to the psychological and finally to the economic. The last of these began in the 1920s and was not replaced by cultural self-perception until the 1980s.[61] The change from a focus on the product during the aesthetic period to a focus on the consumer during the psychological one was accompanied by the embodiment of advertising as a visual sign in everyday life. The site of this development was the city. In the interplay of urban structures and new advertising strategies a system of symbols developed which made the city into a stage, for these signs referred to more than their literal content. Advertising rendered visual the meanings which a product could have. This *Konnotationsystem* was developed on the basis of newly created brand-name products and department stores. Because many of the innovations could not readily explain themselves to the public – as the example of Odol has shown – a forum was created which made it possible to construct symbolic meanings and to offer them to the public. The city was equipped with advertising signs, and the consumer became a *flâneur* in a world of goods, which constantly offered new styles of life.

   This essay is based on the notion that advertising cannot determine the perception of its message, although advertising managers have always dreamed of doing so. I have used a contrasting model, one that takes into account how advertising is received; that is the underlying, though unproven, assumption. The visualization of advertising, in connection with an assumption of appropriately creative work, led to the establishment of a new space where associations could be communicated publicly. This phenomenon is still to a large extent unexplored and can only be touched upon here. It has the fleetingness of images and lacks the seeming clarity of words, and therefore is here denoted a 'visual discourse', a term containing within it both the formulation of the content of the visual advertisements and their reception by each consumer. From this process emerges a picture of the individual's *Lebenswelt*, composed of associations which can always be combined anew. By constantly offering new images, advertising compels city-dwellers to orient themselves actively, because the multitude of impressions makes it impossible for there to be only one effect. From a variety of associations and personal processes, a new, individual, *Lebenswelt* is formed. Because of its super-abundance and its visual qualities, which must continually fight the many layers of meaning of the images, advertising contributes fundamentally to the development of the modern city in which we live. In this regard, the city is a text, which daily offers different concepts of life; the city-dweller moves among these constantly. When this system is established, which is happening now, when the city-dweller can interpret the signs of the environment and has learned to decipher the urban text and to script his or her own role, then the internal and external aspects of this visual discourse, which is a part of a larger urban discourse and of the mental orientation of the individual, begin to blur. The mental model of the city begins to become the place where we live. This is a world that is created by the combination of elements of the different possible meanings of the visual discourse. To orient ourselves in a constantly changing world we must perpetually combine these anew. The passive *flâneur* of the nineteenth century has become an active patchworker. Advertising is one of the paradigms by which this fundamental urban development can be demonstrated.

Notes

1. For a fuller definition of this term, see Edmund Husserl, *Die Krisis der europäischen Wissenschaften und die transzendentale Phänomenologie* (Hamburg: Felix Meiner Verlag, 1982).
2. For the history of advertising see Roland Marchand, *Advertising the American Dream: Making Way for Modernity 1920–1940* (Berkeley and Los Angeles: University of California Press, 1985); Thomas Richards, *The Commodity Culture of Victorian England: Advertising as Spectacle, 1851–1914* (Stanford: Stanford University Press, 1990); Dirk Reinhardt, *Von der*

Reklame zum Marketing: Geschichte der Wirtschaftswerbung in Deutschland (Berlin: Akademie Verlag, 1993); Peter Borscheid and Clemens Wischermann (eds), *Bilderwelt des Alltags: Werbung in der Konsumgesellschaft des 19. und 20. Jahrhunderts.* Studien zur Geschichte des Alltags, vol. 3 (Stuttgart: Steiner, 1995); Stefan Haas, 'Die neue Welt der Bilder: Werbung und visuelle Kultur der Moderne', *Bilderwelt des Alltags,* 64–77.

3. For a new examination of consumption see John Brewer and Roy Porter (eds), *Consumption and the World of Goods* (London and New York, 1993).

4. See especially Richard Sennett, *The Conscience of the Eye: the Design and Social Life of Cities* (New York: Alfred A. Knopf, 1990); Ruth E. Mohrmann, 'Stadterfahrung und Mentalität', *Stadt und Verkehr im Industriezeitalter,* edited by Horst Matzerath (Cologne, Weimar and Vienna: Böhlau, 1996), 261–75.

5. Manfred Smuda, 'Vorwort', *Die Großstadt als 'Text',* edited by Manfred Smuda (Munich, 1992), 7.

6. Reinhardt, *Von der Reklame zum Marketing,* 129–35.

7. Wilhelm Roland, 'Die Aesthetik der Inserate', *Propaganda* 1 (1897–98): 3–9.

8. Stefan Haas, 'Psychologen, Künstler, Ökonomen: Das Selbstverständnis der Werbetreibenden zwischen Fin de Siècle und Nachkriegszeit', *Bilderwelt des Alltags: Werbung in der Konsumgesellschaft des 19. und 20. Jahrhunderts,* Studien zur Geschichte des Alltags, edited by Peter Borscheid and Clemens Wischermann, vol. 3 (Stuttgart: Steiner, 1995), 78–89.

9. For a discussion of the professionalization of advertising, see Carol Hilarius, 'Der Propaganda-Chef', *Mitteilungen des Verbandes der Reklamefachleute* 30 (June 1912), 25–6.

10. Max Poculla, '40 Jahre Reklamefachmann und wie ich zur Reklame kam', *Die Reklame* 2 (1931), 163–8.

11. Poculla, 163–5; Otto Büsser, 'Zwei Erlebnisse', *Die Reklame* 25 (1932), 222–223; A. E. Hörwater, 'Wiener Eindrücke', *Mitteilungen des Verbandes der Reklamefachleute* (1915), 38–9.

12. A. Klein, 'Über das Wesen der Reklame', *Mitteilungen des Verbandes der Reklamefachleute* 34 (October 1912), 17–19; Richard Heinrich, 'Wesen und Zweck der Reklame', *Mitteilungen des Verbandes der Reklamefachleute* 8/9 (September 1915), 243–7.

13. Bernhard Wities, 'Das Wirkungsprinzip in der Reklame: Eine psychologische Studie', *Zeitschrift für Philosophie und philosophische Kritik* 128 (1906), 138–54.

14. Kirk Varnedoe and Adam Gopnik, *High and Low: Modern Art and Popular Culture* (New York: The Museum of Modern Art, 1990).

15. Udo Siegfried Fessel, 'Erst einen Plan machen, dann ausführen', *Mitteilungen des Verbandes der Reklamefachleute* 45 (Oct. 1913): 333–4.

16. Henriette Väth-Hintz, *Odol: Reklame-Kunst um 1900* (Gießen: Anabas, 1985).

17. Oscar Becker, 'Zu Lingners Gedächtnis', *Mitteilungen des Verbandes der Reklamefachleute* (September 1916), 140f.

18. 'Die Weltmarke 4711', *Die Reklame* (1928), 538–42.

19. Martin Henatsch, *Die Entstehung des Plakates: Eine rezeptionsästhetische Untersuchung* (Hildesheim, Zürich and New York: Georg Olms Publishers, 1994).

20. E. Saloman, 'Das Dauerplakat', *Die Reklame* 21 (1928), 121–3.
21. 'Architektur von Reklamebauten', *Die Reklame* 20 (1927), 19.
22. Walter F. Schubert, 'Willy Willrab', *Die Reklame* 21 (1928), 543–6.
23. Roland, 'Die Aesthetik der Inserate', 3–4.
24. Gary Cross, *Time and Money: the Making of Consumer Culture* (London: Routledge, 1993); Daniel Miller, *Material Culture and Mass Consumption* (Oxford: Blackwell, 1987); Robert Fitzgerald, *Rowntree and the Marketing Revolution, 1862–1969* (Cambridge: Cambridge University Press, 1995).
25. 'Berliner Schaufenster', *Propaganda* 3 (1899–1900): 379–81.
26. 'Wert der Schaufensterdekoration [Bericht zu einer Anmerkung des Gewerblichen Ausschusses des Vereins für bürgerliche Interessen zu Krefeld]', *Propaganda* 2 (1898–99), 27.
27. Hans K. Kutschbach, 'Schaufenster', *Die Reklame* 117 (Oct. 1919): 234–8.
28. 'Schaufenster und Ladenfront', *Propaganda* 2 (1898–99): 28.
29. Hanns Kropf, 'Die Reklame des Kaufhauses', *Mitteilungen des Verbandes der Reklamefachleute* 45 (October 1913), 335–40.
30. Alfred Wiener, 'Die Werbekraft des Geschäftshausbaues', *Mitteilungen des Verbandes der Reklamefachleute* (1918), 183–5.
31. Fred Hood, 'Strassenreklame in Paris', *Propaganda* 3 (1899–1900), 325–7.
32. S. Mandelbaum, 'Die Reklame in New York', *Mitteilungen des Verbandes der Reklamefachleute* (April 1914), 139.
33. Ibid.
34. 'Elektrische Beleuchtung', *Propaganda* 3 (1899–1900): 416–17; Ingenieur Gerhardt (AEG): 'Die elektrische Lichtreklame', *Mitteilungen des Verbandes der Reklamefachleute* (July 1914), 252–4; 'Zweckmäbige Schaufensterbeleuchtung', *Mitteilungen des Verbandes der Reklamefachleute* (January 1914), 17–19; 'Eine neue Lichtecke am Kurfürstendamm Berlin', *Die Reklame* (1928), 678–9.
35. Hood, 'Strassenreklame in Paris', 325–7.
36. Ibid., 326.
37. L. Hamel, 'Berlin im Licht: Seine Aufgaben und Ziele', *Die Reklame* (1928), 588–9.
38. A. W. Blau, 'Berlin im Licht: ein mit kritischen Betrachtungen verbundener Bericht über die in der Zeit vom 13. bis 16. Oktober in Berlin stattgefundene Lichtveranstaltung', *Die Reklame* (1928), 795–800.
39. Hamel, 'Berlin im Licht', 588.
40. Gustav Sochaczewer, 'Die Verkehrsreklame und ihre Feinde', *Die Reklame* (1928), 680–81.
41. *Propaganda* 2 (1898–99), 41.
42. Gustav Sochaczewer, 'Uhrensäulen-Reklame', *Die Reklame* 21 (1928), 150–51.
43. *Propaganda* 2 (1898–99), 41.
44. Weidenmüller, 'Eine musterhafte Bearbeitung eines bäuerlichen Kundenkreises', *Mitteilungen des Verbandes der Reklamefachleute* (July 1914), 243–4.
45. John Clifford Savage, 'Die Himmelschrift', *Die Reklame* 20 (1927), 375–7.
46. Uwe Spiekermann, 'Elitenkampf in der Werbung', 126–49.

47. In 1899 a women's clothing shop in Berlin wanted to place a dressed-up mannequin in the local tram by paying the fare. The tram association rejected this request as an affront to their main service, a decision which the advertising managers criticized. 'Schaufenster und Ladenfront', *Propaganda* 3 (1899–1900), 381.

48. Dr jur. Eckstein, 'Das Recht zur Reklame an der Hausfassade', *Mitteilungen des Verbandes der Reklamefachleute* (July 1914), 241–3.

49. Max Hesse, 'Der Entwurf der neuen Berliner Straßenordnung und ihre Einwirkung auf die Reklame', *Mitteilungen des Verbandes der Reklamefachleute* (1914), 100–103.

50. Ibid., 103.

51. 'Berliner Werbearbeit in den Kriegsmonaten September und Oktober 1914', *Mitteilungen des Verbandes der Reklamefachleute* (October/November 1914), 319.

52. Walter Thielemann, 'Reklameplakate für öffentliche Schaustellungen', *Mitteilungen des Verbandes der Reklamefachleute* (1918), 43.

53. 'Die bunte Stadt', *Die Reklame* 112 (May 1919), 112.

54. Max Lang, 'Plakatierung', *Die Reklame* 112 (May 1919), 139–40.

55. Ibid.

56. Walter Heß, 'Die Kultur der Straße', *Die Reklame* 112 (May 1919), 136.

57. Karl Jahnke, 'Berliner Plakatterror', *Die Reklame* 112 (May 1919), 109–11.

58. Ibid., 109.

59. 'Der Werbefilm,' *Die Reklame* (June 1927); Karl Jahnke, 'Berliner Plakatterror', 109–11.

60. Probably the most famous example was Hans Domizlaff, one of the most influential advertising strategists of the 1920s.

61. Michael Schirner, *Werbung ist Kunst*. With an introduction by Hans Ulrich Reck (Munich: Klinkhardt and Biermann, 1988).

CHAPTER FOUR

The Advertising and Marketing of Consumer Goods in Eighteenth-Century London

Claire Walsh

This essay considers the advertising strategies of London shopkeepers in the eighteenth century, placing them within the context of other advertising techniques used at the time. It considers how consumer goods were advertised in newspapers, and questions whether newspaper advertising did in fact constitute the most significant means of marketing consumer goods in the late eighteenth century.

Traditionally, the growth of advertising in Britain has been located in the mid-nineteenth century with the expansion of newspaper distribution, a move towards the use of images in advertising and the application of colour lithography.[1] There has been a tendency to assume that before the mid-nineteenth century advertising played no role, that customers were not enticed to buy or informed about goods on sale. More recently, Neil McKendrick has attempted to shift the origins of consumer manipulation back to the late eighteenth century. Like the historians of the nineteenth century, McKendrick has focused on the use of newspaper advertising to support his argument, examining advertisements placed in the late eighteenth century by particular manufacturers selling on a large scale.[2] This, in conjunction with the manipulation of fashion trends, has been taken as evidence for a consumer revolution linked to the Industrial Revolution in the late eighteenth century, and in this and other studies newspaper advertising has been characterized as a particularly important and powerful force in the increase in consumption of goods and the creation of a consumer culture in Britain.[3]

However, an examination of retail methods and newspaper advertising throughout the eighteenth century rather than simply at its end reveals the limitations of these ideas. Newspaper advertising increased steadily from the mid-seventeenth century onwards, rather than peaking in a revolution at the end of the eighteenth century. At the same time, however, newspaper advertising had very little importance for the sale of domestic products, and hence cannot be held as an indicator of a consumer revolution. The insistence on the importance of newspaper advertisements as the main means of attracting consumers has prevented serious consideration of other forms of advertising and essentially uncritically applies an approach relevant to the nineteenth century to the very different retailing context of the eighteenth century. In addition, this over-emphasis on newspaper advertising in the eighteenth century has drawn attention away from the relationship between marketing goods in shops, urban culture, and the urban environment.

The eighteenth century in England witnessed an increase in both home production and foreign imports, a trend which can already be seen in the seventeenth century. The majority of shopkeepers in London were already pure retailers, no longer craftsmen selling their own wares, and most shops sold goods made at a distance, as well as those produced locally. Fixed retail shops had established themselves as the outlets where most people made their purchases; peddling and purchasing at the market, while still important, were declining gradually at the beginning of the century, and mail-order selling developed only towards the end of the century.[4]

However, while distribution networks for goods across the country were complex, the mediation of information to the consumer about such goods lay not in the hands of the producer but in those of the shopkeeper. Manufacturing enterprises in the eighteenth century ranged from the very small to the very large; some were based on plant production, others on put-out or subcontracted work. Some produced standardized goods, but strict standardization was hard to achieve. Very few goods in the eighteenth century had a brand identity or were marketed by their producers; those that did were items such as proprietary medicines and patented products. As in earlier periods, consumers were used to assessing the different qualities of non-standardized goods (cloth is a good example) by their texture, strength and appearance, and perhaps their region of origin, but not by their association with a particular manufacturer, who might in any case change the type of raw materials used and the workforce employed. In the early twenty-first century, advertising informs consumers about, or seeks to manipulate them into, making choices about whether or what to buy even before they enter a retail outlet. In the eighteenth century, the point of information and persuasion was the shop.

The history of advertising

The regular inclusion (rather than sporadic appearance) of advertisements in English newspapers began in the second half of the seventeenth century.[5] The cost of placing advertisements remained minimal throughout the seventeenth and eighteenth centuries, and by the eighteenth century the number of advertisements had increased to the point where they were gathered together in several pages at the back of the newspaper. In the mid-seventeenth century, a weekly paper was likely to contain at most half a dozen advertisements, whereas by the mid-eighteenth century a daily paper might contain about fifty advertisements of increasing specialization.[6] The increasing importance of advertising to newspaper proprietors is reflected in the fact that several newspapers were circulated for free in the seventeenth century, and that in the eighteenth century advertisements made up over 75 per cent of some publications.[7]

R. B. Walker's excellent study of the advertising in London newspapers from 1650 to 1750 provides a breakdown of the types of advertisements then in use.[8] The wide range of advertisements included lost and found, stolen property, announcements of auctions, arrivals of ships, entertainments, bankruptcies and lotteries; the advertisement of consumer goods formed only one category among many. Within the category of consumer goods, advertisements for books dominated, followed by those for proprietary medicines and other branded consumer products such as refreshing drinks or shoe polish. Together these represented, even in the seventeenth century, between a quarter and a third of the number of advertisements placed. As Walker's study shows, after those for books and medicines, the remaining advertisements for consumer goods were very few indeed, making up between 10 and 50 per cent of advertisements, depending on the newspaper.[9]

It seems likely that the concentration of newspaper advertisements for proprietary medicines was a reflection of the nature of these products. Medicines had few easily ascertainable qualities: their efficacy was mainly a subjective matter and there was little in the actual ingredients or appearance of the various remedies that allowed consumers to distinguish between one and the next. It was the name and the label of the medicines that provided distinction. Persuasion was attempted through claims to efficacy, exoticness of ingredients, scare tactics and testimonials. What was most important to communicate – the brand name and associated qualities – could easily be achieved through the printed word. Warnings against counterfeit products were numerous, and part of the desire to advertise in print must have stemmed from a desire to protect products from imitation.

What is important to note is that the advertisements for these brand-name products were placed by their manufacturers rather than by retailers. Tonics such as Daffy's Elixir were distributed nationally and their success was dependent on their familiarity to consumers as well as their elaborate mixture of ingredients.[10] Such a consistent image could only be achieved centrally, and the same advertisement placed in different newspapers would direct consumers to a range of outlets stocking the product. Advertisements in London newspapers listed outlets both in London and the provinces, but the list could easily be varied from advertisement to advertisement. Tubal-cain Porter's Elixir Salutis was listed as available from thirty-one shops in London and many in the provinces, and the Elixir Magnum Stomachicum at seventeen coffee-houses and two booksellers in London and one bookseller in most towns.[11] Sometimes such products were sold from wholesale warehouses; these would also be listed in the advertisement.[12]

Similarly, advertisements for books, placed by publishers who had acquired their copyrights, aimed to encourage a wide readership of a product available from only one source. Advertisements often offered delivery to consumers and some books were published through subscription. Newspapers aimed at a higher class of reader accepted considerably more book than medical advertisements.[13] Both medicine- and booksellers aimed to achieve as wide a distribution as possible of product information.[14]

Survey of consumer goods advertisements

While Walker has analysed the ratio of types of advertisements placed in London newspapers, there has been no investigation of the make-up of individual categories. By analysing five newspapers preserved in the Burney Collection of the British Library, I hoped to understand more about the nature of advertising consumer goods in the eighteenth century. These newspapers were the *Daily Courant*, the *Daily Advertiser*, the *London Evening Post*, the *General Advertiser* and the *Public Advertiser*. Combined, these newspapers were in publication throughout the eighteenth century, allowing an examination at ten-year intervals from 1721 to 1791.[15] My selection criteria were the devotion of a significant percentage of space (usually between one quarter and two thirds) to advertising and success during publication.

Placing to one side the advertisements for proprietary medicines, patent products and books, which were paid for by manufacturers or wholesalers, and those for auctions, the remaining advertisements for domestic goods were placed by retailers.[16] Here we might expect to find some of the variety of goods and the type of persuasive advertising that is thought to constitute a significant part of a consumer revolution. However, not only were there few such advertisements (in 1731 two appeared in the *Daily Courant* and two in the *Daily Advertiser*; in 1781 two appeared in the *Daily Advertiser* and seven in the *General Adver-*

tiser; in some years no retailers' advertisements appeared), but close examination shows that few of these attempted to persuade customers to buy particular products.

The majority of shopkeepers' advertisements announced a change of address rather than promoting wares. These relocations might be to larger or better premises, the result of a change in partnership arrangements, or simply the opening of a new shop. The language of these advertisements was, above all, polite. John Stanton's advertisement of 1741 was typical: he expressed his hope 'to have the Favours of his Friends still continu'd, which shall always be gratefully acknowledg'd by their oblig'd humble Servant'.[17] Apart from the fact that Stanton was a haberdasher, there was no mention of goods sold. The aim of the advertisement was to inform customers of the change of address while conveying an impression of politeness and gentility and underplaying any references to commercialism.

In the eighteenth century, the middle class was becoming an increasingly wealthy and powerful group, increasingly sensitive to distinctions in politeness and the signifiers of gentility. They shied away from overt references to commercialism, and shopkeepers sought to create images of refinement for their shops and reputations of taste and discernment for themselves, which would draw customers to them without suggesting the pushy selling techniques of the street market or the emotional, repetitive claims of patent product sellers. The shopkeepers placing these advertisements had already built up a network of customers who had visited their shops or received visits from the shopkeepers at home. Passing trade was important to shopkeepers in the eighteenth century, and they spent considerable amounts of money on shop façades and windows,[18] but these advertisements were not intended to encourage passing trade. Advertising a change of address represented a formal, genteel mode of behaviour, designed perhaps to suggest that the shop possessed an élite newspaper-reading clientele rather than to function as the primary means of alerting customers to the change. Occasionally advertisements announcing a change of address did take the opportunity to list the type of goods sold by the retailer, emphasizing those that were most fashionable, but such lists remained short and evocative rather than descriptive, and shopkeepers did not take the opportunity to advertise a second time.[19]

This approach to newspaper advertising by shopkeepers explains Wedgwood's much-quoted dislike of newspaper advertising. In 1771 he wrote to his showroom manager, 'I would much rather not advertise at all if you think the sales are in such a way as to do without it.'[20] This comment from Wedgwood has always sat awkwardly with the fact that he published several 'puffs', or anonymous panegyrics for his wares.

However, 'puffing', because of its anonymity (appearing as an independent newsworthy report) constituted a polite form of promotion
(and also avoided the advertising tax) without the negative associations
of proprietary product manufacturers' advertisements. In his bid to be
considered in the same light as the sellers of the superior and more
expensive imported porcelain, Wedgwood objected to advertising which
would associate him with lower-class retailing or pushy commercialism;[21] he was quite happy to place newspaper advertisements announcing
a change of address or the opening of new showrooms and exhibitions.[22]

The restraint shown by London retailers in promoting their wares in
newspapers underlines their reliance on personal contacts with customers and the use of trade cards and handbills, distributed in hundreds of
thousands each year, to reach a more immediate local clientele. Even an
announcement of the arrival of a special shipment of wares was uncom-
mon in London, although provincial retailers used newspaper
advertisements to alert customers to the arrival of new stock. These
were usually goods arriving from London, and the advertisements pointed
out the fashionability of the shopkeepers' stock and the advantages of
their connections with London suppliers. E. and S. Towsey of Chester
announced in 1790 that they 'Respectfully beg leave to inform their
Friends and the Public, That E. Towsey is just returned from London,
with a new and fashionable assortment of Millinery and Haberdashery
Goods ...'.[23] The reputation of London retailers seems to have rested on
their ability to maintain rich and varied stocks throughout the year.

A second and very small group of advertisements placed by retailers
in London newspapers reflects the belief that newspaper advertisements
were appropriate for drawing customers to a particular event. These
were advertisements announcing the exhibition, for a short period of
time, of a particular product of fine craftsmanship or a new invention.
These exhibitions varied depending on the market level at which they
were aimed. Admission to see the 'most curious CABINET in the World'
was only one shilling and was used to draw potential customers to Mr
Johnson's Cut Glass Warehouse and his wares.[24] This has the hallmark
of the novelty draw, as cabinet work has little connection with cut glass.
At the upper end of the market were exhibitions such as Wedgwood's
display of the Frog Service and the Portland Vase, or the cabinetmaker
Campbell's 'new invented library steps', where aristocratic connections
were played upon as a selling point. Campbell emphasized the fact that
'The original one is in the Possession of the King, and has been highly
distinguished by his Royal Approbation.'[25]

Once again these advertisements offered high-class retailers the opportunity to express politeness and taste as well as to attract potential

new customers. In contrast to the advertisers of proprietary medicines, Wedgwood and Campbell were retailers as well as manufacturers and the item on exhibition was not the sole product for sale. Their advertisements were not intended to work in the same way as advertisements for proprietary medicines; the exhibition, as a transitory example of taste and craftsmanship, was intended to promote the retailer's reputation and encourage contact with his premises.

The final group of advertisements placed by retailers are those placed by large-scale shopkeepers, who advertised large numbers of high-fashion goods sold at reasonable rates and who advertised consistently and regularly in several different newspapers over several months or even sometimes over several decades. A good example of this kind of shop is Briscoe's (Figure 4.1).[26] This group of advertisements represents the type of insistent, informative and persuasive advertising that was developed further in the nineteenth century.

However, these advertisements, unlike those in the nineteenth century, cover an extremely limited range of goods. They are for the most part restricted to metalware and clothing. Metalware retailers offered fashionable tableware and decorative items in low-weight silver or silver plate, and they also sold second-hand goods. The retailers of clothing, who chose to advertise on a consistent long-term basis, were likewise advertising the availability of a wide range of choices and quantities at reasonable prices from their 'warehouses'. They too offered second-hand goods alongside new.

Both metalwork and clothing retailers sold new and old at fixed prices. The usual procedure of haggling over prices was a time-consuming and skilled business requiring close supervision of any staff by the shopkeeper. For large shops needing a high turnover and a quick throughput of customers, fixed prices were a way of speeding up the sales process. Without the need for close supervision of staff, large numbers of shop assistants could be employed, increasing the number of transactions possible. In all probability, fixed prices for goods were accompanied by a greater number of cash sales.

In contrast to the other shopkeepers' advertisements, these were quite lengthy, providing a comprehensive list of the variety and styles of products, emphasizing exotic-sounding names. But again, these advertisements unlike those for patent products and medicines, were intended to draw consumers to a particular shop, not to identify the qualities of a particular product. These shopkeepers were also clearly not involved in manufacturing – the wide range offered made it clear that the retailer had brought in goods made elsewhere or had subcontracted work to a great variety of different craftsmen. In the case of the metalwork retailers, only finished products, rather than commissioned work, were offered.

BRISCOE

JEWELLER and GOLDSMITH,
At the Corner of Friday-Street, Cheapside, *the* GOLDEN
BALL *Only.*

Hath now ready for Sale,

A Complete Service of plain Silver Diſhes,
and a Dozen Soup Plates together or ſeperate, for little more
than the melting Price ; a Table of twenty Inches Diameter, with a
fine chaſed open Border, of moſt exquiſite Workmanſhip ; ſeveral
Ditto, larger and ſmaller, and Waiters of all Sizes ; ſeveral Sets of
chaſed Candleſticks, in the neweſt taſte ; various Terines, Inkſtands,
Tea-Kettles and Lamps, chaſed and plain ; Cups and Covers, Tea
Caniſters, in Caſes, or without ; Cruet Frames and Caſters, Bread-
Baſkets chaſed and plain, Sauce Boats and Pans, Diſh-ſtands, Monumental Candleſticks, a Set of Shaving Plate, Punch Bowls, Decan-
ters, Gold, Silver and Stone Snuff Boxes, Sets of Knives, Forks
and Spoons, Gold, Silver and Metal Watches, by the moſt eminent
Workmen, and all other Pieces of Plate commonly uſed, and at Second-hand, are now to be had at Mr. STAFFORD BRISCOE's Old
Shop, the Corner of Friday-ſtreet, Cheapſide, the Golden-Ball Only,
at Prices extremely low. Likewiſe great Variety of *New Plate,*
finiſhed in the moſt elegant Taſte. He continues to give the moſt
Money for Quantities of Old Plate, Jewels and Watches, and for
ſuch as are pawn'd.

☞ A fine brilliant Solitaire, a Pair of brilliant three-drop Dia-
mond Ear-rings, a chaſed repeating jewell'd Watch, by George Graham, of a middling Size, one plain ditto by George Graham, one ditto
by Tompion, one ditto by Delander, Horizontal, cap'd and jewell'd,
one ditto by Ellicott, a Silver Trumpet, a very curious Silver Watch,
which ſhews the riſing and Setting of the Sun, in five different Parts
of the World, all to be ſold very cheap.

BRISCOE

Now on SALE, and to be diſpoſed on very Cheap, for ready
Money.

THE greateſt Variety of new and old
Plate, chaſed and plain, uſeful or ornamental, by STAFFORD
BRISCOE, at the Three Kings and Golden Ball in Cheapſide, oppo-
ſite to Foſter-Lane, near St. Paul's, who is removed from the Corner
of Friday-ſtreet. Among a great Number of Particulars, are Services
of Plates and Diſhes, a Set of chaſed hiſtorical Dreſſing Plate, ſeveral
Pieces of emboſſed light old Plate, in the fine old Taſte, Epargnes of a
new Faſhion, Terines, Tea Tables, a great Choice of Tea Kettles,
Candleſticks, Canniſters, two Ice Pails, Cups and Covers, a Set of Com-
munion Plate, and ſeveral Pieces of fine Gilt Plate, Caſes of Knives,
Forks, and Spoons, ſeveral Gold Repeating and other Watches, by
the beſt Maſters ; Gold Snuff Boxes, and the moſt Money conſtantly
given for any Quantity of old Plate, Watches, and Jewels.

4.1 Newspaper advertisements for Briscoe's, goldsmith and jeweller

Sources: *Public Advertiser* (20 March 1760), *General Advertiser* (2 January
1750), British Library, Burney Collection

The advertisements constantly emphasize fashionability, but there is no reference to craftsmanship or quality. While the list of products within the advertisements served as an enticement to consumers, its purpose was primarily to establish the particular retail method of these shops – fast-selling, competitively priced and stocking a large selection – in contrast to more service-oriented, traditional or higher-class shops.

Alongside these advertisements could be placed those about tailoring services which likewise presented a lengthy list of the different types of clothing produced, each with its price next to it. Again the emphasis was on speed, cheapness and variety, all suggesting a large, centrally organized workforce. The relative frequency of such advertisements from the time of their first appearance in the 1760s suggests both fairly intense competition for tailoring orders for both male and female clothing and the need to attract customers from further afield than the local area, as that could be achieved with similarly styled handbills.

Newspaper advertising versus marketing through the shop

An analysis of the way consumer goods were advertised in London newspapers in the eighteenth century reveals that advertisements for medicines and patented products sought first to promote specific wares and create a brand identity for them, then to direct purchasers towards retail outlets. Advertisements for other consumer goods sought to promote a retailer and his or her shop by enhancing the chosen image of the shop – either as a genteel environment or as a fast-selling warehouse of goods.

A study of newspaper advertisements is therefore useful in revealing distinct selling patterns in eighteenth-century shops. Retailers responded to different levels of the market and different shopping practices, suggesting sophisticated retail practices which historians of the nineteenth century have not recognized.

The study also reveals that a majority of those goods that were advertised in newspapers were advertised by their manufacturers rather than by retailers. A vast majority of shopkeepers chose not to advertise in newspapers and those who did advertise did not, unlike their nineteenth-century counterparts, promote particular goods. Newspaper advertising proved to be useful for only a few retailers in the eighteenth century, a fraction of the number of shops trading successfully. The range of goods advertised in newspapers, whether by manufacturers or retailers, was extremely limited, especially in comparison with the extremely rich and ever-increasing range of goods commercially available to consumers in the late seventeenth and eighteenth centuries.

Historians of the nineteenth century have taken limited newspaper advertising to mean limited commercial activity, but Mui and Mui have shown that a widespread and important network of shops stretched across Britain in the eighteenth century. Furthermore, economic historians of the early modern period have noted steadily increasing levels of consumption from the seventeenth century onwards.[27] If newspaper advertising was not important to the promotion of goods in new markets, how was this increase achieved?

In eighteenth-century England, newspaper advertising was effective for the promotion of brand-name goods, but non-brand-name consumer goods were promoted through the shop. Shopkeepers' management of the display of goods, of the environment of the shops, and of their sales patterns proved to be highly effective techniques for the sale of non-brand-name goods. The shop was the point of information and persuasion.

Eighteenth-century shops have been characterized as bare and unenticing places, requiring the customer to make a purchase from a limited range of goods kept out of sight and available only on demand. However, contemporary comment draws attention to the bargaining process consumers engaged in. The fact that customers were served by shop staff over the counter meant that the customer was introduced to the goods by physical contact with them and by verbal information supplied by the retailer. The shopkeeper informed, described, unwrapped and displayed his wares, bringing goods down from the shelves around the shop and thus providing unlimited access to the stock. Chairs on the customer's side of the counter symbolized the ease, attention, and service that was due the customer. At the counter, the presentation of goods was active, and interactive, rather than passive. Once the goods were on the counter, the customer handled, compared, considered and selected them, while discussing them with the shopkeeper. A mercer, writing to *The Plain Dealer* in 1727, complained of the way ladies 'tumble over my goods, and deafen me with a round of questions'.[28] Here customers had access to information which would allow them to make effective decisions about the purchase of non-standardized goods and which was not available in printed form. This was also an opportunity for shopkeepers to introduce customers to new goods, or to receive feedback about the quality or fashionability of goods – important information for restocking and for passing on consumer preferences to manufacturers.

The shopkeeper undoubtedly aimed to manipulate his customers into making a purchase: Charles Lilly, a toy dealer, was satirically described by the *Tatler* in 1710 as 'the Orator behind the Counter' who seduced his customers into making a purchase by the sheer power of his rhetoric.[29] But customers were not powerless and were not obliged to purchase.

Retailers complained vociferously that shoppers would rifle through their stock and leave without buying anything, and consumers also acknowledged the practice. A mercer, writing to *The Plain Dealer* in 1727, complained, 'They swim into my shop by shoals, with not the least intention to buy, but only to hear my silks rustle, and fill up their own leisure by putting me into full employment.'[30] Joanna Schopenhauer, a German visitor to London in 1803, stated that shopping meant 'going into at least twenty shops, having a thousand things shown to us which we do not wish to buy, in fact turning the whole shop upside down and, in the end, perhaps leaving without purchasing anything. It is impossible to admire sufficiently the patience of the shopkeepers, who endure this nonsense without ever dreaming of showing annoyance.'[31] Retailers bore the practice because it exposed their stock to potential customers who might buy it later if not at that moment, and customers indulged in it because it informed them about a shopkeeper's stock and gave them pleasure. In many cases, however, it is clear that a good relationship developed between shopkeeper and customer, usually over time, and a balanced consultation could be achieved with the customer drawing on the advice and judgement of the shopkeeper.[32]

The language in the lengthy newspaper advertisements of fast-selling shops, an enticing compilation of fashionable items, perhaps echoes the sales patter of shopkeepers. This could begin even before potential customers entered the shop, as shopkeepers stood at the shop door, inviting people in off the street. Such invitations were made particularly as people stopped to look at displays in shop windows.[33] Although this technique was similar to vendors' cries in a market, it also had a much deeper significance, for the process of understanding and describing goods in the eighteenth century was verbal as well as visual. Orders for bespoke items by customers[34] and manufacturers' instructions often took the form of verbal descriptions.[35] This may in part account for the eighteenth-century emphasis on the printed word rather than images in newspaper advertisements and on trade cards.

The appearance of the shop was as important as the sales language used to creating an appealing atmosphere in which goods could be shown to their best advantage. Lists from shopkeepers' inventories of the interior fittings and furnishing reveal a very high level of spending on and a concern for interior design from the very beginning of the century. As the century progressed, these fittings became more elaborate and numerous, but the significance of presenting goods well and creating an enticing atmosphere had already been established.[36] The details from the inventories accord well with the images of shop interiors portrayed on trade cards, although these obviously represent an ideal rather than an actual shop (see Figure 4.2).

4.2 Trade card for Masefield's, wallpaper and papier mâché seller, *c.*1758

Source: British Museum, Heal Collection

A 1746 inventory of a goldsmith's shop listed carved wooden pillars and arches, painted and gilded mouldings and cornice, and a great deal of glass (a very expensive and prestigious commodity at the time), used on all four sides of the shop (in the shop windows, in extensive show-cases, and between the front and back rooms of the shop).[37] An inventory of a draper's shop in 1721 points to a concern for comfort and exoti-cism conducive to enhancing the display of fine cloth and Far Eastern silks to a clientele which was probably largely female. The shop con-tained 'a pier glass and 3 glass sconces, 4 leather stools, 2 chairs and cushions, a silk curtain and 10 Indian pictures'.[38]

The recording of these fittings and furnishings in inventories (espe-cially the record of non-moveable fittings, which were normally excluded from inventories) underlines how important they were to the workings of a retail business. Shop interiors could be designed to appeal to particular levels of or groups in society, producing an effective market-ing system which drew on customers of the appropriate taste and financial status. This essentially class-specific marketing strategy was supported by the careful design of shop façades which imitated or echoed current trends in domestic and civic architecture as well as the stocking of fashionable windows with a selection of items representing the stock held inside.[39] It was far more effective for shopkeepers to pay significant amounts for the design and decoration of the shop than it was to advertise in newspapers.

Shopkeepers marketed themselves and their wares by creating fashionable shop fronts and enticing interiors. The design of the shop could underline the fashionability of the stock available, suggest financial security to customers ordering expensive items, persuade customers to invest in untried products, or simply lure customers into enjoying the pleasurable environment – and thus into spending more time shopping. The image created by the visible, physical part of the business was a crucial support to the reputation of the shopkeeper.[40] Customers would be drawn to a particular shop because it could provide expert knowledge about the quality, price and type of goods they wanted and had the right trade connections to supply those goods.

Once a shopkeeper had established a reputation and developed a particular identity for his shop, he could use trade cards and handbills to maintain customers' awareness of the business. Distributed in the local area and to customers in the shop, these would reach the shop's target market. Of necessity, if the idea of reputation were to carry weight, this was a local or select market. Trade cards, usually presenting the shop sign, name and address, as well as a list of the types of goods it stocked, were used to reinforce the business image and reputation of the shop rather than to promote particular wares for sale inside. The shopkeeper aimed, by using all of these methods – trade cards, handbills, façade and reputation – to bring the customer to the shop, at which point he would begin marketing specific wares rather than the shop itself.

It was therefore a particular shop, rather than a particular named product, that the customer first identified before making a purchase. In this way, the shop, through its reputation – signalled by its design – was the prime means of marketing for retailers in the eighteenth century. At this time it was, in a sense, the shop which was branded rather than the goods it sold.

Understanding the importance of the shop for the marketing of goods in the eighteenth century leads in turn to consideration of the role of the shop in the urban environment. Growth in the number of shops and increased expenditure on shop fronts and elaborate window displays changed the profile of the street. Shopping became an activity which could be carried out every weekday rather than just on market days, and the street, with its array of shops, replaced the street market as the mental focus of consumers. Some types of shopping became a social activity, especially for the middle and upper classes, who had more time to spare.

London had always been a thriving commercial centre with a rich supply of goods, but by the early eighteenth century shopping had become a much pleasanter experience as pavements were laid, street lighting introduced, streets cleared of hawkers and foul-smelling wastes, and semi-permanent 'bulks', or makeshift wooden shops, removed. In some places markets were even relocated so that the more refined activity of shopping in shops would not be hindered. Shopping in fixed retail shops was associated with the cleaner, healthier and wealthier lifestyle of new developments in city centres. Permanent shops became part of the urban identity; in London, fast becoming the commercial capital of Europe, they were a potent symbol of economic stability and fashionability that in tourist accounts clearly rivalled Paris by mid-century.

High-class shopkeepers, in their choice of architectural styles in both interiors and exteriors, made visual links between shops and other leisure venues such as assembly rooms and theatres, and they became associated with the leisure culture of the city. London shops formed part of a developing urban culture which was well established by about 1760.[41] Shopkeepers played with the variety of cultural values abroad in the city, using them to enhance or promote the goods they sold, and sometimes using them to create lifestyle settings for goods. As soon as the new urban aesthetic – the classical style – was introduced to domestic architecture at the turn of the seventeenth century, shopkeepers eagerly took it up to decorate their shops.[42]

While the attempts of particular entrepreneurs to manipulate fashion in the eighteenth century have been studied, little consideration has been given to shopkeepers, who were in a position to mediate ideas between consumers and manufacturers and hence could promote new ideas or respond quickly to fashion changes. When the importance of the shop as a locus for the exchange of ideas is understood, it becomes clear that consumers in eighteenth-century London were less victims of commercialization than partners in it.

Conclusion

Even though newspaper circulation and advertising increased throughout the eighteenth century, the vast majority of shopkeepers did not use this strategy. Instead, the focus of their marketing was on the immediate urban environment and the reputation or identity of the shop. The majority of domestic goods available to consumers in the eighteenth century were marketed through the shop, using handbills, trade cards, and occasional newspaper advertising to reinforce knowledge of the shop's reputation. Such a marketing strategy, which encouraged customers to identify with the skills of a particular shopkeeper rather than with the qualities of particular products, was effective in the period before the widespread sale of brand-name and standardized products. In the retailing context of the eighteenth century, where non-standardized goods were selected by the consumer based on verbal, tactile and visual information, there was little point in using newspaper advertisements to try to lure distant customers. This effective marketing strategy introduced consumers to new and varied goods and possessed a persuasive power which newspaper advertising would not have had.

This evidence points away from a consumer revolution in the late eighteenth century and towards a steady increase in consumption from the seventeenth century onwards.[43] It challenges the notion of marketing as a modern development resulting only from industrialization and the growth of mass markets. It also encourages us to think of the process of advertising in terms other than those of mass manipulation – in this case in terms of advertising's relationship with the local urban environment and urban culture.

Notes

1. See J. Jeffreys, *Retail Trading in Britain 1850–1950* (Cambridge: Cambridge University Press, 1954); Dorothy Davis, *A History of Shopping* (London: Routledge, 1966); Peter Mathias, *Retailing Revolution* (London: Batsford, 1967).

2. Neil McKendrick, John Brewer and J. H. Plumb, *The Birth of a Consumer Society* (London: Europa Publications, 1982). McKendrick also considers the role of shops, showrooms, and show windows, but his argument concentrates on the newspaper advertisements of entrepreneurs in the late eighteenth century.

3. The other recent key work on eighteenth-century retailing is Lorna Mui and Hoh-cheung Mui, *Shops and Shopkeeping in Eighteenth Century England* (Montreal: McGill-Queen's University Press, 1989). Chapter 12 looks at the marketing of goods mainly through newspaper advertising. Historians of the early modern period have shown how industrialization and consumption increased steadily through the seventeenth and eighteenth centuries rather than suddenly peaking in a revolution at the end of the eighteenth century; see John Styles, 'Manufacturing, Consumption, and Design in Eighteenth Century England', in *Consumption and the World of Goods in the Eighteenth Century*, edited by John Brewer and Roy Porter (London and New York: Routledge, 1993), 527–54.

4. Mui and Mui, *Shops and Shopkeeping*, chap. 1.

5. R. B. Walker, 'Advertising in London Newspapers 1650–1750', *Business History* 15 (1975), 112–30.

6. Ibid., 123.

7. Walker (ibid.) uses examples from the *Daily Advertiser* and the *General Advertiser* in the 1780s.

8. Ibid., tables on 117 and 119.

9. Ibid., tables on 117, 119, 121 and 123.

10. Daffy's Elixir is an example of the successful creation of a brand identity. It was first advertised in the late seventeenth century and was still being marketed in the early twentieth century.

11. Walker, 'Advertising in London Newspapers 1650–1750', 127.

12. Ibid. For example, Dr Godfrey's Cordial sold at wholesale warehouses in Bristol, Norwich, Chester, Newcastle-upon-Tyne, Dublin and London.

13. Ibid., 123 and 126.

14. Ibid., 113–15. Sometimes publishers of newspapers had a vested interest in the goods advertised.

15. The *Public(k) Advertiser* ran weekly from 1657. The *Daily Courant* was published daily from 1702 to 1735. The *London Evening Post* (later the *Evening Post*), a weekly and evening paper aimed at more select readership than the *Public(k) Advertiser*, ran from 1706. The *Daily Advertiser* ran from 1731 and the *London Daily Post and General Advertiser* began publication in 1734 (from 1744 it was called simply the *General Advertiser*). Apart from the *Daily Courant*, these papers were still in publication at the end of the eighteenth century.

16. Announcements of auctions form another group of advertisements for the sale of domestic goods, but these were strictly notices of when and where an auction was to take place. Advertisements for candlelight sales of goods unloaded from ships also acted as announcements and appear to have been aimed at wholesale bulk purchase only. Auctions of the contents of private houses listed the types of goods available and would normally be held on the premises. Sometimes house clearances took the form of sales using fixed prices, presumably to speed up the clearance.

17. John Stanton, *London Evening Post* (2–4 April 1741). Shopkeepers also advertised the sale of stock and fittings when closing their businesses; from the wording, it seems that these were most often aimed at others in their field who might want to take on large quantities of the stock. For an example, see 'Auction King St', *London Daily Post and General Advertiser* (27 July 1739).

18. For further details see Claire Walsh, 'Shop Design and the Display of Goods in the Eighteenth Century', (Master's thesis, Royal College of Art/ V&A, 1993).

19. For example, Benjamin Payne, *London Evening Post* (14–17 May 1737). This tendency increased from the 1770s on.

20. McKendrick et al., *Birth of a Consumer Society*, 123.

21. Ibid. Wedgwood wrote to Bentley, 'We have hitherto appeared in a very different light to common Shopkeepers, but this step (in my opinion) will sink us exceedingly.'

22. Wedgwood placed advertisements in the *St. James Chronicle* in 1768 and 1769, and in the *Public Advertiser* in 1774.

23. Quoted in Mass Observation, *Browns and Chester: Portrait of a Shop 1780–1946*, edited by H. D. Willcock (London: Drummond, 1947), 14.

24. Hildebrand, *Public Advertiser* (14 January 1760).

25. Campbell, *Public Advertiser* (10 February 1775).

26. Briscoe advertised in the *General Advertiser* in the 1750s and the *Public Advertiser* in the 1760s.

27. Mui and Mui, *Shops and Shopkeeping*. On consumption in the early modern period, see John Styles, 'Manufacturing, Consumption, and Design'.

28. *The Plain Dealer*, quoted in Daniel Defoe, *The Complete English Tradesman* (New York: Burt Franklin, 1970), 64.

29. *Tatler* (7 March 1710).

30. *The Plain Dealer*, quoted in Defoe, *The Complete English Tradesman*, 64. See also Defoe, 60–61.

31. Joanna Schopenhauer, *A Lady Travels: Journeys in England and Scotland from the Diaries of Joanna Schopenhauer*, translated and edited by R. Michaelis-Jena and W. Merson (London: Routledge, 1988), 151. See also Defoe, *The Complete English Tradesman*, 61–2.

32. The relationship of Mr and Mrs Vyvyan with goldsmith Joseph Brasbridge is one example. See Joseph Brasbridge, *The Fruits of Experience: or Memoir of Joseph Brasbridge Written in his 80th and 81st Years* (London: self-published, 1824), 172.

33. Evidence from records of court cases, for example *Old Bailey Proceedings*, June 1809, 15.

34. Helen Clifford, 'Parker and Wakelin: the Study of an Eighteenth Century Goldsmithing Business with Particular Reference to the Garrard Ledgers 1770–1776' (Ph.D. diss., Royal College of Art, 1989).

35. Styles, 'Manufacturing, Consumption, and Design', 545–6.

36. Claire Walsh, 'Shop Design and the Display of Goods in Eighteenth-Century London', *Journal of Design History* 8, no. 3 (1995), 157–76.

37. George Braithwaite, Public Record Office, Chancery Masters Exhibits C105/5 Part I.

38. William Morford, Corporation of London Records Office, Orphans Court 3178.

39. Walsh, 'Shop Design and the Display of Goods in the Eighteenth Century', chap. 1.

40. Fast-selling shops, less dependent on reputation and image, could more effectively use newspaper advertising.

41. Peter Borsay, 'The English Urban Renaissance: the development of provincial urban culture c. 1680–1760,' *Social History* 5 (May 1977), 582.

42. Ibid., 588–9.

43. McKendrick et al., *Birth of a Consumer Society*. There has been an over-emphasis on manufacturers' advertising in past research. McKendrick's key examples for evidence of a consumer revolution were Wedgwood, a manufacturer unusually retailing his own products, and Packwood, a manufacturer and distributor of patented razor strops.

CHAPTER FIVE

French Court Society and Advertising Art: The Reputation of Parisian Merchants at the End of the Eighteenth Century[1]

Natacha Coquery

> Take luxury away from France, particularly from the capital, and you will kill off most of its trade and take away its supremacy in Europe. And I ask you: if fashion doesn't come from Paris, whence would it come?[2]

In the city of light at the end of the eighteenth century, the stakes were high: French aristocrats had lost real power and the last weapon that was left to them in order to maintain the upper hand was to make a show of themselves. The élite put great pressure on the fashion industry, both its manufacturers and its merchants, and this industry devoted itself to fulfilling that demand successfully, as the huge growth in production, specifically in textiles, and the birth of a genuine luxury industry, whose greatest creation was the Paris of the eighteenth century, bear witness. The activity which surrounded the fulfilment of these new fashion demands left its mark on the capital city.[3] As skilled manipulators of taste, the merchants took advantage of the various social obligations to which their clients were subject, and strove to invent new products and fashions with which to entice them.

The number of luxury establishments was expanding in eighteenth-century Paris, and a growing number of these moved west in order to follow the city's expansion and the migration of the wealthy. The Palais-Royal and the banks of the Seine, which with its well-known shop, *Small Dunkerque* had charmed Voltaire, overpowered the Palace Gallery (Palais de la Cité), whose commercial bluster had been the great showcase of the city during the time of Corneille. The merchants were genuine masters of making the most of the motivating force of fashion in court society's endless race for distinction: consumption, fashion and glamour were inextricably linked.

What one needs to understand here is the crucial role that merchants played in hastening the advent of consumerism. One method of examining the role of the merchants from the supply side is to analyse their own public presentation by looking at their invoices.[4] By doing so, we can deconstruct various mechanisms of the luxury industry: courtiers' mimicry, the vagaries of fashion, merchants' creativity and the artistry of advertising. Press advertisements, as well as merchants' letterheads, allow us to think about advertisement.[5]

The nobility were masters of the art of consumption. As such, they became the target for those merchants most successful at installing themselves in the luxury market. Such merchants displayed great inventiveness in their attempts to maintain pre-eminence and to keep clients attached to their products. Their success was not based solely on their wares: gold and silk fabrics, English saddles, rosewater. More important were commercial know-how and understanding of the special way in which the court functioned, where the way you are, or even more, the way you appear to be, was determined by competition and mimicry. The merchants cheerfully took advantage of these court dynamics, striving to cajole their customers: shop names, signs, invoices, displays – everything came together to produce a true art of advertising even before the concept existed in language: 'The sign becomes the thing: we see stuffed tongues, laurel wreathed hams, fattened pullets, and bright-red patés, and then displayed in front of us are sweetened cakes; we begin to think they are there just waiting to be picked up ... '.[6] But before studying this kind of eighteenth-century advertising art, it may be useful to define the word 'advertising' in its eighteenth-century context, as distinguished from the more modern meaning that predominated only at the end of the nineteenth century.[7]

During the eighteenth and into the nineteenth centuries, the term 'advertising', according to contemporary dictionaries, referred to the public nature of a thing or something that had a public use.[8] The notion of advertising as a way of exerting influence on the public for commercial ends was a later meaning (*Petit Robert*[9]). For instance, in the *Encyclopedia*, the terms 'poster', 'label', and 'leaflet' were strictly related to printing and not to commercial activity of any kind.[10] At the time we are discussing, posters were conceived of as nothing more than announcements of the availability of goods. One cannot call single- or even limited-copy forms of announcements and publicity, such as signs, advertisement. For these kinds of signs to become advertising, mass forms of communication are required as intermediaries: the press and posters (in the new sense of the word), not to mention twentieth-century audiovisual advertising media.[11] The labels and leaflets of merchants that I have studied addressed themselves to a limited audi-

ence. That is why it would be best to talk about these as the first fruits
of advertising art.

Although the dictionaries of the time did not fully define the term, the
sheer number of articles on words related to *publicité* reveals the important function which advertising began to have during the last third of
the eighteenth century, in commerce and luxury consumption as well as
in the spread of fashion. The proof can be found in the press, especially
the fashion press, but also in merchants' bills. Having the same aim – to
sell – merchants and the press shared the same stratagems.

Fashion magazines, which grew in size and number after 1750, played
the main role of go-between amongst manufacturers, designers and
consumers. They were aware of their position as well as of the economic challenges of fashion, as shown by the preamble of the *Cabinet
des Modes*, the most successful among them:

> *Cabinet* will present, issue after issue, descriptions of every chang-
> ing fashion in all of its details. If French manufactures receive some
> encouragement, if Fashion output ... is up to date and substantial,
> all the Nations of Europe could have the pleasure of being in-
> structed ... Such pleasant labor for Europe, and such favorable
> Commerce for the Capital deserve the expansion for which we
> strive through the Work we now publish.[12]

Given the links among customers, journalists and manufacturers, the
paper spoke directly to creative merchants, irrespective of the branch of
the industry to which they belonged:

> We invite the Amateurs, the Artists, the Artisans, the Manufactur-
> ers and the Handicrafts, to advise Mr. Allemand ... in Paris, of
> everything they invent or improve upon, either in Clothing and
> Finery for both sexes, or in all kinds of Furniture, Decorations,
> Embellishments of Rooms, Coach Styles, Jewelry, Goldsmith Pieces,
> and more generally, of all objects that may provide usefulness,
> comfort, Fashion or pleasure. You are invited to send to the same
> address ... accurate Descriptions, with the drawings and the Plans
> needed for their publication, introducing their merit, and describ-
> ing the advantage we could draw from them. The merchants who
> have already given us such details have profited from the sale of
> some of their articles in a way that perhaps would not have been
> possible without our advertisement.[13]

Production and marketing were intertwined in furthering the growth
of the fashion industry. Together they stimulated both supply and
demand: supply existed only to satisfy a predicted and anticipated
desire.[14] Manufacturers and merchants quickly understood the crucial
importance of this type of magazine in spreading the word. Tradespeople supported it with their advertisements, anticipating a rise in
sales. *Cabinet de Modes* was stuffed with advertisements: fashion and

advertising went hand in hand, both of them continually upping the ante of consumption:

> All of our subscribers could not better apply for those waistcoats …than to Mr. Jubin, silk Fabrics Merchant, from the Palais Royal… He is well known for the integrity of his work and the appropriateness of his prices, which he has reduced to such an extent that he is realizing much more modest profits than other merchants. That is praise that is his due.[15]

> Mr. Bouche, Upholsterer and Mirror Merchant … rue de la Verrerie … owns one of the most beautiful shops in Paris. He offers some of the latest and most fashionable pieces of Furniture …[16]

However, these advertisements were not illustrated, and their layout does not clearly distinguish them from other newspaper articles or bits of information. Only a few tradespeople, particularly the wealthy merchants of Palais Royal, the luxury shopping centre of the capital, built by the enterprising Duke of Orléans in the eighteenth century, are named. Press advertising had in fact begun.

Systematically examining a second source, the letterheads, or invoices, sent by merchants to their aristocratic customers, allows us to take a closer look at this topic. In these, in contrast to newspapers and periodicals, illustration was often present. Fashion merchants and haberdashers appeared much more inventive, though this should not be surprising given their reputation as the kings of fashion. They not only offered some of the most brilliant and seductive arrays of products, but some of the most ostentatious and therefore most subject to change. They were at the centre of the distribution network for objects, taste and manners. When defining fashion, Savary des Bruslons starts with the link between fashion and fabric:

> *Vogue* [Fashion]: retailing of merchandise or fabrics for a limited time only. We use this term for new textiles, attracting one's attention with their color, pattern, or workmanship, snatched up with alacrity but soon replaced by the novel charm of even newer fabrics. We make use of the word *mode* [fashion] for almost everything that has to do with the commerce in wool and silk, be it for garments, finery, or furniture. We say that a fabric is no longer in *mode* [fashion], that it is out of *mode* [fashion], when it is no longer desired, no longer asked for …[17]

And in French the term 'novelties' is used for new fabrics. The merchants of gold, silver, and silk fabrics also gave this name to their taffetas and other light fabrics intended as ladies' summer clothes, hardly worn for longer than three months.[18]

Some letterheads were illustrated, showing earthenware or hats. Most of the illustrations evoked the name of the shop, some with more

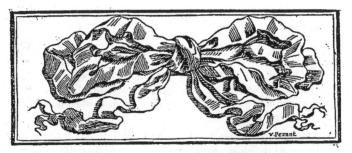

AU NŒUD GALANT,

Rue du Petit-Repoſoir, près la Place des Victoires.

BEAULARD, tient Magaſin de Modes, Corbeilles pour les Mariages & Baptêmes; garnit les Grands-Habits; Robes & Dominos; vend des Gazes, Blondes, Fleurs d'Italie, Eventails, & généralement tout ce qui concerne la Parure des Dames, dans le goût le plus nouveau.

Il fait auſſi la Commiſſion en tout genre pour la Province & le Pays Etranger.

Archives Nationales, T 166 ³⁵

5.1   Letterhead of the fashion merchant Beaulard, 1772

Source: Archives Nationales, T 166.35

creativity than others. Examples include a dove (for a fabric shop called *Holy Spirit*), an ear topped by a crown (for a linen shop called *The Crowned Golden Ear*), a shepherdess among her sheep, giving her hand to her lover (for The Faithful Shepherd confectioner's shop), a bundled-up man warming himself in front of his fireplace (for The Great Winter: a Tiger and a Leopard, a furrier's shop), a young woman in a rustic scene holding a distaff and a spindle (for The Spinner, a fashion merchant), a person dressed Turkish-style standing between two ships (for The Great Turk, a silk merchant), and a monkey playing backgammon (for The Green Monkey, a toy merchant).[19] Sometimes labels were decorated only by a border of flourishes, scallops or lilies, or were not decorated at all.

As in press advertisements, the language of these letterheads focused on different merits of the merchandise, often in conjunction with one other, emphasizing price,[20] quality,[21] quantity and variety, beauty,[22] hygiene, safety, novelty, the distinction of the clientele, how easy it was to deliver the product to the provinces or abroad and, last but not least, the English origin of products. Tradespeople tried every possible strata-

Archives Nationales, T 166 ˢ³

5.2 Letterhead of the silk fabrics merchant Le Normand, 1780

Source: Archives Nationales, T 166.3–5

gem to compete with their rivals in an attempt to control the market. No holds were barred that led to commercial success. Some merchants, however, preferred a more sober style and confined themselves to descriptive advertisements: 'Pinchon, Glover, Purser and Perfumier, Manufactures and Stocks all kinds of Gloves, Powders, Ointments and Perfumes'.

Others, however, adopted the exact opposite technique. Some were very wordy, sparing no details in lists of products of some fifteen lines or more. The four-page letterhead of the glover–purser–perfumer Chafanel Dupon, The Arc,[23] was, without ever being labelled as such, a real brochure (see Figure 5.7). For over three pages, which are illuminating to us because he uses all kinds of selling strategies, the merchant parades his craft and the excellence of his merchandise: gloves, fans, silks, linens, lipsticks, face powders, ointments, perfumes and scents. His list of perfumes blended ordinary cosmetics, such as jasmine water and cucumber ointment, with more extravagant, but highly appealing, concoctions: 'genuine Sultana water, used to whiten the skin, smooth out wrinkles,

BUFFAULT

MARCHAND DE TOUTES SORTES D'ETOFFES, DE SOIE D'OR ET D'ARGENT,

RUE S. HONORÉ,

Au coin de celle des Frondeurs, vis-à-vis la rue de l'Echelle,

A PARIS.

Archives Nationales, T 220 ³⁻⁷

5.3   Letterhead of the silk merchant Buffault, 1769

Source: Archives Nationales, T 220.5–7

and remove freckles and facial blemishes'.[24] This text poses the problem of distinguishing between advertising and charlatanism. The toy merchant, Vaugeois, was also wordy, but his letterhead was one of the most elaborate (see Fig. 5.6).

A close study of the text of these letterheads reveals to us both the specific sales tactics used by tradespeople and their masterful use of flattery for attracting and maintaining a very specific clientele. The diversity of goods stimulated the imagination of salespeople, leading to advertisements abounding in phrases such as 'all kinds of', 'all ways', 'all colours', 'all sizes', 'all tastes', 'made for all uses', and in addition, many end with the all-purpose formula 'and we have everything you could imagine!'[25] Many merchants used prices as their main selling point. The term 'Reliable Shop' existed well before the nineteenth century: 'Bazin ... announces a Reliable Shop with low mark-ups on merchandise, fixed prices ... displayed in a way that nobody could mistake ... '.

The practice of setting fixed prices, which predominated later, was not a widespread commercial practice at that time: prices were not displayed,

Archives Nationales, T 186 ³⁰

5.4 Letterhead of the fabrics merchant Hayet, 1788

Source: Archives Nationales, T 186.50

and purchasing an item required debate and bargaining between salesperson and customer. The Morel silk shop had 'as its main aim to gain the confidence of the public through the use of fixed prices ... '. Likewise, the shop of the very famous jeweller Granchez, The shop of *Small Dunkerque*, was reputed to be one of the first to use this practice.

Always looking for ways to distinguish themselves from their competition, many merchants took advantage of the nobility's attraction to the sciences. Advertisements frequently invoked scholarly authority. For instance, Chafanel Dupon slipped in a line from the very serious Royal Academy of Science in his prospectus about the approval of his lipstick by Lavoisier and Jussieu. Demachy did not hesitate to adopt a lofty title, relating it to the new attraction of botany: instead of using the term apothecary, he chose the designation of Master of Pharmacy, Teacher of Natural History, Member of Several Academies, and Royal Censor. Degournay, the manager of the royal silver-plated china manufactory, quoted the following in support of his manufacturing process of plating copper with silver: 'According to Honourable Representatives of the Academy of Science and the Representatives of the Faculty of Medicine; according to the scientist Macquer in his last Chemistry Dictionary; according again to Mr. Duplanil in his treatise on Home Medicine ... '.[26]

5.5   Letterhead of the furrier Arson, 1780

Source: Archives Nationales, T 166.3–5

Entrepreneurs also used scare tactics to promote the relative advantages of their products, such as, in Demachy's case, the threat of
'poisoning by verdigris'. He praised the safety of his silver-plated products which 'combine the double advantage of cleanliness and the
protection of clients' health from all potential danger'. Mr Clement,
who owned a cistern and stoneware shop, used similar arguments in a
bill dated 1784: 'No one can deny ... the well-known usefulness of
Sandstone Cisterns; it is enough to bring before our citizens' eyes only
one example of the dangerous accidents caused by the use of those
made of copper ... '. The progress made in metalwork production in the
second half of the eighteenth century is well known.[27] We can see here
how tradespeople propelled and promoted that progress.

Haberdashers brandished the theme of novelty to a great extent in
their advertisements.[28] It often appears even in the names of shops, as in
The Basket of New Tastes (Pradel & Co., a fabrics merchant) or The
Novelty Shop (Ibert Beauvais, also a fabric merchant). In the constant
innovations, one finds the link between production and luxury consumption: dealers were destined to satisfy and to tempt anew, boosting

Archives Nationales, T 186⁵²

5.6   Letterhead of the merchant Vaugeois, purveyor of toys, undated

Source: Archives Nationales, T 186.52

their sales and creating new products in the process. These new products, which stimulated demand, in turn led to the development of further innovations. This is the secret of their success. This kind of success is aided by the conspicuous consumption of court society. Fashion spurred supply and demand at the same time. The *Manuel de la toilette et de la mode* (*Handbook of Toilet and Fashion*) stressed this role: 'Nothing is more natural for a human being than the love of change. It is a blessing for the State, because industry and commerce benefit.'[29]

Some suppliers addressed a privileged clientele: dukes and lords, ladies and gentlemen, officers, the royal house, troops and regiments. The merchants, always eager to flatter, used their clients' positions even in the names of their products, selling ointments 'Duchess style' and 'in the style of Maréchal's Wife'. The sign of a wood merchant, *The Lily Flower*, aimed at a very specific public, for this merchant only delivered wood for hothouses. The trump card would be, precisely because he was addressing the court, to have the king and the queen among his customers: royal consumption was crucial for the spreading of product

A L'ARCHE, DUPON, Marchand,

Rue de Richelieu, présentement vis-à-vis la Bibliothèque du Roi,
où est le Tableau de son Rouge Végétal, à côté de l'Épicier.

CHAFANEL DUPON, pere & fils, très-connu pour les beaux Gants très-fins de son Pays de Grenoble, Gants blancs, Gants Danois, Gants de peaux de chien, Gants de Tirol, Gants d'Inspruck, Gants de Castor, Gants glacés de toutes couleurs, Gans en amadis pour les femmes qui montent à cheval, Gans faits pour les mariages, Gants & Mitaines de suif, Gants de peaux de renne pour hommes & pour femmes, les belles Peaux de renne pour vestes, gilets & culottes, & pour faire des draps pour les Voyageurs.

Toutes sortes de beaux Éventails Anglois & de Paris, pour les mariages, des plus à la mode; la vraie Flanelle d'Angleterre, blanche & bleue, bonne pour les rhumatismes, & pour faire des chemises de bain.

Le Tableau d'Angleterre pour les coupeurs & brûleurs.

La belle Cire d'Espagne, à graveur, rouge & noire.

Les étoffes de soie noire, pour les habits d'été; les drap de Minorque & drap de Prince, & les doubles Croisés pour doublures; les Habits tricotés, en soie & en laine, en noir, d'Angleterre.

Les bonnes Étoffes en soie noire pour culottes, qui sont l'Éternelle de Marseille & la Prunelle.

Les Bamboches d'Allemagne, pour hommes & pour femmes, pour garantir du froid aux pieds aux Églises, en voitures & aux Spectacles.

Les belles Couvertures de soie, de toute grandeur.

Il tient aussi les Couvertures de coton ordinaires, en petit gris, pour les lits des garderobes. On trouve aussi les Couvertures en ouvre de soie, petit gris, pour les Domestiques. Toutes ces Couvertures sont très-bonnes pour meubler les Châteaux & les Maisons de campagne & de ville. Il garantit que les vers ne les piquent jamais.

Il tient encore les Capitons de soie pour les Jupons.

2

ROUGE végétal pour la Toilette des Dames.

DUPON à l'honneur de donner avis aux Dames qu'il distribue avec succès son Rouge végétal, dont il est l'Auteur, approuvé par l'Académie Royale des Sciences. Il ne tient que le Rouge très-fin & le Rouge superfin des Indes, dont les qualités en diffèrent les prix de 6 à 12 & à 24 liv. lesdits Rouges sont d'une belle couleur rose vermeille; ils ne contiennent point aucun chaud. Pour qu'il n'y ait point d'abus, lesdits pots sont couverts de l'approbation de l'Académie Royale des Sciences, pour la facilité des Dames de Province ou en Campagne, afin d'avoir l'utile & satisfaction en demandant par les numéros donc ci-après est l'explication.

No. 1. Rouge vif de blonde.　　No. 4. Rouge encore plus vif pour
No. 2. Rouge plus vif de brune.　la nuit, les bals & pour les théâtres.
No. 3. Rouge très-vif pour la nuit.

EXTRAIT des Registres de l'Académie Royale des Sciences.
Du 26 Juillet 1775.

MESSIEURS LAVOISIER ET DE JUSSIEU, le jeune, qui avoient été nommés pour examiner un Rouge végétal à l'usage des Dames, présenté par le Sieur CHAFANEL DUPON, l'ayant fait composer devant eux par le Sieur DUPON, pour s'assurer qu'il ne contenoit rien qui pût nuire à la peau, ni altérer la santé, en ayant fait leur rapport, l'Académie a jugé que ce Rouge, qui ne parolt le céder en rien à celui du Sieur COLIN, approuvé en 1772, & qui, comme lui, ne contient rien de nuisible à la peau ni à la santé, avoit les mêmes droits à son approbation; en foi de quoi j'ai signé le présent Certificat. A Paris, le 7 Novembre 1775. Signé GRANDJEAN DE FOUCHY, Secrétaire perpétuel de l'Académie Royale des Sciences.

DUPON tient aussi toutes sortes de Parfums : Savoir;

Poudre blanche purgée à l'esprit-de-vin, parfumée de toutes sortes d'odeurs & sans odeurs.

Poudre au Jasmin d'Espagne.　　Poudre de Violette.
Poudre à la Fleur d'Orange.　　Poudre à la Franchipane.
Poudre de Mille-Fleurs.

Poudres brunes de toutes les meilleures qualités, à bon parfum double & simple.

Poudre à la Maréchale, double.　Poudre à la Violette.
Poudre à l'Œillet, double.　　　Poudre de Chipre Royale.
Poudre de Mille-Fleurs, double.　Poudre à la Jamaïque.
Poudre de Mousseline, double.　Poudre brune, grise & noire.
Poudre à la Franchipane.　　　Poudre couleur de rose & jaune.

3

Les bonnes Pommades de Rome & de Provence, & de sa façon, de toutes les meilleures qualités, toutes doubles de fleurs & parfums.

Pommade au Citron & à la Bergamote.
Pommade au Jasmin d'Espagne.
Pommade à la Fleur d'Orange.
Pommade à la Tubéreuse.
Pommade à la Rose.
Pommade à la Vanille.
Pommade à l'Œillet.
Pommade de Mille-Fleurs.
Pommade à la Duchesse.
Pommade à la Maréchale.
Pommade à la Franchipane.
Pommade au Thin.
Pommade d'ours à la moëlle de bœuf, parfumée à la fleur d'orange, pour faire revenir & fortifier les cheveux.
Pommade pour le teint.
Pommade au Concombre.
Pommade au Limaçon.
Pommade en bâton de toutes les meilleures qualités, double de fleurs & parfums.

Les bonnes Savonnettes aux herbes de Provence.
Le Savon de Naples parfumé.
Essence de Savon parfumé pour la barbe.
Les Éponges fines de Venise.
Les Éponges préparées au corail pour les de-es.
Les Racines de Guimauve & l'Opiat.
Les Curecuredents à la Cathenne & autres.
Les Houppes de cygne.
Il vient aussi toutes sortes de Quintessences, & de Citron, qui ôte les taches de graisse sur toutes sortes d'étoffes.
Toutes sortes de Pâte pour blanchir les mains.
Pâte d'Amandes amères & Amandes douces.
Pâte à la Reine parfumée, qui se conserve bien.
Pâte au Miel.
Pâte à la Vanille.

Eaux de senteur de toutes les meilleures qualités, pour la Toilette; toutes doubles de fleurs & en bons parfums.

Eau de Jasmin d'Espagne.
Eau de Bergamotte.
Eau de Mille-Fleurs.
Eau Suave.
Eau de Bouquet à la Reine.
Eau au Pot-Pourri.
Eau de Chypre.
Eau d'Œillet.
Eau de Thin & Romarin.
Eau de Cythère Royale.
Eau de Violette au Cédrat.
Eau de Lavande à la Royale.
Eau de Lavande de Trenel.
Eau de Cologne & de la Reine d'Hongrie.

Eau de Mélisse.
Eau de Rose & de Fleur d'Orange.
Lait Virginal pour le teint.
La véritable Eau des Sultanes pour le teint, qui blanchit la peau, efface les rides, les taches de rousseur & les masques du visage.
La Lavande rouge.
Le Vinaigre à la Lavande, distillé.
Vinaigre pour embaumer les Appartemens.
Toutes sortes de Vinaigres à odeur pour la Toilette; comme à la Lavande, à la Bergamotte, &c.

Il tient aussi toutes sortes d'Épingles blanches & noires pour la Toilette.

4

Nota. Le Sieur Dupon ne pouvant pas satisfaire à toutes les demandes d'aller en Ville, prie les Dames de lui envoyer un vice. On ne pout même, & d'avoir la bonté de dire les couleurs; par ce moyen, elles feront bien satisfaites.

Vu & approuvé à Paris ce 30 Juillet 1776.

Vu l'Approbation, permis d'imprimer ce 30 Juillet 1776. LENOIR.

De l'Imprimerie de GRANGE, rue de la Parcheminerie.

popularity and therefore for a shop's success. As soon as the queen, the 'fashion arbiter', as Sebastien Mercier named her, was dressed by a certain haberdasher, court ladies would begin fighting to follow her. Step by step, the court, the town, then the provinces, would imitate royal dress: 'We say of the town that it is the court's monkey.'[30]

The expectation of the workings of court society transformed the aristocracy, as well as the king himself, into tools of advertising. The names of merchants' shops invoked their royal or princely customers: *The Shop of King Louis XV* (Fernandez et Joly, haberdashers), *The Shop of the King of France, Louis XV* (Bellepanne, fireworks' manufacturer), *The Royal Hat* (Desperrelles, hatter), *The Shop of the Queen of France* (Girardin, fabric merchant), *The Royal Toilet* (Delaroue, fashion merchant), *The Crowned Dauphin* (Lacoste, fashion merchant), *The Dauphiness* (Montassier, hosier, and Tempé, embroiderer), *The Count of Artois* (Billard, Estelle, embroiderer), *The Duke of Berry* (Leroux et Delasalle, fabric merchants), *The Duke of Bourgogne* (Rigonot, hosier), *The Duke of Bourbon* (Curner-Neilson, hosier), and so on.

To be able to call oneself the regular supplier of the king or queen was the best advertisement: the spirit of imitation could be allowed full rein. The fortune of somebody like Granchez, Jeweller to the Queen, who owned two of the main china manufactures – those of the queen and of the king's brother[31] – and the fortunes of Beaulard or Bertin, fashion merchants of the queen, could not otherwise be explained. Advertisements, whether for iron merchants or glovers, never failed to call attention immediately to their illustrious protectors.[32] The presentation of merchandise came only afterwards: Ravoise, Confectioner of the Queen for the court sweets; Calteau, Glover–Perfume Merchant, usual supplier, appointed by H.R.H. the Countess of Artois; De la Briere, Merchant, and Perfumier of Madame, the King's brother's Wife … sells the lipstick of Miss Martin; Provost, Button Maker of H.R.H. the Duke of Orléans, First Crown Prince, of Madame, and of the Royal Princes, the Duke of Chartres, the Duke of Montpensier and the Duke of Beaujolais and so on.

The story of this last merchant is a very interesting one. At the end of the 1780s, he moved his shop to the Palais-Royal and, at the same time, changed his written letterhead. Previously he had simply listed his button descriptions on a long notice (twelve tight lines written in small characters). The shop had had a literal and not very attractive title: General Shop for Buttons of Charité-sur-Loire Royal Manufacture. In 1787, he began citing the patronage of the Duke and Duchess of Orléans and their three sons. After this announcement, he put less stress on the description of his products, shortening his advertisement to seven lines. He also chose a new eye-catching title: To the *Town of Birmingham*. He made the most of his opportunity: the Anglomania of the Duke of Orléans and the rest of the court was well known. Between 1779 and 1782, the haberdasher–embroiderer Barnou acted similarly, changing the name of his shop from *The Hood* to *The English Hood*.

These two merchants were not alone. Many shop-owners, well aware of the mechanisms of fashion, and profiting from the industrial and commercial dynamism of England, knew how to exploit Anglomania and thereby contributed to the boom in English products. Vying with each other, they celebrated English products: buttons, porcelain, wallpaper, fabric, ribbon and saddles and so on.[33] Fashion, once again, was used consciously by the merchant world. Merchants whose products came from such places as China and India promoted these origins in their advertisements as well.[34] They took advantage of exotic vogue and of the development of economic trade with Asian countries, coincidentally controlled by England. In France, 'toiles peintes', cotton-print fabrics first imported from India and then copied all over Europe, triumphed in spite of the authorities' efforts to protect domestic factories from their invasion: the customer's taste always won.[35] The development of this Indian fashion was connected with a revolution in customer taste and of social consumption practices, and was provoked by the introduction and imitation of Indian painted clothes. These changes eliminated the primacy of silk in clothing and furnishings.[36] The fabrics' names indicated their faraway origin: Persian, Indian, Chinese, Damask, Cashmere, Muslin and so on.[37]

Some other merchants, a bit less precise in their descriptions, worked with the simple term 'foreign'.[38] Here they still used the shop name as bait: Great Turk (Buffaut, Normand, silk fabric merchants; Bonnot, haberdasher; Grare, cloth merchant; but also Devaux, innkeeper), Great Mongol (Bertin, fashion merchant; Robert, fabric merchant), Chinese Cabinet (Le Bégue, dyes merchant), The King of China (Michel, fabric merchant), To the Eastern Port (Guesnier, silk fabric merchant), The English Shop (Ibert Beauvais, fabric merchant), The Famous English Shop (Chaniaud, saddler), To the Town of Winchester (Tissot, ribbon merchant), The English Glove (Sauvan, fashion merchant). This last advertised itself as a

> Shop for all kinds of English ribbons, plain or striped ones; plain and brocaded Moère; lilac Taffetas; plain single colour Satins; lilac, blue-green, black Velvets; genuine English quilting Piqué; plain and flowered Gauzes for furniture; all kinds of scarves, fine Italian Hats, English cotton Satins; new plain Fabrics of different English colours; small embroidery Ribbons; Indian Fans; English Fans; genuine English Honey Water; Mint and Peppermint Water; excellent Indian liquor.[39]

Granchez owned the 'large and beautiful French and English Shop' called *Small Dunkerque*. Certain changes in that title were significant for the growing importance of the phenomenon of Anglomania. The glover Mignot, cousin and successor to Chafanel, shortened the shop advertisement (to a dozen lines instead of four pages), so that both gloves and perfumes were presented concisely. At the same time, we can note the store's amusing change of name, making use of the glover pun. The shop, situated in rue de Richelieu (in front of the Royal Library), was originally called The Arc;[40] the advertisement began with The Arc, Dupon, Merchant. With Mignot, the new shopkeeper, this sign became *The Large Shop of the Bridge's Arch*. In this way, old customers were not lost. Texts were altered up to the very beginning of the 1780s. Showing the merchant's adjustment to the changing times, as well as the important link between England and horse racing, the advertisement for 'reindeer-skin gloves for men and women' was replaced by 'genuine English reindeer-skin gloves for male and female horse riders ... '.

Far from being confined to the role of passive agents between manufacturers and consumers, merchants of the eighteenth century became designers of their products, revealing themselves as active influences in the changing tastes of the times. Very skilful in detecting and sparking trends, they were instigators of the new, accelerating the evolution of style through the subtle changes that they imprinted upon their wares. Powerfully challenged by their clientele's requirements, they created the fashions of the times and were the inventors of commercial advertising.

Notes

1. Translated from the French in the linguistic seminar of Professor Anne Decrosse (Paris, E.H.E.S.S.), with the assistance of Johanna Dordea, doctoral candidate at the E.H.E.S.S.
2. Baronne Henriette L. D'Oberkirch, *Mémoires de la baronne d'Oberkirch sur la cour de Louis XVI et la societé française avant 1789*, edited by Suzanne Burkard (Paris: Mercure de France, 1989 (originally published in 1853)), 94–5. The *Mémoires* were written in 1789.
3. Fernand Braudel, *Civilisation matériélle, économie et capitalisme, XVe–XVIIIe siècle*, vol. 2 (Paris: A. Colin, 1979), 146–9.
4. This study was based on invoices found among the papers of five aristocratic families: La Trémoïlle, Fitz-James, Coigny, Fleury and the Princess Kinsky – French National Archives, revolutionary sequestration (Set T). These documents principally concerned the second half of the eighteenth century. Among some 1800 merchants and artisans accounted for, 200 were the main suppliers of a large number of these aristocratic families. Mlle Bertin, for example, was the favourite fashion merchant of Coigny, Fitz-James, Fleury and Princess Kinsky. My purpose is to analyse luxury commerce, surveying principally these favoured merchants and artisans.

See my book: 'L'hôtel aristocratique. Le marché du luxe à Paris au XVIIIe siècle' (Paris: Publications de la Sorbonne, 1998).

5. During the eighteenth century, the notion and term of *annonce*, corresponding in English to 'advertisement', prevailed in French. The American term 'advertising' *–art publicitaire* in French, appeared in about 1930.

6. Louis-Sébastien Mercier, *Tableau de Paris* (Genève: Slatkine, 1979 (originally written in 1782–88)), chap. 362.

7. It is our claim that the advertisement as material object bears the seeds of the modern strategy and practice of advertising. In the material we are looking at, we can find clearly expressed the operational notion of advertisement only as object, label, leaflet or poster, but not as a word. In the French of the Age of Enlightenment, the terms 'label', 'leaflet', 'poster' referred exclusively to printing activities and were not related to commercial practice. More recently these terms have developed a commercially related meaning. In the twentieth century, the notion of advertising became an independent activity, but this modern professional notion rests upon the same paradigm. We note the difference in French between the meaning of *publiciste* – the term for journalist in the eighteenth century – and what will become *publicité* – a publicity-related activity, as opposed to English, in which advertisement and advertising developed their connotations together.

8. Dènis Diderot and Jèan Le Rond d'Alembert (eds), *Encyclopédie, ou Dictionnaire raisonné des sciences, des arts, et des métiers* (Stuttgart–Bad Cannstatt: Friedrich Frommann Verlag, 1966 (originally written in 1751–80)). See also Emile Littré, *Dictionnaire de la langue française* (Paris: Hachette, 1873).

9. Although the *Petit Robert* gives 1829 as first date of use.

10. The poster (*l'affiche* in French) 'is a bill or a sheet of paper usually stuck on street corners to announce different public matters of general interest: awards presented, goods for sale, lost and found goods, recently printed or reprinted books, etc ... We understand by "label" (*vignette*), the ornamentation with which printed matter is decorated. They are largely used at the beginning of a work, book, preface, or dedicatory epistle. The labels represent different drawings and have a size commensurate with the drawing's shape.' The leaflet (*prospectus*) 'means the project or program of the work we propose to sign ...'. The neologism first appears in Littré as a fifth meaning: '[advertisement is a] small notice inserted separately from announcements in a newspaper, and referring, in praise, to a book, art object, object of commerce ...'.

11. Marc Martin, *Trois siècles de publicité en France* (Paris: Odile Jacob, 1992), 15.

12. *Cabinet des Modes, ou les Modes Nouvelles* 1 (15 November 1785).

13. *Cabinet des Modes.* 'Paper' is the translation for the French word *annonce*, related to *annonceur*, an advertising-related profession.

14. Braudel, *Civilisation matérielle*.

15. *Cabinet des Modes* 23 (15 October 1786).

16. *Cabinet des Modes* 9 (15 March 1786).

17. Jacques Savary des Bruslons, *Dictionnaire universel de commerce* (Paris: J. Estienne, 1723–30), 'Fashions'.

18. Ibid., 'Novelty'.

19. In France, names were not given to shops based solely on the image that

they conveyed, or on the aesthetic qualities of the names themselves; location also played a role. It is for this reason that many shop names begin with *A la, Au, Aux* (To the ...).

20. 'Everything at the right price', 'very low price', 'very good value', 'at set price', and 'always at the manufacturing price', and so on.

21. 'of first quality', 'the most wanted', 'of all the best qualities', 'in all the best qualities', and so on.

22. 'very pretty', 'beautiful', 'very fine range', and so on.

23. A clever joke: in French, *du pont* means a bridge with arches.

24. T 186/96: bill addressed to the Duke and Duchess of Fitz-James, May–December 1777.

25. We also find 'all sorts of', 'in all types', 'of different sorts', 'all Comestibles of every season', 'all kinds of lines made for all uses', 'very large collection', 'whole and retail sales', and so on.

26. T 1051/52: bill addressed to the Duke of La Trémoïlle, 3 November 1786.

27. 'Josiah Wedgwood and the Commercialization of the Potteries', in Neil McKendrick, John Brewer and J. H. Plumb, *The Birth of a Consumer Society* (London: Europa Publications, 1982), 100–145; Lorna Weatherill, *Consumer Behaviour and Material Culture in Britain 1660–1760* (London and New York: Routledge, 1988), 100; and Daniel Roche, *Le Peuple de Paris* (Paris: Aubier Montaigne 1981), 145–6.

28. 'What art creates as the latest fashion', 'according to the latest taste', 'of the latest taste', 'in the latest taste', 'the latest', 'the new models', 'from all the novelties', 'new models of his own design', 'the newest and the most fashionable merchandise', and so on.

29. C. S. Walther, *Manuel de la toilette et de la mode (Essai d'un petit dictionnaire des modes)*, 3 vols (Dresda: 1771–80).

30. Paul Antoine Saint-Cyr, *Le tableau du siècle* (Geneva: n.p., 1759), cited by Norbert Elias, *The Court Society* (Oxford: Basil Blackwell, 1983), 11. Montesquieu's opinion did not differ: 'The Prince's spirit marked the Court; the Court influenced the Town, the Town sent it to the provinces', Montesquieu, *Persian Letters* (Harmondsworth: Penguin, 1993), 189.

31. The Factory of the Queen was situated in rue Thiroux; the Factory of Monsieur was situated in rue Clignancourt.

32. London commercial practices were similar, as proven by this bill, dated 1785, of a hatter of Pall Mall, London: 'Bought of J. A. Carter, Hatter to Their Royal Highnesses the Princes of Wales, Prince Frederick and Prince Wilh. Henry ... '. (T 166/16–19: bill sent to the Viscount of Fleury on 30 March 1785).

33. 'English wallpaper', 'genuine English flannels', 'English velvet made of cotton', 'English fabrics', 'Rivoire Widow, English silk Manufacturer, manufactures also Yarn to make round point Net, like the English Silk work', 'French and English Horses, Equipages', 'all kinds of English Equipage', 'Steel-made English Snuffers', 'English buttons', and, more generally, 'all sorts of odd objects directly from England'.

34. 'Chinese liquor stands', 'Chinese Screens and Papers', 'genuine Indian Papers', 'Indian chinaware', and so on.

35. At the end of the sixteenth century, Indian painted clothes became fashionable in Europe, but their wider diffusion didn't come until the eighteenth century. According to Bertrand Gille, *Documents sur l'état de l'industrie*

et du commerce à Paris (Paris: Impression Municipale, 1963), 18; Louis Bergeron, 'Paris dans l'organisation des échanges intérieurs français à la fin du XVIIIe siècle', in *Aires et structures du commerce français au XVIIIe siècle*, national seminar of the French Association of Economic Historians, 4–6 October 1973, Lyon: Economic and Social History of the Lyon Country Centre (1975), 253–4. The Mulhouse museum of fabric and wallpaper offers a marvellous range of these textile splendours of the eighteenth century.

36. Pierre Léon, *Histoire économique et sociale du monde* (Paris: Armand Colin, 1977), 3: 362.

37. 'genuine Indian and English Chintz', 'Persian English, Indian, and Jouy Clothes', and so on.

38. 'very important range of foreign fabrics', 'foreign jewelry', and so on.

39. Invoice of the merchant Sauvan.

40. See note 23.

CHAPTER SIX

Commercial Immanence: The Poster and Urban Territory in Nineteenth-Century France

*Aaron J. Segal**

On the quays by Notre-Dame, near the Place du Tertre just west of Sacre-Coeur, along the shopping strip that links Les Halles to the flanks of the Centre Pompidou, upon the walls of the Petit Bistro on La Cienega Boulevard in Los Angeles, in so many sites that seek to embody Paris – in the capital and abroad – the bright tones of posters and poster reproductions evoke a *fin-de-siècle* Paris envisioned as the capital of a *belle époque* of pleasure expressed in paper and ink. As early as 1901, the Vicomte Georges d'Avenel wrote, 'Thus Paris develops in an indistinct fresco, on fences or cracked plaster, the allegorical figuration of its spectacles, its styles, its life.' Historian, economist and journalist, d'Avenel was not the first to analyse the turn-of-the-century poster as an avatar of the great city itself. Later scholars and others have investigated the relationship of posters to Parisian culture and society through the paintings of Toulouse-Lautrec, Seurat and Picasso, music-halls, bicycles, a plethora of products, and the cityscape itself. Indeed, historians have helped to contextualize the advertising poster by reintegrating it into the politics of the Third Republic. Studies have analysed how republican critics embraced the poster as a vehicle of aesthetic, social, democratic and moral reform, while cultural conservatives decried it as an emblem of seduction, prostitution, excessive democratization and a capitalism antithetical to small shopkeepers. In short, research has tried to correct what might be termed 'commercial memory'.[1]

At the same time, scholars of other cities have increasingly encountered the phenomenon of commercialization in their efforts to interpret the uses of streets, walls and public spaces in the late nineteenth and early twentieth century. Although posters mobilized vast resources, they integrated poorly into a society which purported to divide money and art, the commercial and the aesthetic, into opposing camps. Commercial publicity blurred the guarded boundaries of culture and commerce. This essay will explore the tensions in responses to the poster grounded in its dual aesthetic and commercial nature. After examining the aesthetic consecration of the poster in the context of naturalism, the decorative arts reform movement, nationalism and attitudes towards popular imagery, I trace how French officials in a number of cities sought to regulate and quarantine public advertising as part of a broader campaign of republican social and political landscaping.

By highlighting the French context – a newly created republican regime with older administrative traditions and a deep-seated concern for the vulnerability of the will – I demonstrate how efforts to circumscribe commercial messages embodied a particular conception of France and its citizens at the end of the nineteenth and the beginning of the twentieth century. The spread of posters into towns and cities has implications for the periodization of advertising and the commercialization of cityscapes, for an understanding of republican citizenship and for an interpretation of urban policy during the first decades of the Third Republic.[2]

By the mid-1890s, posters crafted to capture the attention of urban viewers and manufactured by the millions covered buses, stations, kiosks and walls in cities and towns across France. My ultimate concern here is the meanings and power attributed to advertising posters and efforts to regulate them during the first decades of the Third Republic. None the less, as basic questions of when, where and to what degree posters appeared on provincial walls, façades, pillars, fences, columns, kiosks and parapets in the nineteenth century have not been answered, I will begin by briefly sketching out that development. My comments will be based primarily on data gathered by the municipal governments of five cities – Nantes, Bordeaux, Lyons, Marseilles and Paris – as they recorded disputes, contemplated lawsuits or established bargaining positions.

Of course, the history of posters pre-dates the final decades of the nineteenth century. Deployed by Church, State, revolutionaries and businessmen under the *ancien régime*, they covered the walls of Paris by the 1830s at the latest, when satirists caricatured 'poster-mania'. During the last two decades of the century, city advertising concessions for Paris omnibuses, municipal walls, pillars, lamp-posts, controller booths, post boxes, decorated poles and kiosks, some created under the Second Empire, multiplied in scope and value until they probably generated over half a million francs per year in revenue for the city alone.[3]

In the provinces, the poster industry developed in the largest cities in the 1840s and expanded into large towns by the end of the century. Under the Second Empire, Parisian posting agencies promised to deliver posters to every community in the nation in a matter of days, no doubt exaggerating resources and failing to take into account the conditions of highways, waterways and railways. According to municipal poster contracts, a more reliable index, city walls acquired value as poster supports soon after the fall of the Second Empire at Sedan. Bordeaux and Lyons began to lease posting space in the mid-1870s. By the mid-1890s, wall-space prices had climbed to 20,000 francs per year in Lyons, 6,170 in Marseilles, 5,000 in Nantes and 3,500 in Le Hâvre, although Lille and Rouen bartered posting rights on kiosks and toilets for the cost of constructing and maintaining them and posting municipal advertisements. Values dipped with the market crash of 1882 and slumped in 1897, when the Agence Dalziel, a major player with contracts across France, failed at the end of two decades of recession, after having driven local competitors out of business. However, prices recovered. Furthermore, those figures hint at a growing provincial industry. In 1913, the largest advertising business in Lyons paid 18,790 francs for city walls, over 28,640 francs for municipal columns, 11,336 francs for municipal urinals, and 21,000 francs for private wall space.[4]

The value of city walls is one measure of the expansion of provincial advertising; the expansion of advertising companies is another. In the final decades of the century, firms multiplied and spread. According to the local business directory in Marseilles, a single company placed posters on walls, fences and kiosks in 1878; in 1890, six did so. By 1896, poster-mounting and conservation enterprises operated in towns and cities in fifty-two departments in every region. They were scarce in the impoverished south–centre, from the Creuse to the Aveyron, and plentiful along the Normandy coast. In 1898, the Société générale de publicité, O. Zucca, boasted concessions for tramway and omnibus advertising in over forty locations including Marseilles, Bordeaux, Lyons, Elbeuf, and even Aniche, with a population under 10,000; 50,000 meters of wall space in major municipalities; 200 advertising wagons; 500 sandwichmen; restroom concessions in a dozen towns; and more. By 1913, the letterhead of the Agence nationale d'affichage listed seventy-six branch offices in the provinces. A trade sheet, *La Publicité moderne*, estimated that roughly three times as much area was covered by posters in 1908 as in 1897. Those figures suggest that poster businesses emerged in even medium-size towns, and wall space was commodified in larger regional centres during the final three decades of the nineteenth century. To interpret the significance of that development, it is necessary to turn from figures to images and words.[5]

Naturalist criticism

During the early 1880s, or perhaps earlier, in the rue Legendre in the Batignolles district near Montmartre, the symbolist writer Joris-Karl

Huysmans came upon a shop laden with the busts of mannequins. Struck at first by the impression of a morgue with decapitated cadavers, he soon warmed to what he saw. Comparing that 'museum of breasts' to the sculpture galleries of the Louvre, he contrasted the uniform, studied, dismal beauty of statues of Venus to the necks and chests of the couturiers. The suggestive power of the marbles was dead, he wrote, when contrasted with the fabric-covered busts of the dressmakers. By looking up the street mentioned by Huysmans in a catalogue of the period, it is possible to suggest where he viewed his mannequin – in the display window of the largest manufacturer of the period, Fréd Stockman, who developed anatomical casting at the end of the Second Empire.[6]

Huysmans' confrontation with the puzzling figure of the mannequin clearly mocked academic tradition, but it also suggested an aesthetic in which commercial display objects, by virtue of their verisimilitude, novelty and, perhaps, crudity, could convey more sensation than the artefacts of classical culture. In praising the mannequin, Huysmans suggested that manufactured objects designed for commercial display could be considered works of art and questioned the classifications of museums. Huysmans' description of the mannequin was part and parcel of a naturalist effort to invert aesthetic categories despite the incipient critique of naturalism it contained.[7]

Huysmans' comments are of particular importance for an analysis of aesthetic responses to advertising. For Huysmans pronounced on commercial images in another context: his review of the 1880 Salon. There he urged the disheartened to step outside and gaze at the works he described – the posters of Jules Chéret – as displaying a thousand times more talent than most of the canvases he had critiqued. He thus inaugurated a new branch of criticism.[8] Before the end of the decade, in an attempt to shape an aesthetic suited to a democratic society, critics would consecrate the poster as a new genre, weakening the distinction between the commercial and the aesthetic, reshaping the boundaries of the artistic and paving the way for future artistic revolutions. By the First World War, posters had been incorporated into the national cultural patrimony.

The valorization of the poster in the mid-1880s developed in response to the work of a single artist: Jules Chéret. By 1884, Chéret's workshop was producing nearly 200,000 posters per year. Exhibited at the Galerie Vivienne that year, included in Beraldi's *Graveurs du XIXe Siècle* in 1885, forming the basis of Maindron's *Affiches illustrées* in 1886, exhibited at the Exposition universelle and then the Théâtre de l'Application in 1889, the work of Chéret and his promoters had created the modern poster as a new genre replete with collectors, critics and historians by the final decade of the century. Critics have

6.1   Bonnard-Bidault

Source: Bibliothèque Nationale de France, Print Collection

described the consecration of mass-produced prints as works of art in the context of the decorative arts reform movement and sought to describe a radical strain in poster production, but they have neglected to place that development in the context of national ideologies of culture and commerce which welcomed the poster as a synthesis of innovation and tradition.[9]

In *Art Nouveau in Fin-de-siècle France*, Debora Silverman describes how the promotion of the unity of the decorative and fine arts and an eighteenth-century aristocratic rococo tradition corresponded to an attempt to rally left and right to the Third Republic during the final decade of the nineteenth century. She also traces the complex relationship of new concepts of consciousness and urban reality to interior decoration. Unlike late nineteenth-century decorative craft objects, the poster was flimsy, mechanically reproduced, and designed for public commercial display. None the less, many of the concerns which shaped the decorative arts revival informed efforts to promote the poster as a modern manifestation of French cultural tradition. Aesthetics, industry and power were bound up in the creation of a new genre.[10]

The crucial figure in that development was Roger Marx, an inspector of provincial museums and the author, in 1913, of *L'Art social*. He penned the introduction to Chéret's exhibition catalogue in 1889 and promoted his work over the next decade. Marx viewed the poster as a popular medium arising from new social conditions which could transform and uplift broad segments of the population. But his work marked the culmination of a tradition rather than its inauguration. The changes he wrought in that heritage illustrate important attitudes toward the poster and the decorative arts revival in the late nineteenth century.[11]

The poster, a vehicle of propaganda during the Reformation and an instrument of royal authority under the *ancien régime*, was envisioned as a tool of enlightenment and persuasion well before the Third Republic. During the Revolution of 1848, Jules Michelet advocated illustrated multicolour posters with large type as a means of educating the public. Under the Second Empire, to cite one case, a museum conservator argued for the use of posters to educate and enlighten peasants, workers and children. Posters in the classroom could teach rural hygiene in the countryside, home economics in girls' schools and geography to boys; workers could learn about the metric system or the lives of great inventors from factory walls. For children and labourers, wrote the author, shied away from books but devoured posters. Sébastien Mercier first gave wide currency to the notion that posters could form the basis of popular education. In his 1783 *Tableau de Paris*, reprinted and cited throughout the century, he suggested that posters could offer political, literary and moral education for a broader public and likened them to 'open-air libraries'.[12]

For Marx, the visual aspect of Chéret's work was of the utmost importance. Whereas Mercier had spoken of 'open-air libraries', Marx spoke of an 'open-air museum' and compared the posters of Chéret with tapestries for religious processions which exemplified their period and educated taste. Other advocates described commercial images as immediately accessible to the public. As Gustave Geffroy, a critic and future director of the Gobelins tapestry manufacture, declared, they required no printed invitation, had no gold frames and required no catalogues to be deciphered. Throughout the 1890s, journals such as *Le Livre et l'image*, *L'Estampe et l'affiche* and the *Journal des arts* devoted regular columns to what they termed the 'Salon of the Streets' – posters glimpsed on the streets of Paris.[13]

Poster design competitions resonated within the artistic community. Sponsored by design magazines, by chicory, soap, liquor and typewriter manufacturers, by expositions, and even by tourist sites, they promised fame and communication with a broad public and drew hundreds of submissions. The major academic artists of the day – Jean Léon Gérôme, the military painter Edouard Détaille, and others – reigned over the first juries, and some contests attracted the patronage of arts organizations and the State. At the opening of the exhibition displaying the results of the competition for the journal *L'Eclair,* the Minister of Public Instruction and the Fine Arts, Alfred Rambaud, gave voice to the hopes of Marx and the decorative arts movement by exalting the role of beautiful quotidian objects in the education of 'the race' and heralding the poster as an ephemeral fresco which both turned the street into a museum and recalled an age before the separation of artists from artisans. The *Concours* implied a democratic faith in public taste: some sponsors let contestants participate in jury selection; others submitted works to the judgement of consumers in an aesthetic plebiscite.[14]

The movement to transmit a new aesthetic via the poster was echoed in the radical press. While *La Fédération lithographique*, the journal of the lithographers' union, saluted Chéret's posters as democratic art available to workers as well as to capitalists, *L'Egalité* praised him for choosing walls for his canvases and the crowd as his critic. The most extraordinary article appeared in the anarchist journal, *Le Père peinard*, in which the *avant-garde* critic Félix Fénéon urged anarchists to steal posters to decorate their homes.[15]

For Marx and others, the work of Chéret humanized the vista of the urban landscape with images of festive unity. Chéret's images often fused peasant fertility dances – the *ronde* and the *farandole* – redolent with associations of community, celebration and tradition – with figures from the *commedia dell'arte* and the cabarets of Montmartre in modern dress. That curious *mélange* of urban and rural, popular and aristocratic, which seemed to unite all France in a continual celebration, was executed with shadowy figures elevated into space, whose outlines seemed to blend with the colour layers that surrounded them.[16]

Proponents of the poster recognized that Chéret's work was advertising. Paradoxically, the relationship of the poster to economic needs made it seem all the more potent as a force for aesthetic and social transformation. Advocates of *l'art social* believed that art would spring directly from society and the people, as they imagined it had in the medieval period. Posters promised for a time to be that form. John Grand-Carteret, no proponent of *l'art social*, wrote that Chéret's images gave form to the needs of the age and defined him as one of the 'aesthetic labourers of the present'. To some, the artisanal and industrial character of Chéret's work made it an appropriate vehicle for change. For many it was a manifestation of national glory.[17]

An *art social* designed to uplift and to harmonize class tastes was entirely compatible with a national aesthetic concerned with observers as members of a political community. Nationalism, with or without

6.2   Carnaval

Source: Lucy Broids, *The Posters of Jules Chéret* (New York: Dover Publications, 1997), plate XVII

economic reform, was a heritage of the revolutionary tradition as well. For Marx, in 1889, the posters of Chéret 'revealed the character of a race'. Another critic declared that Chéret, like Puvis des Chavannes and the Impressionists, had 'resoak[ed] the faded tonalities of our school in gold and sunlight' and rendered a patriotic service to 'the national art'.[18]

Critical praise for the work of Chéret was linked to an explicit concern for the relationship among national taste, national industry, national forms of symbolization and national identity. Silverman has demonstrated that the promotion of the unity of the arts and rococo corresponded to an ideology of social solidarity. At a time when aesthetic conservatives castigated Impressionists and post-Impressionists as anarchists, and innovators condemned official art as reactionary, both left and right saw the work of Chéret as the incarnation of a French *joie de vivre* exemplified by the eighteenth-century *fêtes galantes* of Jean Honoré Fragonard and Antoine Watteau. Indeed, the view that Chéret's work incarnated French identity was so widespread that an 1890 reviewer in *Art et critique* protested that the work of Chéret was the work of an individual and not the product of a 'national taste'.[19]

Here the important case of Frantz Jourdain, champion of decorative arts reform and architect of the Samaritaine, must be considered. Between 1889 and 1891, Jourdain, a disciple of the *communard* Jules Vallès, praised Chéret as the embodiment of a national decorative movement free of foreign symbols, a modern creator informed by recent developments in painting, but gifted with a personal vision. Jourdain wrote that he had transformed decoration by 'bringing art into the street and democratizing talent'. Yet, like many contemporaries, he associated Chéret with a gracious and witty aristocratic tradition exemplified by Watteau, translated in a manner acceptable to a broader French public. Jourdain also associated Chéret with a blood-like embodiment of French soil, spirit and cultivation: wine.[20]

The national aesthetic revival envisioned by Jourdain disowned alien models – including Greco-Roman allegory. In proposing Chéret as a model for boutique designers, he wrote that the lithographer had enlivened the dullest subjects by studying the women and children of the age without resorting to Greek or Italian models or 'rummaging among ashes'. He also argued that Chéret's decorative panels could rescue French wallpaper from a pastiche of the Japanese. 'We are French, let us remain French,' Jourdain wrote, 'and finish once and for all with that unfortunate mania of painfully stripping labels from foreign rags, when we possess such fine rich linen close at hand.'[21]

Interest in the national character of Chéret's work was shared across the political spectrum. On the left, the radical avant-garde Brussels review, *L'Art moderne*, demonstrated a desire to naturalize a foreign medium when it praised Chéret by declaring, 'the poster has been renewed, purified of the blinding flashiness (*tape-à-l'œil*) imagined by Yankee puffery'. On the right, the *Action française* linked Chéret to a national tradition of pleasure visualized in his posters: 'He is of the *Moulin rouge*, he is of the *Moulin de la Galette*, he is of Paris and he is of France. Beneath his fingers he has not the lyre of Greece, but rather a guitar made in France (*de marque française*) that he strums with stunning brilliance'. In remarking that Chéret prints covered street walls with delicate tones, 'seductive' colours and 'gallant' design, a journalist for the *Journal des arts* declared, 'one begins to yield to a quite understandable burst of patriotic pride. Indeed, one can be proud to be French without regarding the Vendôme Column.' Thus aesthetic nationalism could supplant monuments and their factious significance with new forms of culture. Twenty years after Gustave Courbet and his Communard colleagues toppled the Bonapartist column in protest of its association with an imagined imperial heritage, French men and women could embrace a form of outdoor public culture devoid of factional connotations: the poster.[22]

After Chéret supporters – who included artists on the margins of official culture such as Albert Besnard and Eugène Carrière, academics such as Jules Dalou, Alfred Philippe Roll, and Albert Ernest Carrier-Belleuse, symbolists such as Huysmans and Félicien Rops, establishment critics such as Arsène Alexandre and Roger Marx, the conservative critic Jules Lemaître and others – petitioned the government, the artist received official recognition. On 6 April 1890, Léon Bourgeois awarded Chéret the Legion of Honour as a 'Lithographer–Painter'. An article announcing Chéret's receipt of this award proclaimed that his name would have a special meaning in the history of the arts: the close collaboration of art and industry for the production of 'veritable masterpieces'.[23]

By 1891, posters had become a collecting phenomenon and were well on their way to official recognition. Although he did produce occasional works later, Chéret decided to renounce posters for pastels and painting in the mid-1890s. Before the end of the decade, through the influence of the lithographer and critic Félix Bracquemond and the critic Philippe Burty, Chéret's poster-honed art was commissioned to decorate a meeting room in the Hôtel de Ville, the Paris city hall destroyed by arson during the Commune. That 'definitive consecration' helped to complete an edifice whose reconstruction was intended to embody national reconciliation. There Chéret's images – designed to create an atmosphere of 'pleasure and festival' – joined what the arts administrator Marius Vachon lauded in an official tome as an 'imposing museum' of contemporary art, a synthesis of the past, present and future glory of Paris, and a 'shining act of patriotic faith'.[24]

By the end of the century, Marx called for the creation of a poster museum with a 'survey' which aroused broad support. The national tapestry manufacture at Gobelins converted a Chéret poster into a tapestry, then commissioned decorative panels and upholstery designs translated into cloth. After protracted legal campaigns, posters, once disdained as industrial drawings, were safeguarded as elements of a national cultural patrimony. Commercial art, seen as the basis for a national culture free of the symbols of left and right, became official art.

Posters were also incorporated into the unofficial culture of urban carnival, balls and street life. As commercialized Mid-Lent festivals (Mi-Carême) and Carnival shifted from custom to committee-run festivity, posters boarded floats in the cavalcade. Publicity loomed large in Parisian celebrations well before the twentieth century. As early as March 1889, one writer noted that carnival parading was 'dead, dead and buried' except for mothers and children in costume and 'the inevitable advertising wagons'. At the Paris Mid-Lent festival of 1909, women dressed in the uniforms of billposters stuck up oversized feminist posters while riding a float shaped like a gigantic glue-pot to promote the posting firm of Gabert.[25]

At Montmartre and society balls, revellers embraced the poster as a medium of expression and play. A participant at a masked ball of the *Incohérents*, whose painted caricatures savaged artistic conventions in the mid-1880s, dressed as a poster kiosk. At a society gathering in Dinard in the Ille-et-Vilaine in the summer of 1907, four women dressed as the subjects of posters for cigarettes, soap, medicinal wine and Chéret's *Saxoléine*. On 27 February 1909, at one of the costume balls that accompanied Carnival, guests disguised as popular posters were greeted by hosts bearing glue-pots and brushes.[26]

Poster-bearing wagons and billposters continued the traditions of barkers and mountebanks, gathering crowds to watch commercial spectacles intended to sell goods. By the early 1880s, carts and wagons shaped like newspaper kiosks or pyramids, illuminated or plain, drawn by horses harnessed without ornament or in rich livery, travelled the streets of Paris day and night. 'In the Moorish, Egyptian, Gothic, Renaissance, etc., styles, always sober and in good taste,' one promoter described his teams. Advertising dromedaries drew crowds estimated by police at 250, while billposters duelling to cover one another's posters became a feature of the urban landscape, in one case attracting crowds estimated by police at about 200. We know of such incidents through the records of police and other authorities who monitored their disorder with displeasure. Circulation was one, but not the sole, concern. When viewed as the embodiment of commercial forces disruptive of a republican political and cultural project, posters met with concern, wariness and surveillance.[27]

The contaminating advertisement

An uneasiness toward commercial publicity pre-dated the proclamation of the Republic in 1875. In 1866 in 'A Victim of Advertising', the young Émile Zola told the story of a youth educated from birth via street signs, posters and newspaper announcements. Dulled, maddened, drenched, driven bald, poisoned, drowned and dropped in a ditch to rot by the age of twenty-one, Pierre Landry or Claude, as different versions named him, 'the deplorable victim of advertising', showed 'what we will become … if we have the naiveté to live the sweet and happy life promised by ads'. Zola's dark vision of a boy educated by means of advertisements may be seen as a male version of his 1883 novel *The*

Ladies' Paradise, which portrayed a department store that ravaged the will of female consumers. Zola took his inspiration from a piece by Philarète Chasles, but he darkened the critic's tale by rejecting his source's emphasis on the hope and sensation provided by publicity and raising the spectre of socialization by a force divorced from a humanist cultural tradition: commercial advertising which appealed to desire in order to encourage consumption.[28]

Critiques of the will

In the wake of the resounding defeat of France at Sedan in 1870, problems of individual will became national problems. From the beginning of the Third Republic, intellectuals and municipal authorities feared that commercial forces would socialize new generations in manners and values alien to their parents and leaders and so subvert tradition. Advertising seemed to threaten the reason and judgement assumed necessary for republican government grounded in majority rule. Inspired by new theories of psychology and state tradition, officials issued decrees and promulgated legislation to shield the eyes of town- and city-dwellers from commercial contamination. They thus sought to safeguard the role of family, school and nation in the communication of knowledge and values. In the process, they hoped to mould republican subjects. After considering theories of attention and perception, I will focus on four sites of conflict: monuments, the urban landscape, urinals and schools.[29]

Academic artists, attuned to problems of vision and perception, critiqued the power of posters to corrupt. The female painter Georges Achille Fould's 1889 Salon canvas, *Parti pour l'école*, represented the problem of visual socialization with a depiction of a boy gazing at a poster (Figure 6.3). His blond curls peeking from beneath his dark cap, he stands before a wall covered with posters, his umbrella hooked beneath his arm, his satchel ignored on the curb. He stares at an image of geese flapping on the wall. Beneath his line of sight a municipal proclamation announces mandatory schooling, while two circus horses rear on a poster to his right. At the top centre of the canvas, on the wall above, a macabre clown's face laughs and stares.

Fould's work was the subversion of a sub-genre – the depiction of children setting off for, or en route to, school. Her mesmerized child, her circus-pasted walls, her obscured official proclamation – all warned of the power of commercial images in secular republican society. The canvas was reproduced in the conservative *France illustrée* with a gibe at secular education and a plea that new generations be shown 'that God forbids the disfigurement by contortions of what he made in his

George Achille Fould, *Parti Pour l'École* (1889).

6.3   *Parti pour l'école*

Source: *La France Íllustrée*, 15 March 1890, 180 Bibliothèque Nationale de France

own image'. To one critic, the poster, icon of a fallen world, exemplified the dangers that a republican society without God posed for new citizens. Fould's image implied a critique of the republican regime, but government officials shared her fear that commercial posters would divert attention from education to frivolity in an age when liberty and licence could commingle and merge.[30]

The concept of attention, a major concern of physiological psychology, became an increasingly politicized issue as republican officials and social commentators strove to shelter vision and volition from unwanted appeals. Jonathan Crary has described a dynamic, temporal, synthetic notion of attention as a fundamental concern of the 1880s and 1890s, related to the rise of 'a social, urban, psychic, industrial field increasingly saturated with sensory input' and the attempt to make the 'seeing body' a productive student, worker, consumer or patient. Théodule Ribot, who founded the *Revue philosophique* with Taine in 1876 and joined the Collège de France a dozen years later, described attention as a physiological state of heightened activity in his extremely popular work on the subject. A disciple of Ribot, Jean-Paul Nayrac, won the prize competition on that subject sponsored by the Académie des Sciences Morales et Politiques in 1906 by extending his scientific hypotheses. The term was also used to urge students to concentrate on their studies in a less august context – in an 1887 address, professor of rhetoric Léon Quid'beuf told pupils at a secondary school in Le Mans that attention to their tasks was the key to their success in modern democratic society.[31]

Advertisers, too, explicitly used the language of attention. As early as 1878, the author of the first advertising guide argued that the poster should 'first, attract the eye, second, hold it, and finally, captivate the passerby, in a manner which completely absorbs his attention ... '. An article on advertising in the twenty-seventh volume of the *Grande encyclopédie*, published between 1898 and 1902, declared that 'advertising works only by retaining the attention, and having arrested it, only by doing violence to it'.[32]

But it was a politicized version of the notion of attention as a physiological response to external stimuli that had the broadest social ramifications. For physiological theories of attention combined with psychological models which described the power of images to transform consciousness to provoke particular concern regarding posters. During the early 1880s, both Jean-Marie Charcot at the Salpêtrie and Hippolyte Bernheim at the Faculté de Médecine conducted experiments which emphasized the visual receptivity and visual projections of patients. But whereas Charcot identified visual sensitivity as pathological, Bernheim emphasized the vulnerability of all consciences to suggestion and visual projection. 'Poor human reason has taken flight,' he wrote in 1884. 'The most ambitious spirit yields to hallucinations and becomes ... the plaything of dreams evoked by the imagination.' The symbolist novelist and critic Paul Adam compared the poster explicitly to the treatment of Charcot and feared an élite would yield to vignettes, colour arrangements and decorative frames, which he termed the 'forces of hypnotism'. By 1912, advertising theorists themselves cited Bernheim and announced that 'in the grand scheme of their operating modes, suggestion in medicine and suggestion in advertising move in absolute parallel'. Both Charcot and Bernheim disseminated their findings widely. Concerns for perception and attention would be incorporated explicitly into attempts to protect the gaze of urban viewers.[33]

City and state

The new psychology reinforced a tradition of state concern about the exhibition of imagery. At mid-century, under the monarchy of Louis-

Philippe and the Second Empire, officials monitored both republican and commercial images.[34] Writing in 1878, a Controller-General of Police who had served under both Louis-Napoléon and the Republic, noted that the courts had always distinguished between the right to print and the right to exhibit. In recommending that the caricaturist André Gill's *La Lune rousse* be prohibited from using sandwichmen bearing illustrations to advertise, he declared:

> Illustrations have more drawbacks than writing; they strike the intelligence in a more vivid, more lasting manner. In exhibiting a drawing, especially in circulating it on a public street, one ad-dresses people as a group; one speaks to their eyes; there is more there than the expression of an opinion; there is a fact, a putting into action, a life.[35]

Historians have described the aestheticization of the interiors of dwell-ings in the late nineteenth century as a bulwark against the overstimulation of modern urban life. During the same period, city administrators, police officials and members of parliament strove to demarcate public and private space and regulate public advertising. Those efforts have received limited scholarly attention. Following the passage of legislation mandating freedom of the press on 29 July 1881, republicans attempted to control streets and city walls not only to thwart revolution, but also to promote and preserve symbols of republi-can authority, shield the gaze of city-dwellers from appeals to the subconscious, and govern the morality of public expression. Those policies coincided with a movement to preserve landmarks, monuments and cityscapes as artistic treasures, embodiments of a national heritage and models of taste and culture. Such urban political landscaping fo-cused primarily on visual phenomena, which were believed to confront citizens with a greater threat to the will.

Parliamentary debates over government posting on church walls at the time of the press laws of July 1881 exemplify efforts to expand republican space in towns and cities across France. The republican sense of embattlement in a France that had been governed almost entirely by royal houses or Bonapartes since the Revolution should not be underestimated. If the first elections of the new Republic returned decisive republican majorities in the Chamber of Deputies in 1876 and 1877, it was only in the elections of 9 January 1879 that they wrested a decisive majority in the Senate. Soon after, the heirs of an anti-clerical tradition dating to the Enlightenment, grouped behind Jules Ferry, prom-ulgated a series of measures aimed at the Church: free, compulsory lay primary education, salary reductions for bishops and archbishops, the abrogation of work restrictions on Sundays, the suppression of army chaplains, the transfer of the authority to ring the church bells to mayors, and so forth. Efforts to authorize the apposition of official proclamations on church façades fell squarely into that tradition. Although pro-Catholic legislators and centrists managed to block what they saw as the defacement of church exteriors with republican proclamations, in the years that followed deputies on the left continued to propose measures to consolidate control over enemy territory by turning monuments to Catholicism into republican signboards.[36]

I mention political posting here solely to illustrate republican efforts to control posting in public space. During the late 1880s, republican police placed under surveillance posting by supporters of the charismatic General Georges Boulanger, who challenged the parliamentary system with an extensive publicity campaign funded from monarchical coffers. When the Duke of Orléans placed legally stamped portraits on the walls of Paris in 1897 announcing his imminent return, presumably to claim the throne, the Prefect of Police had agents lawlessly shred them. In both cases, officials expressed concern over the deployment of posters.

By the end of the century, only private firms and the government had the resources and the will to appeal systematically and continually to viewers in public space. Although Catholics sympathetic to anti-republican parties controlled great wealth, they funded few extensive poster campaigns. Manuals written by Catholic strategists betray the inequality of the struggle between the State and religious propagandists. Writing in Montpellier, the Abbot Fourié even taught the faithful how to soak and cook flour to make glue with which to post notices. By the twentieth century, revolutionary syndicalists also used posters as an arm against the State in Paris and certain provincial cities by systematically placing unstamped posters on monuments. Other groups did launch periodic or episodic appeals: electoral campaigners, including such polemicists as Dreyfusards and anti-Dreyfusards, and temperance reformers. Those efforts were significant, but they can only be noted here. The power and wealth needed to appeal to public consciousness on a regular basis with messages uncongenial to republican officials was held neither by the syndicalist Congrès Général de Travail nor by the Church. After the waning of the old right, republican fears focused not only on socialist propaganda, but also on a ubiquitous threat: commercial imagery propagated in massive quantities by new methods of reproduction.[37]

Posters competed for attention in a cityscape charged with meaning. Maurice Agulhon has described the spread of political statues over the course of the nineteenth century. That development began in earnest under the July Monarchy after 1830 and culminated under the Third Republic. Grounded in humanism, the erection of new forms in homage to secular figures was seen by Catholics such as Louis Veuillot as the consecration of 'new gods'. The erection of sculptures and fountains in city plazas and town squares was part of a profound battle over symbols and memory and a drive to conquer or reconquer public spaces for republican, clerical or imperial traditions.[38]

Preservation

The construction of statues and edifices coincided with the redefinition of the vestiges of the past as monuments and landmarks. In France, a preservationist movement emerged during the early Third Republic in part to check the threat posed by commercial placards to public taste and the national patrimony. Concern over the effect of advertising on the urban landscape certainly pre-dated that moment. In 1859, for example, Viollet Le Duc claimed to have received a letter from a Spanish canon who complained of feverish dreams after wandering in a cityscape where colossal painted advertisements for teeth and shoes obscured landmarks. Despite a belief in the didactic potential of cityscapes, organizations dedicated to translating those concerns into law emerged only later. Founded in the mid-1880s by Charles Normand, the Société des amis des monuments parisiens and L'Ami des monuments et des arts parisiens et français sought to preserve the architectural vestiges of Catholic, royal, aristocratic and commercial edifices both as artistic treasures and as monuments to a national past. Normand proclaimed that 'patriotism consists of memories as well as hopes', and later urged his collaborators to protect a 'clear French spirit' menaced by exaggerated utilitarianism, speculation and exploitation. The Parisian association turned to advertising as one of its first targets. Their drive was spearheaded by Charles Garnier, designer of the Opéra and the Casino at Monte Carlo, who urged that streets, plazas and towns should educate, and warned that posters threatened to pervert national taste with the baroque, the bizarre and the impudent. The group succeeded in banishing posters from many landmarks in 1886.[39]

Council members and law-makers reacted to the infringement of posters on monuments and landmarks intended to embody republican and national memory with resolutions, committees and legislation. Preservationist calls for a cityscape that embodied the vestiges of tradition in a harmonious whole echoed within the Paris municipal council, where Adrien Lamouroux, a radical from Les Halles with nationalist support, sponsored the creation of the Commission du vieux Paris in 1897. When an advertising pole obscured the face of Dalou's Republic, the Municipal Council recommended its removal. After numerous façades and sculptures were covered, the Chamber forbade posting on monuments in 1902. The effort to shelter republican monuments and their didactic functions from the ravages of posting demonstrates a conflict between the intentions of official power and new commercial forces.[40]

Officials became increasingly concerned that posters were debasing not only monuments, but also the Parisian character of the cityscape. Public parks remained free of advertisements, although the director of the Service des promenades and socialist councillors had to battle to table proposals by horticultural firms to promote their names in return for maintaining squares. François Levée, a councillor and wallpaper manufacturer representing the Palais-Royal district, complained that the authorization to raise roof levels had led owners to erect scaffolding for billboards and that the most beautiful streets had begun to resemble those of New York and Chicago. From 1909, Bonapartists and royalists representing the affluent wards to the west echoed resolutions of the Commission du vieux Paris in an effort to preserve scenic vistas from billboards. After Parliament taxed billboards which disfigured natural sites in 1912, Adrien Mithouard, an anti-Dreyfusard lawyer and poet representing the École Militaire district, warned of an 'invasion' of the capital by advertisers and proposed a prohibitive levy to sweep advertising from its walls. But the tax was co-opted by the budget committee, and anti-advertising legislation yielded to fiscal need.[41]

Preservation was one element of a municipal aesthetic that promoted alternatives to modern advertising. The Paris city council sought not only to safeguard monuments and vistas, but also to revitalize façade designs and illustrated shop signs emblematic of traditional small-scale commerce. Emulating efforts in Brussels by Eugene Broerman and *L'Art appliqué à la rue* to promote aesthetic reform via urban landscaping, the municipality sponsored a competition for façade designs along the Rue Réaumur in 1897 and created a city-wide annual competition the following year. A signboard contest spearheaded by the nationalist military painter Edouard Detaille, intended to turn the capital's streets into a 'permanent and democratic exhibition', according to the Prefect de Selves, followed in 1902. Paris, however, drew the line between façades and signboards and posters. A suggestion by the radical–socialist photographer Victor Louis Pannelier for a contest to beautify the city walls with posters for the 1900 Universal Exposition was rejected by his colleagues, who reasoned that market forces would produce aesthetic images and who probably preferred stone to paper and ink anyway. Other councillors on the left proposed the extension of posting concessions on aesthetic grounds.[42]

Quarantine

Where poster concessions were granted, they raised fears over the information conveyed. Urinals and lavatories were constructed by advertising firms in exchange for posting rights. They proved unsavoury to officials concerned with moral hygiene, as posters disseminated unsanctioned knowledge to satisfy a demand for cures for venereal disease. The caricaturist Frédéric Bouchot equated posters and bodily excretions around mid-century, when he quipped: 'What are those little monuments ... where I see people stand inside and read little posters? – Of course ... it's quite simple ... they are new ... literary ... exhibition rooms/toilets (*cabinets*) ... which correspond to a need of the century.'[43] In 1889 in Paris, Dr Gillebert Dhercourt, chief physician attached to the police, noted that posters there exposed young girls 'to initiation into the mysteries of secret diseases, shameful flows, etc.', while scrapings and scrawlings created obscene phrases and designs. Problems surfaced elsewhere. In Lyons in the late 1880s, the mayor complained that posters soiled urinals and promoted graffiti; in July 1897 in Nantes, a squad of officers lacerated 865 posters in an eight-day operation. In each case, the city was obliged to take further action.[44]

Authorities attempted to create a protective zone free from commercial and moral contamination around schools as well. In March 1897, within a week after a teacher at a girls' school in Lyons complained that posters lining the school gate threatened to undermine morality lessons, the mayor withdrew the walls from the city-posting concession. At Nantes, to head off a ban, the municipal poster contractor suggested limiting such advertisements to official pronouncements. The worst case was the capital, where, in 1912, a member of the municipal council warned that pharmacies were using posters bearing the words 'Municipality of Paris' to advertise venereal remedies on school walls. In 1913, the Prefect of the Deux-Sèvres warned mayors of the dangers which posters depicting scenes of violence and passion, designed to 'strike hard' and grip the attention in passing, posed to the impressionable imagination of children and adolescents. He suggested that they apply statutes outlawing the sale of alcohol near schools to hoardings.[45]

Fears for the will extended to a broader public. By the prewar era, theories of cognition developed by the psychologists Charcot and Bernheim during the 1880s were translated into legislative initiatives to control advertising. In the winter of 1908–9, the deputy Maurice Viollette authored measures to modify free press legislation to forbid the public display of visual representations of murder. Viollette's proposition was directed specifically against forms of advertising which, he argued, speculated on trauma to maintain a nervous fever. He traced a chain of sensations beginning with fright which would end in misery and crime. What particularly unnerved the legislator was the involuntary perception of images. Media that demanded no 'act of will' from the public were 'particularly dangerous': 'The poster ... strikes the eyes of the passerby like it or not; he is forced to look at it; his eyes cannot turn away until after they have perceived its pleasant or painful sense, but the impression is made and the imagination is struck.' Such language expressed fears regarding the breakdown, in the face of commercial imagery, of an Enlightenment-derived liberal conception of a rational citizenry. A parliamentary commission concluded that the reproduction even of imaginary crime scenes in posters should be forbidden.[46]

Despite official concern, posters became a fixture of the urban landscape as cities across France turned over their walls to contractors. Provincial wall space, once free, became a commodity. By the eve of the Great War, Lyons alone earned close to 60,000 francs per year and Paris over half a million for walls, urinals and columns maintained by contractors. Town planners everywhere registered their protests concerning those arrangements: 'in principle there are always difficulties'; 'neither dignified nor appropriate'; 'profoundly regrettable, from all perspectives'. However, they continued, with important modifications. From the 1880s, departments and municipalities distinguished public and private wall spaces. Nantes and Lyons began to restrict posters to designated locations in the immediate prewar era, quarantining a dangerous force, consecrating a new power.[47]

In a debate over popular culture, Nathalie Zemon Davis called for the study of unresolved conflicts and 'unpopular culture' to identify patterns of meaning characteristic of an epoch. Posters fused the antithetical – the commercial and the aesthetic – and appealed to a broad public without the sanction of educators, writers or authorities. By transgressing deeply held boundaries, advertising constituted what the anthropologist Mary Douglas has termed a 'dirty' power – the consecration of the poster as a genre 'enshrined corruption ... in sacred places'. That has implications for what happened to French cities at the end of the nineteenth and the beginning of the twentieth centuries.[48]

Across Western Europe and North America, following the example, if not the spirit of Haussmann, urban officials transformed streets into thoroughfares and promoted circulation and cleanliness at the expense of what some have seen as popular or working-class sites of community and trade. During the first decades of the Third Republic, police, municipal councillors and city administrators struggled with advertisers for control of walls and streets, not only to sanitize cities and towns, but also to impose a conception of self and state on public space. Republican positions were not uniform: anti-capitalist fears inherited from Catholic and conservative opponents competed with concerns for a rational citizenry, labour and small business, and a democratic aesthetic. However, in the context of dynamic psychology, the Franco-Prussian War and state concern over visual imagery, officials sought to protect the attention of citizen-subjects from appeals to desire in order to enforce morality, and to shield symbols of republican and national authority from commercial messages.

The rise of a national industry funded by tremendous capital and intent on appealing to consciousness confronted administrators and legislators with a power they deemed incompatible with civic and national traditions. As advertisers employed posters to capture the gaze of city-dwellers, authorities landscaped the urban environment to preserve the attention of citizens for political ends. To do so, they banished posters from the vicinity of monuments and schools and demarcated their place in the cityscape.

Notes

*   I would like to thank Debora Silverman, Eugen Weber, Mary Anderson, Lesley Walker, Claudio Fogu and Lori Weintrob for their comments on earlier versions of this paper.

1.   Georges d'Avenel, 'Le Mécanisme de la vie moderne: la publicité', *Revue des deux mondes* (January–February 1901), 655; for a small selection of the literature, see, in addition to the works cited later in this chapter, Jean-David Jumeau-Lafond, 'L'*Enfance de Sainte-Geneviève*: une affiche de Puvis de Chavannes au service de l'*Union pour l'action morale*', *Revue de l'art* (1995), 63–74; Kirk Varnedoe and Adam Gopnik, *High and Low; Modern Art and Popular Culture* (New York: The Museum of Modern Art, 1990); Jeffrey Weiss, *The Popular Culture of Modern Art: Picasso, Duchamp, and Avant-Gardism* (New Haven: Yale University Press, 1995); Eric Darragon, 'Pégase à Fernando: A propos de *Cirque* et du réalisme de Seurat en 1891', *Revue de l'Art* (1989), 44–57; Segolène Le Men, *Seurat & Chéret: le peintre, le cirque et l'affiche* (Paris: CNRS éditions, 1994); Réjane Bargiel-Harry and Fabrice D'Almeida, 'Eléments pour une bibliographie générale de l'affiche', *Degrès* (winter 1989–spring 1990), 24.

2.   For a review of recent American scholarship on French urban life, see Leslie Page Moch, 'Pushing at the Margins of French Urban History', *Journal of Urban History* 22 (March 1996), 377–83; for insightful treatments of teleological and ideological uses of the categories 'nation' and 'national identity' in a French context, see Steven Englund, 'The Ghost of Nation Past', *Journal of Modern History* 18 (June 1992), 299–320; Carla Hesse and Thomas Laqueur, 'Introduction: National Cultures Before Nationalism', *Representations* (summer 1994), 1–9; for a critical comparative

perspective, see Prasenjit Duara, *Rescuing History from the Nation* (Chicago: University of Chicago Press, 1995).

3. I reached that figure by totalling the amounts paid by various contractors.

4. For Lyons, see *Procès-verbaux d'adjudication, 1877–1897* in Archives municipales (hereafter, AM), Lyons, 923 WP 250; for Bordeaux, see *Procès-verbaux, Conseil municipal de Bordeaux*, 8 August, 1873, 14 November 1873, 19 November 1875, 199; Chief Litigator, 'Concession du droit d'affichage', 25 September 1896, AM, Nantes, I2 c. 28 d2; 'Cahier des Charges', 19 February 1885, AM, Marseilles, 2 D 347, n. 872; *Procès-verbaux d'adjudication*, 24 September 1897, AM, Marseilles, 1 D 155, 117–9; *Procès-verbaux d'adjudication, murs de Lyon*, 1 March 1913, 923 WP 51; Engineer, Highway Department, 'Rapport: Projet de résiliation de concession de l'Agence Fournier', 21 August 1916, AM, Lyons, 923 WP 251.

5. AM, Marseilles, 2 D 507, n. 4369. *Ministère du Commerce, de l'Industrie, des Postes et des Télégraphes. Direction de l'Office du Travail, Service du Recensement Professionnel. Resultats Statistiques du Recensement des Industries et Professions. Dénombrement général de la population du 29 March 1896* I–III (Paris, 1899–1900); *Ministère du Commerce, de l'Industrie, des Postes et des Télégraphes. Direction du Travail, Service du Recensement. Resultats Statistiques du Recensement Général de la Population effectué le 24 March 1901* I–III (Paris, 1904–6); Letterhead, to Mayor of Marseilles, 8 September 1898, AM, Marseilles, 2 D 507, n. 4369; *La Publicité moderne* (March 1908), 10.

6. Joris-K. Huysmans, 'L'Etiage', *Oeuvres complètes* 8 (1928), 137–40. 'L'Etiage' first appeared in the 1886 edition of *Croquis parisiens*. Léon Riotor, *Le Mannequin* (Paris: 1900), 74–89; Stockman, *Catalogue des bustes et mannequins de mode* (1894, 1896); Nicole Parrot, *Mannequins* (Paris: Editions Colona, 1981). Stockman also supplied dummies to expositions and museums.

7. Huysman's pronouncements had an ironic edge. Thus the description of a body cast as a work of art by the author of *A Rebours* (Paris: 1883) may imply an ironic commentary on the aspirations of naturalism to represent an objective reality. None the less, his comments can be seen as part of a romantic tradition of aesthetic inversion that passes through Baudelaire.

8. Joris-K. Huysmans, 'Le Salon Officiel de 1880', *Oeuvres complètes* 10 (1929), 186.

9. See Bradford Collins, 'Jules Chéret and the Nineteenth-Century French Poster' (Ph.D. diss., Yale University, 1980); Lucy Broido, *The Posters of Jules Chéret* (New York: Dover Publications, 1992); Gustave Fustier, 'La littérature murale', *Le Livre, bibliographie retrospective* (1884), 354; I have referred to the chronology of Meredith Clausen, 'Toward a redefinition of the Art Nouveau', *Gazette des beaux-arts* (September 1985), 83; Collins, 'Jules Chéret', 158–83; Madeleine Rebérioux, 'De l'art industriel à l'art social: Jean Jaurès et Roger Marx', *Gazette des beaux-arts* (January–February 1988), 155–8; Clausen, 'Toward a Redefinition of the Art Nouveau', 81–94; Marcus Verhagen, 'The Poster in *Fin-du-Siècle* Paris: That Mobile and Degenerate Art', in *Cinema and the Invention of Modern Life*, edited by Leo Charney and Vanessa Schwartz (Berkeley and Los Angeles: University of California Press, 1995), 103–29; and Miriam Levin,

'Democratic Vistas – Democratic Media: Defining a Role for Printed Images in Industrializing France', *French Historical Studies* (spring 1993), 82–108.

10. Debora Silverman, *Art Nouveau in Fin-de-Siècle France* (Berkeley and Los Angeles: University of California Press, 1989). For a thorough analysis of the cultural ideologies of republican officials, see also Miriam Levin, *Republican Art and Ideology in Late Nineteenth-Century France* (Ann Arbor: University of Michigan Press, 1986).

11. Roger Marx, *L'Art Social* (Paris: Bibliothèque-Charpentier, 1913).

12. Letter to Béranger, 16 June 1848, in Paul Villaneix, *La voie royale* (Paris, 1971) in Chantal Georgel, *L'Enfant et l'image au XIXe siècle* (Paris, 1988), 8; Louis Revon, *L'Enseignement par les affiches et les tableaux* (Annecy, 1867), 5–9; Mercier cited in Georgel, 60–61; for posters and popular culture in the eighteenth century, see Daniel Roche, *The People of Paris* (New York: Aubier Montaigne, 1981), 228–33.

13. Gustave Geffroy, 'Chronique: Jules Chéret', *La Justice* (8 July 1888).

14. See Roussignann Jamakorzian, *De la publicité commerciale en France* (Paris, 1911); *L'Estampe et l'affiche* (15 July 1897), 148; Réjane Bargiel (ed.), *Byrrh: L'Affiche imaginaire. Le Concours d'affiches vers 1900* (Union des arts décoratifs, 18 février – 3 mai 1992), 19–20; *Le Figaro illustré* (September 1895), xxxv; and Jean Grand-Carteret, 'Napoléon par l'image', *Le Livre et l'image*, (1893–94); Edmond de Crauzat, 'Murailles', *L'Estampe et l'affiche* (February 1898), 61. Anonymous, 'L'Affiche de l'Eclair', *L'Eclair* (10 February 1897, 8 March 1897), 1. For the *Eclair* contest, see Georges Montorgueil, 'Introduction', *Les Affiches illustrées. Concours organisé par le journal 'L'Eclair'* (L'Eclair, [1897]); *L'Estampe et l'affiche* (15 October 1897), 202.

15. 'L'oeuvre d'un maître', *La fédération lithographique; organe officiel de la corporation lithographique et de toutes les partis similaires. Union-Force-Resistance* (February 1890) in Bibliothèque National, Cabinet d'Estampes, Yb-3–1657, II. (Hereafter Yb-3–1657. Yb-3–1650 and Yb-3–1657 contain unpaginated, imprecisely dated newspaper clippings. Neither authorship nor pagination is indicated consistently.) Anonymous, 'Variétés: Chéret', *L'Egalité* (13 February 1890); Félix Fénéon, 'Chez les barbouilleurs: les affiches en couleur', *Oeuvres plus que complètes,* II (Geneva, 1970).

16. Roger Marx, 'Les papiers de teinture de Jules Chéret', *Le Voltaire* ([December 1891]?) in Yb-3–1650, II; of course, peasant 'folk' culture was seen across nineteenth-century Europe as the embodiment of national tradition.

17. Jean Grand-Carteret, 'Chéret et l'affiche illustrée', *Le National* (31 December 1889) in Yb-3–1657, I. For Grand-Carteret's reactionary politics and their relationship to Boulevard culture, see Philip Nord, *Paris Shopkeepers and the Politics of Resentment* (Princeton: Princeton University Press, 1986).

18. *L'art dans les deux mondes* (4 April 1891), in Yb-3–1657, II.

19. Debora Silverman, *Art Nouveau in Fin-de-Siècle France*, 9 and 51; 'Exposition Jules Chéret', 1889–90 in Yb-3–1657, II.

20. Debora Silverman, 'Frantz Jourdain: Rococo and Art Nouveau', *Macmillan Encyclopedia of Architects* (New York: Free Press, 1982); Arlette Barre-Despond, *Jourdain* (New York: Rizzoli, 1991); Meredith Clausen, *Frantz Jourdain and the Samaritaine* (Leiden: E. J. Brill, 1987).

21. Frantz Jourdain, 'Jules Chéret', *La Revue illustrée* (15 February 1889) in Yb-3–1657, II; Frantz Jourdain, 'La Décoration des boutiques', *Revue des arts décoratifs* 14 (1892–93): 263; Frantz Jourdain, *L'Art chez soi* (1891), in Yb-3–1650, II.

22. 'Affiches illustrées', *L'Art moderne* (9 September 1891), Yb-3–1657, II; 'Galerie Devambez', *Action française*, misdated 1890 in Yb-3–1657, II (1893–1902); *Journal des arts* (8 December 1890) in Yb-3–1657, II.

23. Unattributed clipping, (5–12 April 1890), in Yb3–1650, II.

24. Paul Berthelot, *La Petite Gironde* (28 May 1892), in Yb-3–1657, II; Achille Ségard, *Peintres d'aujourd'hui* (Paris, n.d.[1913]), I, 251; Marius Vachon, *L'Hôtel de Ville de Paris, 1835–1905* (Paris, 1905), i–iv, 136.

25. For the shift in Carnival, see Maurice Crubellier, in Georges Duby (ed.), *Histoire de la France urbaine*, vol. 4 (Paris, 1983), 410; Anonymous, 'Un Peu de tout', *L'Egalité* (7 March 1889), 1; Gabert in Arren, *La Publicité lucrative*, 284–7; Joseph Denais, *Conseil municipal. Procès-verbal du 12 avril 1911*, 658.

26. *La Publicité moderne* (September 1907), 4–5; *Atlas* (April 1909), 21–2.

27. Baron de Vaux-Cassilon to Prefect of Police, 20 October 1876, APP, DA 127; 'Maugras & Montant, publicité orientale', 29 September 1881, APP, DA 127; 16 October 1898, APP, BA 1557.

28. Émile Zola, *Contes et nouvelles* (Paris: Gallimard, 1976), 299–301 and 1313–17; Philarète Chasles, *Études contemporaines: voyages, philosophie et beaux-arts* (Paris, 1866), 52–69.

29. The bibliography on decadence and degeneration – not unrelated to concerns for the will – is extensive. See Robert Nye, *Crime, Madness and Politics in Modern France* (Princeton: Princeton University Press, 1984); Robert Nye, *The Origins of Crowd Psychology* (London: Sage Publications, 1975); Susanna Barrows, *Distorting Mirrors* (New Haven: Yale University Press, 1981); and, of course, Max Nordau, *Degeneration* (New York: D. Appleton, 1895).

30. C.G., 'Parti pour l'école', *La France illustrée* (15 March 1890), 180.

31. Jonathan Crary, 'Unbinding Vision: Manet and the Attentive Observer in the Late Nineteenth Century,' in Leo Charney and Vanessa Schwartz (eds), *Cinema and the Invention of Modern Life* (Berkeley and Los Angeles: University of California Press, 1995), 47–9, 68; Théodule Ribot, *La Psychologie de l'attention* (Paris, 1889); Jean-Paul Nayrac, *Physiologie et psychologie de l'attention* (Paris: F. Alcan 1905); Léon Quid'beuf, *L'Attention, discours prononcé à la distribution des prix du collège Notre-Dame de Sainte-Croix* (Le Mans, 1887). Marjorie Beale, 'Advertising and the Politics of Public Persuasion in France, 1900–1939' (Ph.D. diss., University of California, 1991), 27–8, contrasts spontaneous and voluntary attention in the thought of Ribot.

32. Emile Mermet, *Guide Mermet: la publicité en France* (Paris, 1878), 66; L.S., 'La Publicité,' *La Grande encyclopédie*, vol. 27 (Paris, [1898–1902]), 909.

33. *De la suggestion dans l'état hypnotique et dans l'état de veille* (Paris, 1884), 89–90, in Silverman, 86–8; Paul Adam, *Les Disciplines de la France* (Paris: Vuibert and Nony, 1908), 187–8; Octave-Jacques Gérin and C. Espinadel, *La Publicité suggestive: théorie et technique* (Paris, 1911), 72.

34. See Miriam Levin, 'Democratic Vistas – Democratic Media: Defining a

Role for Printed Images in Industrializing France', *French Historical Studies* (spring 1993), 82–108.

35. Inspector General Marseille, 29 April 1878, APP, DB 203, no. 70906. Thus caricature was censored more than the written word. See Robert Justin Goldstein, *Censorship of Political Caricature in Nineteenth-Century France* (Kent, Ohio: Kent State University Press, 1989), 258.

36. *Bastid, Député, n. 620, Chambre des Députés. 3e Législature. 1882. Annexe au procès-verbal de la séance du 18 mars 1882*; for the anti-clerical measures of the early 1880s, see Guy Chapman, *The Third Republic of France* (London: 1962), 210–11.

37. Abbé Fourié, *De l'affichage politique; conseils pratiques pour la rédaction, l'apposition et la protection des affiches* (Paris, 1903), 7–12; Ballot, 'Préface', *De l'affichage politique* (1903), v; Police Commissioner Soullière, 'Rapport', 8 July 1908, Anonymous, 4 July 1910, and so on, APP, BA 1557.

38. Maurice Agulhon, *Histoire vagabonde: ethnologie et politique dans la France contemporaine* (Paris: Gallimard, 1988), 101–85, esp. 150–51; Maurice Agulhon, *Marianne au pouvoir* (Paris: Flammarion, 1989).

39. Viollet Le Duc, *Gazette des beaux-arts* (1859), 168; Charles Garnier, *La Construction moderne* (13 November 1886), 49; Charles Normand, 'A Nos Lecteurs', *L'Ami des monuments* 1 (1887), 4.

40. Hattat, *Conseil municipal. Procès-verbal du 16 Juin 1897*, p. 1006; Alfred Dodanthun, *Des Affiches électorales: étude de droit public* (Paris, 1903), 94–5.

41. See the Paris Municipal Council, *Conseil municipal. Procès-verbal du 25 novembre 1881, Conseil municipal. Procès-verbal du 20 Juillet 1883* and *Rapports* (1883), n. 35, 52 in Florence Baker, 'Parisians and their Parks' (Ph.D. diss., University of California at Los Angeles, 1994), 35. Levée, *Conseil municipal. Procès-verbal du 16 novembre 1908*, 350. Quentin-Bauchart, *Conseil municipal. Procès-verbal du 21 Juin 1909*, 1067–68; Froment-Meurice, *Conseil municipal. Procès-verbal du 28 Novembre 1910*, 395–6. Adrien Mithouard, *Conseil municipal. Procès-verbal du 12 Juillet 1912*, 1681; Camille Rousset, *Conseil municipal. Procès-verbal du 12 Juillet 1912*, 1677; *Conseil municipal. Procès-verbal du 31 décembre 1913*, 1538–43 and 1616–18.

42. Anthony Sutcliffe, *The Autumn of Central Paris: the Defeat of Town Planning, 1850–1970* (London: Edward Arnold, 1970), 194; Félix Régamey in *La Revue des arts graphiques* (2 November 1895): 6; see Nord, 'Paris Shopkeepers', 452; *Conseil municipal, procès-verbaux* I (6 and 27 June, 9 July 1902): 849–51 and 1074; *Conseil municipal, procès-verbaux* II (29 October and 5 November 1902), 132, 379 and 476; Normand, 'La Beauté de Paris: idées pour le concours des enseignes de la ville de Paris', *L'Ami des monuments et des arts* 16 (1901?), 163; Pannelier, *Conseil municipal, procès-verbaux* (12 and 17 May 1899), 722 and 777.

43. *Les Grands boulevards* (Musée Carnavalet, 25 June – 20 October 1985), 206–7.

44. 23 July 1883, AM, Paris, VO nc 16; Dr. Gillebert Dhelcourt, 15 May 1889, AM, Paris, VO nc 16, A.968. A police sergeant to police headquarters, 25 July 1897, Chief of Police to Mayor, 27 July 1897, AM, Nantes, I2, c.28, n.1.

45. Hirsch, the city planner, to the Mayor, 16 March 1897, 'Affichage sur les

murs de la ville', AM, Lyons, 923 WP 250; Georges Delanoë to Mayor, 26 February 1913, AM, Nantes, I2 c.22 d.5; Levée, *Conseil municipal de la ville de Paris. Procès-verbal du 4 mars 1912*, 75–8; 'Notes & Echos', *La Publicité* 11 (1913), 160–61.

46.   *n.2240. Chambre des Députés. 1909. Annexe au procès-verbal de la séance du 15 Janvier 1909. Rapport fait au nom de la commission de la réforme judiciaire et de la legislation civile et criminelle chargée d'examiner la proposition de loi de M. Maurice Viollette, tendant à compléter l'article 38 de la loi du 29 juillet 1881 sur la presse.* Viollette, Député, 3.

47.   Hirsch, City Planner, to Mayor, 'Affichage sur les murs de la Ville', 16 March 1897, AM, Lyons, 923 WP 250; City Manager to the Engineer in Chief, 26 August 1881, AM, Lyons, 923 WP 250; 19 June 1907, AM, Bordeaux, 3280–I-1, n.1251–19; *Cahier des charges; affichage sur divers batiments et murs communaux et murs de refend*, 21 September 1912, AM, Lyons, 923 WP 251; Mayor to Edmond Lemeignen, agent of Courbet & Cie, 7 March 1914, AM, Nantes, I2 c.22 d3.

48.   Mary Douglas, *Purity and Danger* (New York: Praeger, 1966).

CHAPTER SEVEN

Display Windows and Window Displays in German Cities of the Nineteenth Century: Towards the History of a Commercial Breakthrough[1]

Uwe Spiekermann

Advertising has, in the last twenty years, become an increasingly important topic in international social and economic history.[2] As a result, we can now better explore topics with public appeal, and at the same time can better study the origins of modern consumer society. Yet the growing number of relevant publications should not conceal the fact that there is a dearth of primary research on advertising, especially in Germany. Advertising can only be understood adequately in the context of consumption, retail trade and the production of consumer goods – and this is exactly where valid studies are very rare.[3] We know even less about the newly emerging world of objects of the nineteenth century. What products were advertised and bought, where they were purchased and how they were evaluated – such fundamental questions, especially when asked about Germany, are almost impossible to answer. Nevertheless, we must pose these questions. Only recently has anthropologist Bruno Latour pointed out to us the fundamental relevance of consumer goods to understanding the modern age.[4]

One of the crucial innovations of early consumer society was undoubtedly the shop window. The items for sale were displayed behind it and the window thus created an artificial space for the merchandise. But like so many other things, its impact depended on its being part of a whole. 'Shop windows became urban attractions, forming the main centres of interest of the street; they were like magnets, casting a spell over the crowds of people.' The public's curiosity coupled with the shopkeepers' and manufacturers' pride in their merchandise came together in one and the same place:

> Detached from the sphere of immediate consumption, the goods appear as objects in a transparent artificial space; they do not

provoke interest because of their utility or exchange value, but, it seems, only for their own sake: the object should not be used or bought, but looked at and admired. The shop window, by allowing a better view of the goods, inspires an aesthetic epiphany.[5]

The shop window transformed fast-growing cities into places of signs and significations and thus formed the beginning of a modern lifestyle, which we still share, albeit in somewhat modified form.

Such general characterizations are common, but only rarely does one find the various developments clearly delineated in their proper historical sequence. Rarer still is any attempt to provide empirical evidence for them.[6] In what follows, I will try to begin that task. Generally speaking, the shop window and its form of advertising in German cities of the nineteenth century developed in four distinct stages. Until 1835 or so, the display window was a means of presentation for only a few shops with luxury goods; between then and the 1870s, it caught on everywhere in the larger cities of the German Empire. Subsequently, the display window and its decoration changed fundamentally. 'Glass palaces' and window display art peaked and reached a turning point at the start of the twentieth century. Finally, advertising extended into the shop and has now become emblematic of how merchandise is generally presented. I will conclude with some observations on the importance of this development for the history of advertising, the economy, and the society of the German Empire.

The display window before 1835

We cannot imagine a shop window without a shop. The shop, however, whose history goes back to the Middle Ages, initially had no windows.[7] Its forerunner was the *Bude*, a market stall, which protected seller and merchandise from the rigours of the weather. The *Bude* usually consisted of two wooden shutters, one of which was folded up and the other folded down. Two shutters made a shop. The merchants thus had a counter on which some of their goods could be displayed while the upper shutter provided shelter from rain. The simple wooden booth combined free access to the goods during the day with appropriate protection at night.

This principle was maintained even when trade gradually moved indoors. Here the traders could store greater amounts of merchandise and craftsmen could combine production and sales. The buyer always remained outside, and viewed the available goods from the public street. In Germany, unlike in France, Great Britain and Austria, this model survived until the late eighteenth century. The so-called bull's-eye windows, which existed from the sixteenth century on, served only to provide light, not to draw attention to the merchandise.[8] They were too small for commercial purposes and allowed only a blurred view of the products displayed behind the glass. The same was true of sliding and removable windows. Even when the Frenchman Lucas de Neheon developed a commercially viable process for the production of rolled cast glass in 1688, it had no effect on German retailing. On the other hand, Coulage glass windows (measuring 2 by 1.2 metres) allowed a clear and unblurred view of the merchandise, in contrast to that permitted by blown glass.

The large time lag between the invention and the general use of this glass for display windows not only resulted from its high price; mirror glass, after all, although expensive, had quickly become a significant characteristic of aristocratic architecture. The up-market shops of the late seventeenth century which could have afforded to install this glass did not yet need to display their merchandise publicly. The nobility demanded custom-made goods, and their demands were met as quickly as possible. The situation changed only with the emergence of a wealthy bourgeois clientele. It created a new political and commercial public. Correspondingly, British and French luxury stores were the first ones to use cast glass. In Germany the first such shops can be traced to Würzburg in 1725 and Augsburg in 1740, but they were truly exceptions.[9] Even though cast glass became more readily available by the early nineteenth century, it was still a rarity in shop windows.[10]

Yet the display of merchandise in German cities in the eighteenth century did develop further. Inside, shop counters, which were placed in the sales room, emerged and the larger stores had folding doors which helped to attract customers. The tables on which expensive goods were displayed now served as the lower shutters the medieval stall once had. They usually stood in the middle of the room, evoking their origins. The art of merchandise display, which was to have great impact in the later shop window, came into being in the sales room. The façade, on the other hand, was now dominated by the store sign, and most shopkeepers relied on its effect to lure customers.[11] The merchandise itself attracted people only after they entered the room. Luxury shops were a space where the bourgeoisie were consumers, and where the poor were excluded. Only those who could afford expensive textiles, furniture and other paraphernalia could enter the sales rooms.

The establishment of the display window in German cities (1835–70)

The growing significance of retailing was most important to the development of the shop window. To identify its origins as early as 1830 is unusual in German historiography; the focus is usually on the changes within the production sector.[12] The frequent overlap between production and sales, the above-average growth in the number of efficient shops, as well as the pressure of having to provide goods for the people working in the production sector, have usually been ignored. In view of laws regulating commerce that were still in effect in many places, scholars have tended to locate the long-lasting retail boom – and with it the growth of modern consumer society – in the 1870s, or even as late as the 1890s.[13] According to current scholarship, the development of the department store was primarily responsible for setting important standards for advertising and window displays.[14]

If one looks, however, at the various earlier changes in retail trade, one finds a new perspective on the history of advertising and of display windows: 'If business history research is able to come to terms with consumer sales then the early history of advertising will have to be reconsidered.'[15] And so it appears that in Germany, the city became a place of merchandise display and of consumer shopping much earlier than scholars have suggested.

In Germany, from the late 1830s on, the sale of consumer goods in small- and medium-sized shops had increased greatly. For example, in Prussia in 1837 there were 21,782 retail merchants who owned shops; by 1858 this number had risen to 48,625. To put these figures into perspective, this is an increase of 76.4 per cent over the growth in population in only twenty-one years, whereas the importance of grocers (most of whom did not own shops) and of peddlers decreased significantly, rising by only 10.1 per cent in absolute terms (from 89,149 to 98,158) during the same period.[16]

Shopkeepers usually worked in the larger cities. Despite guild regulations, they succeeded in improving upon the traditional supply system that had so far been influenced primarily by the weekly and yearly markets, as well as by the hawkers, peddlers and craftsmen. And in more and more places shops came to dominate the retail market, and an increasing number of these new shops had display windows. By the time of the founding of the German Empire in 1871, these windows had become the most effective means of advertising in an increasingly competition-oriented retail trade.

The textile business pioneered not only production techniques, but also retail methods. Berlin is an excellent example. Until the beginning of the nineteenth century, it was common practice in Berlin either to sew clothes at home or to have them tailor-made. Although from the beginning of the eighteenth century there had been tailors and merchants who also sold ready-made clothes, and although they became increasingly important, the used-clothing trade remained more popular.

Only at the beginning of the nineteenth century did this change dramatically. The growing number of single (and wealthy) men, rapidly increasing tourism in Berlin, and the growing importance of fashion which required a faster change in individuals' wardrobes combined to trigger the rise of the *Magazin*. This term describes a retail shop which handled merchandise produced by homeworkers or craftsmen, but whose main business was sales. At first, trousers, waistcoats and gowns were the items most frequently offered; from the 1820s on the collection included dressing-gowns, jackets and coats, shirts and collars.

The growing supply and variety led to an increased degree of specialization. Separate gentlemen's shops emerged from clothes and linen shops. Data from city directories show the radical change. In 1830 there were only 54 linen and clothing shops in Berlin, but by 1838 there were already 116, and by 1847, 158. In 1838 20 men's clothing shops were listed for the first time; their numbers rose to 66 by 1847.[17] And Berlin was not an exception: in Hamburg the number of clothes shops went from 10 to 39 between 1800 and 1822, the fashion shops from 19 to 31 and the shops with manufactured goods from 10 to 91.[18] In these large cities the shops turned the display window into a common phenomenon; as early as 1830 the Hamburg police believed it was their responsibility to take action against those retailers who protected their window displays from the sun with low-hanging awnings.[19]

The *Magazin* not only represented a new type of business within the retail trade but stood out above all because it introduced a new type of advertising. Here Hamburg is the best example: the city centre was almost completely destroyed by a fire in 1842, and the newly rebuilt streets were captured in an extensive series of lithographs. Figure 7.1 shows the façade of two *Magazine*. Both have display windows and skilfully present their merchandise. It is remarkable that a *Magazin* in a street was not an unusual sight. They were framed by the display windows of other specialty shops, all selling ready-made goods. We will now leave this main street and focus on a side street of the city centre.

Here as well we find, to our surprise, that all the shops have display windows, although many differences catch our attention. Almost all of the shop windows are smaller than those on the main street and they mostly consist of less expensive lattice windows. The oriel windows, the so-called *Ausbauer* which were mostly used before 1842, are missing, since after the fire of Hamburg their use was prohibited.[20] Figure 7.2 also shows that not only textile shops displayed their merchandise prominently. Even before the middle of the century, shoes, leather goods, and even meat products were presented through glass. It is noteworthy that even small entrepreneurs like cobblers and glove-makers found it necessary to have stores with shop windows. Even during the early

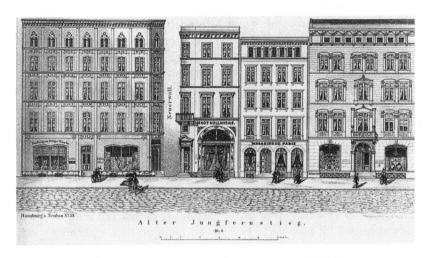

7.1 Shop windows in Hamburg (*Alter Jungfernstieg*), 1846/47

Source: *Hamburgs Neubau. Sammlung sämmtlicher Façaden der Gebäude an den neubebauten Strassen*, Hamburg: Charles Fuchs (reprint 1985): Th. Schäfer: Hannover, folio 39

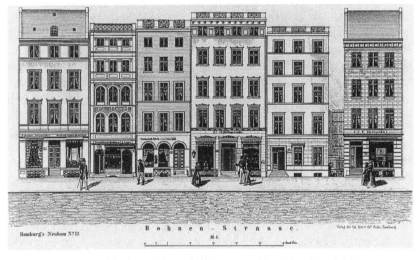

7.2   Display window in Hamburg (*Bohnenstrasse*) 1846/47
Source: *Hamburgs Neubau*, folio 17

period of industrialization, the production of goods was not an end in itself, but gained its real meaning only through sales. The Hamburg lithograph series contains views of a total of 218 shops in the centre of the city. There are shop windows almost everywhere, and a few shops even display their merchandise in front of four large plate-glass windows. In some cases there is even rudimentary lighting equipment. So in Hamburg, before the middle of the century, flickering light invited people to do their window shopping in the evening.[21]

We now return to the developments in the Prussian capital of Berlin. In the late 1830s more *Magazine* emerged there than in Hamburg, along with the first larger retail stores, even if their shop windows did not stand out. Hermann Gerson's *Modewaarenlager* (Fashion Depot), founded in 1836, employed a large number of people (eight supervisors and between 120 and 140 workers in two separate branches, 150 masters with about 1,500 journeymen as delivery men, and about 100 people in the two-storey store), but the *Magazin* that was lit by 120 gas flames attracted its customers with two five-foot wide plate-glass windows. This very clearly showed the loyalty of a wealthy clientele to the luxury shops.[22] Rudolph Hertzog, a store founded in 1839 that sold manufactured goods and which later became the largest German department store and one of Europe's leading mail-order houses, had only average-sized displays, concentrating instead on strategically planned print advertising.

Other *Magazine*, however, took advantage of the display window as an advertising medium. Evidence of this is provided by Louis Landsberger's clothes shop. Not two, not four, but ten large plate-glass windows decorated the shop's two sales floors. Display windows filled with merchandise surrounded the shop, their large number attesting to the size and range of the inventory.

As shops grew larger, window displays became more common, larger and more elaborate. The lighting which drew attention to the *Magazin* at night also attracted customers. Landsberger's shop was only the tip of the iceberg.[23] Consider the following quotation from a city guide in 1861:

> Our well-fed forefathers, who only enjoyed true pleasures, did not know the shimmer of plate-glass windows and of bronze, nor the blaze of colour, the magic of luxury and the appeal of the arts. We, on the other hand, appreciate those modern inventions. The difference between past and present becomes most obvious in the shops ...
>
> If we now look at those shops ... where the merchandise, arranged by artful hands, fascinates the eye! My ladies, over there you see sparkling windows, which have been decorated with Jakona and Organdis, with long shawls, with which you sell your smile,

with Venetian lace, which you trade in for your love! And look here, you dandies from the provinces, the most elaborate piqué vests. Descend to that subterranean place where Bärenschinken is served and the Cliquot is on ice. Here are shining hats at your disposal, delicate Anere watches, velour blankets, gigantic mirrors in golden frames; over there artistic bronze goods, valuable oil paintings, buffets with marble plates, magnificent dinner services; flower bouquets more beautiful in colour than the presents of the Flora Cypris; here you see the beautiful scholarly anthologies in deluxe bindings, Zahn's ornaments from Pompeii, the most wonderful photographs of the reliquary of Bruges.

What richness of splendour, pleasure and glamour for that special mortal who is endowed with a zest for life and equipped with the wherewithal to enjoy it.[24]

In Berlin, window-shopping was possible well before 1871. The travel guide concentrates on expensive, exclusive products, which remained beyond the means of the majority of inhabitants of the capital. A few shops, however, started to concentrate on a simpler range of merchandise in the 1860s, and many grocers also changed their shopfronts or installed new ones. During this process, many shopkeepers compromised:

Very often ordinary windows are used for the display and the only difference is the introduction of larger window panes. It is very obvious that such construction fulfils only the simplest requirements; the display is very much restricted, and the high position of the windows disrupts it even more. A single window does not permit a vast display of merchandise, of course, and for this reason such a window is only useful to show what kind of shop it is.[25]

The shop windows of these small and medium-sized shops can hardly be compared to those of the larger stores. But we should note that even established shops tried to expand or, failing that, to change the configuration of their display windows. It also became very common in the 1860s to include shop windows in the building design at the time of construction. Essays in the architectural press of the time consider the display window an integral part of the shop:

The windows for the display of the goods must be as wide as possible; and generally one uses iron columns and supports to carry the upper floors instead of stone columns and arches, because this increases the usable space. In many cases one designs different axes in the upper floors without any concern that they do not match those of the ground floor, since the axis division of the lower floor is almost invisible and practically disappears due to the small dimension of the iron, and only a glass surface is visible.[26]

This increasing use of steel and glass created completely new possibilities for the design of the façade, so that by the early 1870s two-storey

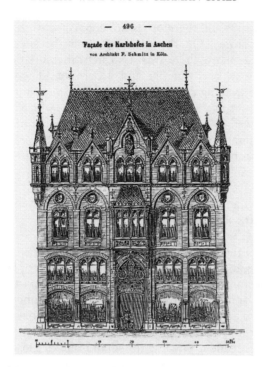

— 496 —

Façade des Karlshofes in Aachen

von Architekt F. Schmitz in Köln.

7.3   Façade of the Karlshof in Aachen, 1869

Source: 'Fassade des Karlshofes in Aachen', *Deutsche Bauzeitung* 3 (1869),
496. Many further examples can be found in *Köln und seine Bauten*,
edited by Architekten- und Ingenieur Verein für Niederrhein und
Westfalen (Cologne: self-published, 1888)

window displays were being built in Berlin.[27] Shops with display windows, which were rented by the majority of small and medium-sized
shop owners, started to be part of the usual design of newer, larger
buildings. Unfortunately, there are no reliable data, and so we cannot
verify whether there really were '3,000 impressive display windows' in
Berlin in 1880, as one contemporary claims.[28] Yet there is no doubt that
in Berlin, in the business sector that dealt with luxury items and with
non-durable goods, the display window was common before the
Reichsgründung in 1871. The small grocery store definitely lagged behind, but the delicatessen and finer groceries shops often had glass
fronts.[29]

The display window had already established itself in the provinces as
well. Figure 7.3 shows a 'characteristic example of the façade construction of private buildings' in the Rhineland. Again, there are four large
display windows, which show that the emergence of display windows

pre-dates the 1890s and therefore is not connected to the establishment of department stores. On the contrary, after the shop window had developed in Germany, there was a strong differentiation of the windows according to size, number and decoration. These variables not only reflected prevailing taste and design, but also created an important distinctive element in a competitive society, one which was shaped by production as well as distribution. German cities had become places of bourgeois consumption long before the turn of the century, and the display windows promised a world of wealth and progress.

Universalization and differentiation of the display window in a competitive market society (c.1870–1900)

The founding of the German Empire in 1871 was not only a moment of political change; it also led to a general liberalization of laws regulating commerce. Liberalism and a free market had already existed in a number of the German states, but now these principles triumphed throughout. Cities continued to grow and now began to resemble modern urban spaces. The large numbers of people with purchasing power in these expanding cities made it possible for small trade to grow more quickly. The social division of labour became more rigid, and it became obvious as early as the 1873 depression that the growing production of merchandise was dependent not only on the availability of liquid capital, but also and particularly on secure and stable sales. The turnover of goods could only be guaranteed through an efficient retail system, in which shop owners competed for customers, and sold them both established and new merchandise. The problems created by the beginning of competition demanded new approaches to sales from the small shops; they now had not only to supply but also to sell an increasing number of newly emerging brand names. Small shopkeepers thus had to modernize their sales techniques, their window displays, and even the shops themselves. It was necessary to show the customer the efficiency of the shop in some tangible way.[30]

Retailers competed not only for the best selection of merchandise, but also for the limited attention of a volatile public. In view of the rapidly growing importance of pleasing the customers in the cities, the display window was critical for success, particularly in shops which sold non-essential items. At the same time the display window was the appropriate advertising medium of a society in which the quality of the presentation of the merchandise was more important than that of the merchandise itself. It would be useful to distinguish a number of distinct but related factors that went into the general development of the display window.

The variety of shop window advertising increased everywhere. Alongside the sophisticated advertising of the majority of shops, which focused on the goods themselves, came some bright and loud advertising posters which were mounted on the façades. This phenomenon can be illustrated with the example of a new type of establishment, the 'bazaar', which developed from the *Magazine* in the late 1860s. Initially, the bazaars also sported spectacular decorations, but unlike the *Magazine*, they usually did not produce their own goods. During the Depression a number of so-called 'junk bazaars' developed which, with the aid of a huge advertising effort, sold cheap products at low prices. The term 'bazaar' thus acquired a negative connotation; this was reinforced by those bazaars that sold a variety of merchandise all at the same price (*Einheitsbazare*), and which emerged in the 1870s and expanded enormously in the 1880s. These fairly small shops used not only display windows but the whole façade for their shrill advertisements. The itinerant stores (*Wanderlager*) (that started to develop in the 1860s) as well as those bazaars that offered credit (from the late 1870s) relied on such shrill advertisement and thus quickly provoked comments about the degradation of the inner cities.[31]

While the small bazaars of the class-based German Empire met the needs of customers from the lower-middle and upper-lower classes, a parallel development occurred in the form of the *Kaufhäuser*, which also grew out of the *Magazine* and catered to the middle and upper classes of society. Most of these, too, were not involved in the production of merchandise, but instead concentrated on the sale of goods. But due to their size they usually had considerable power to stimulate demand, which reinforced their direct influence. Their shop window displays were generally more sophisticated, modest and neutral than those of the bazaars.

Kaufhäuser at the same time pioneered the general enlargement of shop window surfaces. To achieve this, improvements in glass casting technique were necessary. Plate glass became smoother and more transparent, and the individual glass pieces became larger. More importantly, however, the *Kaufhäuser* started to use new building materials like iron and steel for more impressive shop window fronts in the 1870s and 1880s – at a time where there were not yet any department stores in Germany.[32] It was at this time that purely functional business buildings emerged that were used for apartments only very occasionally. The development of display windows and that of cities as a whole were closely interrelated.

Figure 7.4 shows the façade of the *Kaufhaus* Rosipal in Munich after it was rebuilt in 1884. Within the shop manufactured goods, fashion

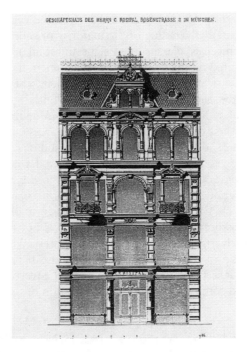

7.4 Façade of the Rosipal department store in Munich, 1884

Source: 'Waaren- und Kaufhaus des Herrn C. Rosipal Rosengasse 3 in München', *Zeitschrift für Baukunde* 7 (1884), 147–8

items and cloth were sold on three floors around a lighted inner court-yard, while the administrative office was located on the fourth floor. The shop windows on the first two floors were decorated, and the large windows on the third and fourth floors were also used for advertising purposes. Ascher & Münchow, in Berlin, used a similar technique, as we can see in Figure 7.5.

Ascher & Münchow, completed in 1887, had eleven large and well-decorated display windows on the two lower floors. This was clearly not sufficient, however, since even on the third floor twelve smaller windows were used for the presentation of modern home furnishings. These advertisements in the windows on the third and fourth floors were designed to attract the attention of the customers in the Leipziger Straße from a distance. The glass surfaces of the *Kaufhäuser* grew until they reached the top of the building in the 1880s; they were also trying to imitate the grandeur of the shopping arcades and luxury store boule-vards. In the late 1890s the principle of glass façades reached its climax in the newly emerging large-scale department stores.[33] They

7.5   Upper floors of the department store Ascher & Münchow in Berlin (1886/87)

Source: 'Kaufhaus Ascher & Münchow in Berlin, Leipzigerstr. 43', *Blätter für Architektur und Kunsthandwerk* 4 (1891), 14, illustration 27

distinguished themselves through their display of a broad range of all kinds of merchandise, due to the consistent use of inner courts and other new interior concepts as well as a façade design that was strongly oriented towards vertical pillar constructions. Their architecture was original and innovative, but as far as the arrangement of goods in the shop window was concerned, they followed the tradition of the German *Kaufhäuser* as well as that of the much more luxurious French *grands magasins*.[34] The Wertheim emporium built by Messel in 1897 and the Hermann Tietz emporium built in 1899–1900 on Leipziger Straße (which had two huge shop windows, each 460 square metres) are the most famous examples of this type of construction. The Kander emporium, however, built in 1900 in Mannheim, was even more impressive (Figure 7.6).

More adamantly than their Berlin counterparts, the architects refused to consider any notion of a decorative façade or even some sort of topping-off of the roof construction in the case of this 'glass palace'. Iron and glass architecture here reached a unique climax: the emporium

7.6   The department store Kander in Mannheim in 1900

Source: Barbara Kilian, 'Die Mannheimer Warenhäuser Kander, Schmoller und Wronker: Ein Stück Mannheimer Wirtschafts- und Architekturgeschichte', *Mannheimer Geschichtsblätter* 1 (1994), 336

seemed entirely transparent and completely open to the curious glances of the customers. However, aesthetic, architectural and fire safety considerations led to the end of the road for this form of monumental display window.[35]

Before we continue with the great department stores, we need to ask ourselves if the shop window also became common in ordinary shops. As we have already seen, in the 1860s, small- and medium-sized businesses also redecorated their display windows or rented sales rooms, which usually had glass fronts. This is also evident in the consumer trade, in particular with groceries and delicatessens; however, it is impossible to quantify this development. Liberal politician Eugen Richter, who was a member of the cooperative movement, emphasized as early as 1867 that consumer cooperatives should have high-quality furnishings similar to those of competing grocery shops, but also wrote, in apparent contradiction to this: 'All consumer cooperatives, according to the English model, should refrain from a display of goods in the shop windows solely to attract customers.'[36] In photographs from the nineteenth century one can find continuous shop window fronts from the 1860s onwards; established, settled groceries also adopted these continuous shop window fronts no later than the 1880s.[37] Only the consumer cooperatives defied this trend until the turn of the century, confident of the loyalty of their membership.[38]

At the same time one cannot neglect to mention their counterparts in private commerce. Retail chains emerged in the semi-luxury food and food sectors' in particular in the 1870s. Their success not only depended on centralized purchasing and administration but also on the fact that the individual stores had a uniform look, whose main attraction was usually one or more large shop windows. Even though the boom of this new type of business can be traced to the 1890s, the big chains usually began to develop earlier out of small retail shops – for example, *Kaisers Kaffeegeschäft* had 667 individual branches by 1900.[39] It therefore seems plausible that knowledge of the advertising power of an attractive display window was firmly established and very common in the grocery business even before the turn of the century.

This universalization of the display window as a crucial means of advertising among the small, independent retail shops was combined with different ways of presenting merchandise. As we have seen in Figures 7.1 and 7.2, the usual method was to pile up as much merchandise as possible in the window display. According to general opinion, this was the best way to present the efficiency of the shop. But mass availability held only limited attraction for customers. For this reason, the practice of arranging unusual or spectacular displays of fanciful design had begun by the early 1870s.[40]

The criticism of these overly decorated shop windows – most of the displays had little connection with the goods being sold – appeared very soon, focused especially on manufactured and baked goods or meat products. The display of fresh meat (Figure 7.7) caused particular offence, even though it had been common practice until the turn of the century.[41]

The criticism that was already prevalent in the 1870s is hardly identical to the picture of display window advertising that has been drawn by scholars so far.[42] The transition from the fantastic window display to the standard of stacked merchandise is always linked to the discourse of the turn of the century's élites. But long before programmatic slogans like 'The new shop window wants to be functional'[43] appeared, the majority of the shop windows had already been decorated 'functionally' anyway. Urban shop window fronts became the normative place for the presentation of modern merchandise. The increasing specialization of the retail shops turned display windows into both the epitome and message-bearer of a merchandise-centred supply: 'More eloquently than

Hans (vor dem Wurstladen): „Du, Mama, das ist aber
sonderbar, daß der Gärtner da seinen Blumenladen mit Schweins-
köpfen und Knackwürsten verziert?!"

7.7   Window display of a south German butcher's shop in 1877

Source: 'Mißdeuteter Schönheitssinn', *Fliegende Blätter* 66 (1877), 207; see
also the caricature 'Ein Zartes Herz', *Fliegende Blätter* 76 (1882), 46

newspaper advertisements it invites people to buy, since it shows off the
merchandise itself and thus often reminds the interested customer of
needs which he would not have thought of without the display window
as a reminder.'[44]

Urban store windows presented the achievements of technological
progress in a simple and unpretentious way:

> Through huge mirror glass windows the viewer sees the most
> colourful splendour and variety, and a stroll through the main
> shopping streets of Berlin is like a walk through a small-scale
> international exhibition. There every merchant portrays the most
> characteristic picture of his field with a lot of effort and decorates
> it to the point of overkill with a sea of bright lights.[45]

Very early on, window display was regarded as a commercial form of
art, which served as entertainment to a growing number of consumers:

> The view of a shop through the window lit in the evening is one of
> the most wonderful spectacles offered by large cities. And if the
> marble warehouse, where sculptures are displayed, attracts the

appreciation of art even more than the sales halls, which are dedicated to the products of manufacturers, then the majority of these
works are brought closer to the art sphere through the spirit. This
spirit can nowadays also be found in the manufacturer's craft.
Looking at manufactured goods is therefore a pleasure which can
truly be described without exaggeration as art appreciation.[46]

In this respect it seems inappropriate, not only because of the small
amount of detailed research, to accuse the retail trade of immoderation
and lack of artistic sense before the turn of the century. Similarly, for
many small stores, symmetrically proportioned stacks of goods were
commonplace, as was placing the merchandise in the centre of the
windows – it was definitely not the exception.

As the complexity and artistic quality of window displays grew, so
did the number of goods whose prices were plainly displayed in those
windows. The window displays in the *Magazine* had earlier provided
much informational value through this practice.[47] This definite state-
ment of price was not only a sign of an honest business practice. In the
1870s one-price bazaars and itinerant stores started to advertise their
low prices as a means of competition. This created a price pressure
amongst competitors which was further reinforced by the large department stores in the 1890s. Consumer obsession with prices was in many
cases fed by price displays in smaller and medium-sized shops:

> If we walk through the streets of Berlin and see an enormous
> crowd of people in front of a store window, I would bet that in
> this window display the merchandise carries price tags. The price
> display attracts the attention of a lot of people, even those who
> are not in the process of doing their shopping. The attention the
> salesman draws to his products does not cost him anything, but it
> is advantageous for him, since people will say when they get
> home: 'I saw a certain product at a certain price!' which is the
> first step towards developing a new customer base. There is no
> way to placate suspicious and hesitant customers, except by pre-
> senting them with price labels in the window. That reassures even
> the uninformed and inexperienced customer and gives him the
> certainty that he does not have to pay more than the savvy
> customer.[48]

The fundamental changes in window display were also reflected in both
the development of a new profession, the decorator (who was sometimes only a semi-professional),[49] and the increasingly important supply
of decorative products. Frames, racks, *etagères*, tailor's dummies, shelves,
mirrors, posters and many more products were made especially for
window displays. An 1895 textbook lists a total of 103 German companies that specialized in these products.[50] In the early 1890s mechanical
figures were invented, which, however, like the vending machine business, made very little headway.[51] Mechanical buttons, which were

attached to the shop façade, were another invention which did not develop much further. More important were rolling racks and tailor's dummies that allowed a true-to-life presentation of clothes. Wax mannequins only emerged after the turn of the century and were an instant success with the larger shops.[52] All these devices helped to make the windows altogether more attractive. High costs, however, were responsible for the obvious differences in the attractiveness of various store displays.

Even though the window display in German cities and towns was very common before the turn of the century, it should not be forgotten that the technique of presenting the merchandise was not yet very refined. It required a great deal of effort for the retailers to make window shopping enjoyable for customers. After all, the glittering world of merchandise had to be seen from the street. Therefore, one had to take precautions in order to make the shop window attractive in all weather conditions. The most obvious means for this was the awning.[53] It was usually made out of canvas and had blinds on the side. The marquee protected shoppers and merchandise from bright sunlight and light rain and, in the summer, against heat outside and to some degree inside as well. The awning also forced people to get closer to the shop, since it obstructed the view from a distance.[54] Rolling blinds obstructed the view of the merchandise on Sundays and holidays. But these common wooden, and later steel, grates were mostly a trade mark of small- and medium-sized shops. Larger shops, on the other hand, left their shop windows unobstructed, since their high-quality window glass also protected against burglaries. Only the art dealers and jewellers installed additional removable iron bars, so that the merchandise was protected and yet could still be seen.[55] However, we must remember that in most cities the shop window had to be covered or closed during the main church services. In some places such laws remained on the books until the end of the German Empire.[56]

Extreme heat and cold were also problems. The display usually consisted of heavy wooden cases that were difficult to ventilate; the small holes for air circulation did not make much of a difference. Condensation was produced, which turned to steam in the summer and frost in the winter if no preventive measures were taken (see Figure 7.8). Each decade more and more new means to solve this problem were invented, but none was entirely effective. Since open gas flames in the window case were extremely dangerous, window glass was regularly coated with glycerin or other strong chemicals to reduce the risk of fire. As a result the customer's view of the merchandise was frequently blurred.[57]

Darkness posed an especially difficult problem. Window displays had to be lit in order to be attractive in the evening too. There were very few

Im Frühling 1888.

Schneidermeister (zum Lehrjungen): „Schlag' einmal die Eiszapf'n
weg, damit die Herrschaften die Frühjahrauslag sehen können!"

7.8   A frosted-over shop window

Source: *Fliegende Blätter*, 88 (1888), no. 2230, Suppl., 5

laws governing business hours until the 1890s, and so many shops
remained open in the evening. Therefore, many shop windows were
initially lit with candles and petroleum lights, later with gas burners.
There was always the danger of fire, and open flames steamed up the
glass. Especially affluent shops relied on the exterior lighting of the
shop windows at an early stage, but street lights were not always
sufficient for the shop window and often blinded the customer. Gas and
oil light were both yellow in tone, so that the look of the goods on
display was often drastically altered. From the late 1880s on, electric
arc lamps appeared; gas glow lamps were introduced in the late 1890s.
Both produced white light but lent the merchandise a chalky character.
For this reason strong colours were necessary and the colour design of
the window displays sometimes seemed unnatural.[59] Even though window display innovations were important, there were aspects of the
shopping experience of the time that have to be taken into consideration in order not to project our present ideas onto the past. Back then
commercial dream worlds also had their limitations due to natural
conditions.

These limitations remind us not to posit the existence of a fully developed urban consumer society. The glass shop windows definitely attracted more and more people but, despite increasing real income, the barriers of class and income were less permeable than the shop windows were transparent.

Display window and store as commercial ensemble after 1900

The development of display windows had reached its quantitative limits around the turn of the century. New innovations, which had followed one another in rapid succession before 1871, now failed to appear. However, we can posit that in the 1890s at the latest, shop windows emerged not only in average-sized towns, but frequently in smaller towns as well.[60] Shopkeepers on the urban outskirts also believed that glass fronts were absolutely indispensable. Still, the development of the display window continued unceasingly, for the domestication of the shop window in German cities around the turn of the century caused a qualitative improvement in sales techniques and the stores themselves: the principles of window design were also applied in the salesroom; the 'display window quality of things'[61] was prevalent in the whole shop, shaping both design and staff.

The background to this change was a general and qualitative growth of the German small retail business, effected by the beginning of the 1890s. Intensive competition led to smaller trade margins, but at the same time increased the general costs of running the enterprise. The display window was primarily responsible for these changes:

> The modern shop window requires enormous sums of money. You cannot imagine how many different items, from the huge plate glass to the practically invisible merchandise racks, are required and how many people and how much work are necessary for the set-up and maintenance of an acceptable window display. Just the decoration of such a shop window alone costs on average 150 to 200 marks for smaller sizes and 1,000 marks or more for the larger ones. On top of that we have to add the salary for the *arrangeurs*, i.e. people who decorate it.[61]

As early as the beginning of the 1890s window displays were changed, on average, every two weeks,[62] even in medium-sized shops, so overhead generally increased. The rapid change became financially necessary to lower the burden of fixed costs. At the same time the standards of window design were rising. Fashions replaced seasons and the decoration materials industry continually offered new and ever more expensive products. Larger businesses could employ their own staff to decorate their windows, the decorators thus replacing the decorating shop owner or his assistant. Textbooks and retail trade journals offered a steadily growing knowledge and information base for the decoration of display windows which would be attractive and would meet the current criteria for good taste.[63] These tasks, however, could not be easily delimited. The customer was not simply supposed to be attracted to the shop to look at the pretty display. He/she was expected to enter the shop to make a purchase. Therefore, he/she had to be presented with an ambience inside the shop commensurate with the progress of decoration technique, an ambience which must at least keep pace with the shop window. The exterior of the shop became the model for the refurbishing of the interior.

New architectural techniques were required for this development. Very early on the *Kaufhäuser* had huge sales counters: Herzog boasted 3,710 square metres in 1878 and the Berlin *Kaufhaus* Heinrich Jordan reached 8,000 square metres by 1893.[64] Only the use of reinforced concrete made it possible to build even larger sales rooms, as partition walls were no longer necessary and the number of supporting pillars could be greatly reduced. Up to this point the furnishings of the larger shops consisted of counters, racks and shelves; now there were big sales and display tables placed in the middle of the rooms. At the same time central heating replaced the hearths in the stores, and larger staircases, galleries and balconies were built. Thus customers could see not only the merchandise from a distance, but the other customers' purchases as well.[65] Store owners faced new problems when it came to decorating the interior of their stores and the display of merchandise, which they solved by reverting back to tried and well-established window decoration practice. In the largest department stores, it is easy to see this trend,[66] but it was more prevalent in medium-sized and larger *Kaufhäuser*, which raised window display advertising to a new, more inclusive level.

The sales rooms of the Berlin firm Esders & Dyckhoff were not only significantly larger and better lit than those in stores of an earlier era (Figure 7.9). They also contained totally new furnishings, including display cases (often with glass fronts), which stood in the middle of the floor. Shelves were inappropriate for large salesrooms and display tables did not offer enough space for the merchandise. Therefore, the shop was refurbished and decorated with mirrors and the merchandise was permanently visible to the consumer. Self-service as a concept did not yet exist. Just as in the display windows, items were to be looked at, but not touched, unless a shop assistant were present.

The continually growing range of industrially produced items favoured the presentation of merchandise within the shop. The display of new hats and blouses in the salesrooms of the Berlin firm Kersten &

Geschäftshaus der Firma H. Esders & Dyckhoff in Berlin, am Dönhoffplatz.
Innenansicht.

7.9   Salesrooms of the Berlin firm H. Esders & Dyckhoff, 1901

Source: *Der Manufacturist* 24, no. 23 (1901), 9

Tuteur was not done with the kinds of mannequins and other props used in window displays (Figure 7.10). Display tables and glass cabinets made another kind of window-shopping possible inside the shop itself.

The presentation of beds in the department store Weddy-Ponicke shows broader possibilities for interior design (Figure 7.11). The decorated merchandise could not only be looked at, but regained its quality as something displayed in a room, became more approachable and could be experienced. Dream worlds could now be built away from the narrow construction of the display window, and their 'natural' appeal increased.

This development of interior decoration was furthered dramatically by the improvements in lighting techniques. No longer were oil or simple gas lights used; bright electric arc lamps, and in particular the new gas glow light, replaced them. Thus the shop could be completely lit and the merchandise and decoration could show their splendour. At the same time, the big hearths disappeared from the shops and were replaced by central heating. This was another way of gaining display room and the ambience was made more pleasant. Structurally necessary pillars were still an irritation; but in new buildings the brick support

7.10   Salesrooms of the Berlin firm Kersten & Tuteur in 1914

Source: *Berliner Architekturwelt* 16 (1914), 148

Für den „Manufacturist" phot. von Fritz Möller-Halle.

Geschäftshaus der Firma H. C. Weddy-Pönicke in Halle a. S.

7.11   Salesrooms of the firm of H.C. Weddy-Pönicke in Halle in 1901

Source: *Der Manufacturist* 24, no. 25 (1901), 13

pillars were increasingly replaced by smaller cast-iron columns or iron supports, which gave medium-sized shops more usable space.[67]

Tasteful interior design was enhanced by the use of colour. Some store owners coordinated the colours of ceilings, walls and window panes. Art nouveau was especially successful in selling up-market consumer goods.[68] After the turn of the century the shop developed, at least as far as the consumer business was concerned, into a functionally designed art environment – functional for the purpose of sales. Even if the majority of the smaller shops could not quite keep up with the exemplary large department stores, one also had to recognize their efforts and their changes – which influenced the smaller stores on a smaller scale. Like the window display, the shop itself became an increasingly reflexive and calculated sales technique and changed its decoration accordingly.

Only when these developments had occurred did window-shopping become a true shopping experience for the majority of consumers. Class barriers were consciously transgressed in order to attract customers who could not normally afford the displayed goods. Thus new commercial 'sensual horizons' were created, as evidenced by the sudden increase in shoplifting incidents.[69] The term 'democratization of consumption' had only limited validity, since despite increasing real wages, high-quality consumer and utility goods were only partially available to the majority of people. In the upper middle class, however, there emerged a new urban consumer culture in which the display windows were still attractive, but in which the salesroom, designed according to the model set by the windows, was the main focus.

> What downside does an otherwise dreary and unbearable winter day have in the face of the lit shopping streets in the large city with their enticing displays of many beautiful and precious items? A hail storm, wet feet? One walks into the first best shop, pleasant warmth, bright unobtrusive light, positive impressions everywhere! One imagines oneself to be the owner of soft carpets, glamorous mirrors, pretty and comfortable furniture, one knows that the tasteful arrangement of merchandise is solely directed at the customer. All other pleasures are at his unlimited disposal. Why not buy something small? Maybe one does not need anything. On the other hand, what is there to do at home on such a day where it is not half as pretty or as modern, where there is not anything new and exciting; what does one do on the street in such nasty weather?[71]

The expansion of the window display into the interior of the shop made it possible for the front of the store to be considered more in terms of quality. Thus a process of mutual coordination began, encouraging uniform advertising by individual shops.

First, the time of the glass palaces ended quickly; they were replaced by shops with smaller display window fronts. Several department store fires showed the limited heat resistance of pure steel and iron constructions, so that the vertical pillars were now almost always covered with stone facing. The number of two- and especially three-storey display window constructions decreased, since windows so high up were hardly noticed.[71] After the turn of the century new possibilities arose, and one of the reasons was curved plate glass. Thus the way from the street into the shop could be framed by display windows and up-market speciality shops took advantage of these new developments.[72] At the same time the windows were adapted more to the displayed goods:

> The type of goods will determine whether a large shop window is appropriate or if a small section of the window is sufficient. Window design requires different considerations for the fashion shop as far as the merchandise display is concerned, as opposed to the jeweller's shop, where the value of the piece lies in it uniqueness. And by pursuing the theory of the pictorial unity of the goods, the idea of concentration and isolation, of framing of the 'still life' in the shop window was introduced. The framing of the window simultaneously became the framing of the merchandise.[73]

A second example of the growing importance of strong qualitative interest is the use of light. The shining façades of the big houses provoked increasing criticism of a 'craze for light'. This criticism started to be met with a weaker, but more strategically applied kind of lighting.[74] An indirect interior lighting took the place of the exterior lighting. Set behind refracting glass, these electric lamps hardly produced any condensation, but created a 'mystical magic' for the merchandise.[75]

Finally, the position of the merchandise within the display changed. The exceptional role played by individual products, which was supposed to make huge piles of merchandise look even more impressive, disappeared in favour of a sales ambience, which was generally supposed to encourage customers to purchase items and which formed the frame for the purchase of a single product. As a considerable percentage of the lower classes suffered from malnutrition and the standard of living of the majority of customers was repeatedly reduced due to rising food prices, the abstract power of the advertisement started increasingly to dominate the displays of the big shops: 'Today's shop window display has become an advertisement to such an extent that many shops have stopped showing the products for sale.'[76] In this context the shop window had only an appellative character and had become a non-specific undifferentiated part of a larger advertising system. In retrospect, there is no longer a single item for whose attraction the shop window provided a visual frame. At the end there is a commercial cult about the merchandise itself. The big stores became cathedrals of consumption, the decorators priests of the new cult, and the displays were their altars:

The merchant who wants to sell his goods cannot be satisfied with
a mass of people passing by fascinated only by the atmosphere of
glamour and light. He wants to grip and impress them, mesmerize
them; the merchandise is supposed to become important for them,
to dominate everything and make one forget the whole enthralling
glamour and become one with every man. It has to create a soli-
tude in which the magic suggestion spins its threads and which the
spellbound cannot get rid of the thought: I have to own you! But
this sacred process of the unification of buyer and merchandise
requires a lot of concentration. A lot of effort is necessary to
isolate the merchandise. Most importantly the window needs a
frame. Endell, the most famous magician amongst the window
dressers in Berlin, understood this necessity. Whenever he had the
chance to design the façades of stores, he put thick pillars between
the windows and ornamented the windows with expensive frames,
so that we experience something like a miracle when we get closer
to the windows. It was also Endell who found the best solution for
the lighting. Long before him the outer arc lamps, which blind the
customer instead of illuminating the merchandise, had been removed. The hidden lighting, which conceals the light source from
the viewer, in order to emphasize the goods even more, had been
introduced to the window displays by the theatrical stage. Endell's
contribution now was a light with its mystic magic. With sparkling
surfaces of coloured glass it sealed the lighting cases against the
street, the light playing down from above onto the merchandise.
Name brands, almost like magic symbols, shine brightly inside.
The scene is filled with the atmosphere which every child experiences in front of the curtain which is to open up a dream world for
the first time. Whatever is offered in this magic shrine is something
precious, even if it is only a pair of black leather boots.[77]

What I have described above allows for various conclusions, for the
display window is only representative of some more general questions
about advertising and the consumer. If we were only to consider this
phenomenon from the perspective of the cultural critical theorists, we
would lose sight of the positive aspects of advertising which are so
strongly expressed in the above quotation: the modern consumer standing empowered and ennobled before the powerful show of goods that
were apparently produced only for him. The merchandise became god-
like, creating a new sacred space of omnipresent and transcendental
power, first within the framework of the display windows, and then later
within the store itself. The rationality of a modern presentation of merchandise created the irrationally rational aspect of modern consumption.
The loss of mystery about this world paradoxically found its counterpart
in the widespread enchantment of the display windows, shops and merchandise. But the notion that advertising and consumption might be the
substitute religion of a capitalist society does not do justice to the attractive aspects of purchase and purchasing, of looking and discovering.

In the development of the window display we find not just alienation, but also the attempts by many people to domesticate the power of nature and to create, by human art alone, a world in a small glass room. Consumption, especially mass consumption in the nineteenth century, was often perceived as an expression of man's ability to progress. The acts of purchasing, acquiring and possessing confirmed his status as the master of the world and, when gazing into the shop window, even a person with little income believed that the world was at his feet. The self-consciousness that makes this notion possible is now lost, but it was definitely part of the fascination that surrounded the display window in the nineteenth century. As we draw our conclusions, maybe we should also think about the achievements of the retailers, who are so often neglected in historical research. After all, it was their efforts and love of detail which created commercial dream worlds and thus they who shaped important elements of the modern city. With the help of a simple, transparent window pane they separated buyer and merchandise, thus creating uncertainty, and bestowing upon the products an element of mystery.

We could assume other roles, for example that of the historian, who would probably be surprised about the new periodization that has been presented in this work. If it is valid, and much seems to support this assumption, the bulk of existing research has had the wrong focus. In the middle, rather than at the end, of the nineteenth century, important changes within window advertising and consumption took place. This hypothesis would question the widely accepted picture of a consumer society that developed only in the 1890s, since in German cities a bourgeois style of consumption emerged much earlier. Furthermore, the prevailing idea that a new visual culture emerged only at the turn of the century would, at the very least, be dated incorrectly. One should ask about the causes of these changes – independent of whether these causes were manufacturers, shop owners or consumers, or, on the other hand, shops, display windows or products. People and things belong together despite their individuality. Maybe the picture of industrialization, which has been so completely dominated by manufacturing, would develop another focus to do justice to the cities as business and consumer centres. And as for the rise of the German Empire as a European economic power, we would probably also be confronted with some surprising perspectives. There are many possible conclusions to be drawn, which you can develop further, and to which you can definitely add a few more. You should try it. It will be worth the effort.

Notes

1. The author would like to thank Regine Wieder for translating this essay from German.

2. Compare Peter N. Stearns, 'Stages of Consumerism: Recent Work on the Issues of Periodization', *Journal of Modern History* 69 (1997), 102–17; Karin Hausen, 'Werbung. Vorbemerkung', *Jahrbuch für Wirtschaftsgeschichte* (1997) 1, 9–10; Jürgen Bolten, 'Werbewandel – Wertewandel. Werbegeschichte als Kommunikationsgeschichte', *Universitas* 51 (1996), 127–42; Peter Borscheid and Clemens Wischermann (eds), *Bilderwelt des Alltags. Werbung in der Konsumgesellschaft des 19. und 20. Jahrhunderts*, Studien zur Geschichte des Alltags, vol. 3 (Stuttgart: Steiner, 1995).

3. Compare Klaus Tenefelde, 'Klassenspezifische Konsummuster im Deutschen Reich', in *Europäische Konsumgeschichte. Zur Gesellschafts- und Kulturgeschichte des Konsums (18.–20. Jahrhundert)*, edited by Hannes Siegrist, Hartmut Kaelble and Jürgen Kocka (Frankfurt and New York: Campus, 1997), 245–66; Uwe Spiekermann, *Basis der Konsumgesellschaft. Entstehung und Entwicklung des modernen Kleinhandels in Deutschland 1850–1914* (Munich: C. H. Beck, 1999); the current authority is Dirk Reinhardt, *Von der Reklame zum Marketing: Geschichte der Witschaftswerbung in Deutschland* (Berlin: Akademie Verlag, 1993). Reinhardt's study, unfortunately, looks at advertising only from the inside.

4. Bruno Latour, *Wir sind nie modern gewesen: Versuch einer symmetrischen Anthropologie* (Berlin: Akademie Verlag, 1995); see also Detlef Stender, 'Vom Leben der toten Dinge: Schränke zum Kühlen als historische Quelle', in *Alltagskultur, Subjektivität und Geschichte: Zur Theorie und Praxis von Alltagsgeschichte*, edited by the Berliner Geschichtswerkstatt (Munster: Verlag Westfälisches Dampfboot, 1994), 157–73.

5. This and the preceding quotation are from Hans-Walter Schmidt, 'Schaufenster des Ostens: Anmerkungen zur Konsumkultur der DDR', *Deutschland-Archiv* 27 (1994), 364–72.

6. Negative examples are Württembergischer Kunstverein (ed.), *Schaufenster: Die Kulturgeschichte eines Massenmediums* (Stuttgart: Dr. Cantz'sche Druckerei, 1974); Heidrun Großjohann, 'Die Karriere des stummen Spektakels: Zur Geschichte des Schaufensters', in *Der neuen Welt ein neuer Rock: Studien zur Kleidung, Körper und Mode an Beispielen aus Baden-Württemberg*, Forschungen und Berichte zur Volkskunde in Baden-Württemberg, edited by C. Köhle-Hezinger and G. Mentges, vol. 9 (Stuttgart: Konrad Theiss, 1993), 252–6.

7. Compare Johann Georg Krünitz, 'Kauf-Laden', in *Oekonomisch-technologische Encyclopädie*, edited by J. G. Krünitz, vol. 36 (Berlin: Joachim Pauli, 1786), 482–6; Margot Aschenbrenner, *Buden und Läden* (Biberach and Riss: n.p., 1992); Gerhard Kaufmann, 'Alte Läden' in *Vom Charme der alten Warenwelt*, edited by M. Galli (Dortmund: Harenberg, 1992), 115–53.

8. Compare Heinrich Sasse, 'Das bremische Krameramt', *Bremisches Jahrbuch* 33 (1931), 108–52, n. 1. Also see H. W. Bahn, 'Studienbeitrag zur Entwicklungsgeschichte des Schaufensters in Deutschland', (Ing. diss., Braunschweig, 1923).

9. Compare Bahn, 'Studienbeitrag zur Entwicklungsgeschichte'; Hermann

Weidemann, 'Skizze zur Geschichte des Glases', *Prometheus* 24 (1913), 340–42, 358–61, 378–81, 394–5.

10. Compare Josef Kirchner, 'Münchener Kaufläden von einst und jetzt', *Münchener Rundschau* 4 (1907), 1–5; *Die Malerische Topographie des Königreiches Bayern* (Munich: Hermann & Barth, 1830) which contains several sketches of shops in Munich with display windows.

11. Compare Boris Röhrl, 'Ladenbeschriftungen des 19. Jahrhunderts: Versuch einer Systematisierung', *Volkskunst* 13, no. 3 (1990), 39–43.

12. Spiekermann, *Basis der Konsumgesellschaft*, presents evidence for a new perspective on these changes.

13. For a different view, see Ulrich Lange, 'Krämer, Höker und Hausierer. Die Anfänge des Massenkonsums in Schleswig-Holstein', in *Mare Balticum. Beiträge zur Geschichte des Ostseeraums im Mittelalter und Neuzeit*, edited by W. Paravicin, Kieler Historische Studien, vol. 36 (Sigmaringen: Jan Thorbecke 1992), 315–27; as well as Heidrun Homburg, 'Werbung – "Eine Kunst, die gelernt sein will." Aufbrüche in eine neue Warenwelt 1750–1850', *Jahrbuch für Wirtschaftsgeschichte* (1997), 1, 11–52.

14. In *Von der Reklame zum Marketing*, Reinhardt emphasizes that 'until the 1890s large and modern shop windows remained very rare in German cities' (271). In contrast, he asserts in his 1995 essay, 'Vom Intelligenzblatt zum Satellitenfernsehen: Stufen der Werbung als Stufen der Gesellschaft', that 'As early as the 1870s the *Gründerzeit* had changed the looks of the streets with its refurbishing of shop fronts' (Peter Borscheid and Clemens Wischermann (eds), *Bilderwelt des Alltags: Werbung in der Konsumgesellschaft des 19. und 20. Jahrhunderts* (Stuttgart: Steiner, 1995), 144–63). It is necessary to consider that this periodization only makes sense if the department store is narrowly defined as 'a capitalist retail trade company which deals with goods of different kinds in uniform sales-rooms' (Uwe Spiekermann, *Warenhaussteuer in Deutschland: Mittelstandsbewegung, Kapitalismus und Rechtsstaat im späten Kaiserreich* (Frankfurt a.M.: Peter Lang, 1994), 29). A broader definition would place the beginning of the history of German department stores during the early phase of industrialization.

15. Wilfred Reininghaus, review of *Bilderwelt des Alltags: Werbung in der Konsumgesellschaft des 19. und 20. Jahrhunderts*, edited by Peter Borscheid and Clemens Wischermann, *Vierteljahresschrift für Sozial- und Wirtschaftsgeschichte* 83 (1996): 239–40.

16. Figures taken from F. C. W. Dieterici, *Statistische Uebersicht der wichtigsten Gegenstände des Verkehrs und Verbrauchs im Preußischen Staate und im deutschen Zollvereine in dem Zeitraume von 1837 bis 1839* (Berlin, Posen and Bromberg: Ernest Siegfried Mittler, 1842), 399–400. Ernst Siegfried Mittler, *Tabellen und amtliche Nachrichten über den Preussischen Staat für das Jahr 1858*, edited by the Statistisches Bureau zu Berlin (Berlin: R. Decker, 1860) 322–3.

17. Figures taken from H[ans] Grandtke, 'Die Entstehung der Berliner Wäsche-Industrie im 19. Jahrhundert', *Jahrbuch für Gesetzgebung, Verwaltung und Volkswirtschaft im Deutschen Reich* 20 (1896), 587–602. The window of a linen shop was portrayed by Johann Erdmann Hummel in the late 1820s (*Westermanns Monatshefte* 147 1929/30): s.p.

18. My own evaluation of the *Hamburgisches Adress-Buch auf das Jahr 1800*

(Hamburg: J. H. Hermann); *Hamburgisches Adressbuch für das Jahr 1822* (Hamburg: Hermann's Erben).

19.   'Polizey-Bekanntmachung, die bequemere Passage der Strassen betreffend v. 15.05.1830', in J. M. Lappenberg, *Sammlung der Verordnungen der freyen Hanse-Stadt Hamburg seit 1814* vol. 4 (Hamburg, 1832), 170–71.

20.   W. Melhop, *Alt-Hamburgische Bauweise: Kurze geschichtliche Entwicklung der Baustile in Hamburg*, 2nd edn (Hamburg: 1925), 326 (reprint of an earlier publication by Kurt Heymann (Hamburg, n.d.)). It contains several exhibits as well as photographs from the 1870s.

21.   It needs to be pointed out that a simple and fairly plain design of the shop windows was common in Hamburg. See Robert Geissler, *Hamburg: Ein Führer durch die Stadt und ihre Umgebungen* (Leipzig: J. J. Weber, 1861), esp. 53.

22.   'Das Gerson'sche Modewaaren-Lager zu Berlin, Werderscher Markt No. 5', *Zeitschrift für Bauwesen* 1 (1851), col. 131–7; Gustav Schmoller, *Zur Geschichte der deutschen Kleingewerbe im 19. Jahrhundert: Statistische und nationalökonomische Untersuchungen* (Halle: Buchhandlung des Waisenhauses, 1870), 646.

23.   See also Elisabeth von Stephani-Hahn, *Schaufenster-Kunst: Lehrsätze und Erlauterungen*, 3rd rev. edn (Berlin: Schottländer & Co., 1926), 9–10; according to von Stephani-Hahn, the first specialized shop window decorators were employed as early as the middle of the nineteenth century.

24.   Springer, *Ein Führer durch die Stadt und ihre Umgebungen*, 330, 332–3.

25.   Stock, 'Ueber Schaufenster-Anlagen', *Zeitschrift für Praktische Baukunst* 24 (1864), col. 9–20.

26.   'Ueber Kaufläden', *Zeitschrift für Bauhandwerker* 7 (1863), 132–6, sheet 17.

27.   Weidemann, 'Skizze zur Geschichte des Glases', 341. London, by contrast, counted only 2,000 similar shop windows, Paris 1,500 and Vienna 1,000.

28.   Compare 'Geschäftshaus in Berlin', *Unter den Linden*, no. 13, für den Kaufmann Kohn, *Zeitschrift für praktische Baukunde* 31(1871), col. 151–2, illustrations 17–20.

29.   This is evidenced by various caricatures; for example, 'Illustrationen zu schönen Worten', *Fliegende Blätter* 37 (1862), 40.

30.   Compare Bischoff et al., *Das Manufakturwaarengeschäft: Fabrikation und Vertrieb*, 2nd edn (Leipzig: Otto Wigand, 1869), 479.

31.   Compare Uwe Spiekermann, 'Elitenkampf um die Werbung: Staat, Heimatschutz und Reklameindustrie im frühen 20. Jahrhundert', in *Bilderwelt des Alltags: Werbung in der Konsumgesellschaft des 19. und 20. Jahrhunderts*, edited by Peter Borscheid and Clemens Wischermann (Stuttgart: Steiner, 1995), 126–149, esp.

32.   For information on the technical issues see J. Schuh, 'Der moderne Ladenbau', *Süddeutsche Bauzeitung* 2 (1892), 222–4, 234–5, esp. 222.

33.   Even the first department store, the Kaiser-Bazaar, founded in 1891, had 130 shop windows ('Vom Kaiser-Bazar in Berlin', *Wiener Bauindustrie-Zeitung* 8 (1891), 323–4.

34.   Similarly, A. L. Plehn, 'Zur Entwicklung der Warenhausfassade', *Deutsche Bauhütte* 8 (1917), 113–14, 127–7, 129. For a French example see Christine Schramm, *Deutsche Warenhausbauten: Ursprung, Typologie und Entwicklungstendenzen* (Aachen: Shaker, 1995), 28–41; Siegfried Gerlach and Dieter Sawatzki, *Grands magasins oder Die Geburt des*

Warenhauses im Paris des 19. Jahrhunderts (Dortmund: Harenberg, 1989), 5–38.

35. Compare Hugo Koch's 1842 criticism, 'Schaufenster und Ladenverschlüsse', in *Handbuch der Architektur* 3 no. 1 (Darmstadt: Arnold Bergsträsser, 1896), 357–8. Hans Schliepmann, 'Das moderne Geschäftshaus', *Berliner Architekturwelt* 3 (1901), 423–5. A positive note is struck by Leo Nacht, 'Moderne Schaufensterauslagen', *Berliner Architekturwelt* 6 (1904), 337.

36. Eugen Richter, *Die Consumvereine: Ein Noth- und Hilfsbuch für deren Gründung und Einrichtung* (Berlin: Franz Duncker, 1867), 95.

37. There is some good evidence for Munich, for instance. See Richard Bauer, *Das alte München: Photographien 1855–1912*, collected by Karl Valentin (Munich: Schirmer Mosel, 1982).

38. Compare Uwe Spiekermann, 'Medium der Solidarität: Die Werbung der Konsumgenossenschaften 1903–1933', in *Bilderwelt des Alltags: Konsumgesellschaft des 19. und 20. Jahrhunderts*, edited by Peter Borschied and Clemens Wischermann (Stuttgart: Steiner, 1995), 150–89; Michael Prinz, *Brot und Dividende: Konsumvereine in Deutschland und England vor 1914*, Kritische Studien zur Geschichtswissenschaft, vol. 112 (Göttingen : Vandenhoeck & Ruprecht, 1996), 263–4.

39. Julius Hirsch provides the best overview in *Die Filialbetriebe im Detailhandel* (Bonn: A. Marcus and E. Webers, 1913).

40. Uli Huber, 'Die Geschichte des Schaufensters', in *Werbende Fenster*, edited by Eugen Johannes Maecker, vol. 1 (Berlin: Kulturbuchverlag), 15.

41. Hermann Kind, *Die Fleischerei in Leipzig* Untersuchungen über die Lage des Handwerks in Deutschland, Schriften des Vereins für Socialpolitik, vol. 67 (Leipzig: Duncker und Humblot, 1897), 55–6. See also the 'artistic' decoration of pig halves in Stephani-Hahn, *Schaufenster-Kunst*, 28 and the exhibit in S. Thron, 'Der Weihnachtsmann in der Großstadt', *Die Woche* 6 (1908), 2237–42.

42. Christiane Lamberty, 'Die Kunst im Leben des Buttergeschäfts: Geschmacksbildung und Reklame in Deutschland vor 1914', *Jahrbuch für Wirtschaftsgeschichte* (1997) 1, 53–78.

43. Karl Ernst Osthaus, 'Das Schaufenster', *Jahrbuch des Deutschen Werkbundes* (1913), 59–69.

44. Bischoff et al., *Das Manufaktuwaarengeschäft*, 472.

45. 'Schaufenster-Decorationen einst und jetzt', *Der Manufacturist* 16, no. 16 (1893), 7.

46. Bischoff et al., *Das Manufaktuwaarengeschäft*, 476–7.

47. Geissler, *Hamburg*, 53.

48. 'Soll man an den Waaren die Preise deutlich mit Ziffern bezeichnen, so daß Jedermann sofort weiss, was das betreffende Stück kostet?', *Der Manufacturist* 16, no. 10 (1893), 5.

49. Respectable training institutes emerged even before the turn of the century. See 'Decorationsschule für Frauen', *Der Manufacturist* 16, no. 4 (1893), 9.

50. J. Erhart, *Der Schaufenster-Dekorateur: Lehrbuch zur zweckmäßigen Dekoration der Schaufenster für sämtliche Modebranchen mit über 300 Illustrationen* (Frankfurt: A. Blazek, Jr, 1895), 215–20.

51. See the advice in 'Wie mache ich Reklame', *Der Materialist* 21, no. 40 (1900), 12.

52. See 'Die Anziehungskraft des Schaufensters' 36, no. 5 (1913), 40; von Stephani-Hahn, *Schaufenster-Kunst*, 149–192, esp. 21.

53. R. Goldschmidt, 'Kauf-, Waaren- und Geschäftshäuser', in *Baukunde des Architekten (Deutsches Bauhandbuch)*, vol. 2 p. 5, 2nd edn (Berlin: Verlag Deutsche Bauzeitung, 1902), 71.

54. See exhibits of the 'Friedrich- and Leipzigerstraße' in *Berliner Architekturwelt* 16 (1914), 193–4.

55. See Koch, 'Schaufenster und Ladenverschlüsse', 364, 370–76; 'Neue Schaufenster-Rouleaux', *Der Materialist* 20, no. 40 (1899), 2; Goldschmidt *Kauf-, Waaren- und Geschäftshäuser*, 69–71; Franz Woas, 'Praktische Neuerungen im Ladenbau', *Bauzeitung für Württemberg, Baden, Hessen und Elsaß-Lothringen* 11 (1914), 170.

56. Dirk Reinhardt, 'Beten oder Bummeln? Der Kampf um die Schaufenster-freiheit', in *Bilderwelt des Alltags: Konsumgesellschaft des 19. und 20. Jahrhunderts*, edited by Peter Borscheid and Clemens Wischermann (Stuttgart: Steiner, 1995), 116–25. The essay, however, overestimates the influence of the churches and does not address the background of the conflicts at the turn of the century.

57. Of the enormous quantities of relevant literature, I recommend the following titles: 'Gefrieren der Schaufenster', *Der Manufacturist* 16, no. 3 (1893), 9; 'Gefrorene Schaufenster', *Der Manufacturist* 16, no. 44 (1893), 8; Goldschmidt, *Kauf-, Waaren- und Geschäftshäuser*, 362; 'Das Beschlagen der Schaufenster', *Der Materialist* 21, no. 1 (1900), 2; 'Das Beschlagen und Gefrieren der Schaufenster', *Der Manufacturist* 24, no. 46 (1901), 12.

58. See on this theme in the history of everyday life: 'Ueber Schaufenster-Beleuchtung', *Der Manufacturist* 16, no. 17 (1893), 3; 'Schaufenster-Beleuchtung', *Der Materialist* 21, no. 16 (1900), 2nd page after 12; Carl Zaar and August Leo Zaar, 'Geschäfts-, Kauf- und Warenhäuser', *Handbuch der Architektur*, T. 4, half volume 2, vol. 2, (Stuttgart: Arnold Bergsträsser, Verlagsbuchhandlung, A. Kröner, 1902), 20–24.

59. See on this topic Max Schröder, *Das Geschäftshaus der Kleinstadt* (Strelitz: M. Hittenkofer, 1911).

60. Georg Simmel, 'Berliner Gewerbe-Ausstellung', *Ästhetik und Kommunikation* 18, 67–8 (1987–89), 105. Originally published in 1896.

61. Dora Feigenbaum, 'Die Reklame: Ihre Entwicklung und Bedeutung', *Deutschland* 7 (1905–6): 427–36, 589–602.

62. Felix Steinl, 'Die Reklame des kleinstädtischen Manufakturwaaren-händlers', in *Moderne Reklame*, edited by Robert Exner (Zittau: Verlag der Expedition der Fachzeitschrift 'Die Reklame', 1892), 7–10.

63. Good examples from the grocery trade are Fritz Grossmann, 'Schmücke Dein Schaufenster: Handbuch der Schaufenster-Reklame', in 'Wort & Bild' (Magdeburg: Hermann Teubner, 1901), and Gustav Teller, *Die Schaufenster-Dekoration für Kolonialwaren-Handlungen und verwandte Geschäftszweige* (Leipzig: Jüstel & Göttel, 1909).

64. For details on new and renovated rooms, see 'Heinrich Jordan, Markgrafen-strasse 105–107', *Deutsche Bauzeitung* 27 (1893), 317–21. Paul Lindenberg, 'Berlin und das Haus Rudolph Hertzog seit 1839', in *Agenda Rudolph Hertzog 1914* (Berlin: self-published, 1913), 13–96.

65. See Erwin Paneth, *Entwicklung der Reklame vom Altertum bis zur Gegenwart: Erfolgreiche Mittel der Geschäfts-, Personen und Ideenreklame*

aus allen Zeiten und Ländern (Munich, Leipzig: R. Oldenbourg, 1926), 161.

66. Compare Alfred Wiener, *Das Warenhaus: Kauf-, Geschäfts-, Büro-Haus* (Berlin: Ernst Wasmuth, 1912).

67. Karl Ross, 'Neubau und Umbau von Geschäftshäuseren und Kaufläden', *Der Manufacturist* 24, no. 27, 5–6, no. 29, 5–6, no. 32, 5–6, no. 35, 5–6, no. 40 (1901), 5–6, here no. 29 (1901), 5.

68. See Rogs, 'Neubau und Umbau' no. 40 (1901), 5. On ceiling decoration, see August Endell, 'Ladeneinrichtungen,' *Jahrbuch des Deutschen Werkbundes* (1913): 58.

69. For more detail see Uwe Spiekermann, 'Theft and Thieves in German Department Stores, 1895–1930: A Discourse on Morality, Crime, and Gender', in *Cathedrals of Consumption: The European Department Store, 1850–1939*, edited by Geoffrey Crossick and Serge Jaumain (Aldershot: Ashgate 1999).

70. 'Die innere Ausstattung: Vom Werke der Raumkunst für das offene Ladengeschäft', *Der Manufacturist* 36, no. 8 (1913), 36.

71. B. Haas, 'Das Schaufenster in ästhetischer und betriebstechnischer Beziehung (Schluss.)', *Deutsche Bauhütte* 10 (1906), 221–3. Compare Hans Schliepmann's critique of this architectural change, 'Das moderne Geschäfthaus (Schluss.)', *Berliner Architekturwelt* 4 (1902), 135–59.

72. Compare 'Ein schmales Bremer Geschäftshaus', *Deutsche Bauhütte* 5 (1901), 266–7; Goldschmidt, 'Kauf-, Waaren-, und Geschäfthäuser', 60; *Berliner Architekturwelt* 16: 68 (the new wing of Hermann Gerson); Woas, *Praktische Neuerungen im Ladenbau*.

73. Kurt Pallmann, 'Künstlerische Ladengestaltung als Aufgabe des Architekten', *Deutsche Bauhütte* 18 (1914), 108, 110, 113, 122–3.

74. 'Neue Wege', *Der Manufacturist* 36, no. 5 (1913), 15, 17.

75. Pallmann, 'Künstlerische Ladengestaltung als Aufgabe des Architekten', 108.

76. Osthaus, 'Das Schaufenster', 60. See also Stephani-Hahn, *Schaufenster-Kunst*, 10–11.

77. Osthaus, 'Das Schaufenster', 62–3.

CHAPTER EIGHT

Surrounding the Consumer: Persuasive Campaigns and Dutch Advertising Theory of the 1920s and 1930s[1]

Esther Cleven

Since the turn of the century, outdoor advertising with illustrated posters has been considered central in the Netherlands. Especially during the 1920s and 1930s, most Dutch cities had to deal with what seemed to be a wave of outdoor advertising. In that period, the Bond Heemschut, the Dutch association which since 1912 had, following the example of the German Heimatschutz, dedicated itself to the protection of the national heritage, successfully started to organize action against the visual pollution of the cityscape.[2] From 1928 to 1935, for instance, no fewer than 500 frames supporting electrical and neon signs were removed from the typical houses lining Amsterdam's canals.[3] None the less, this figure indicates that in the 1920s there was a craze for neon signs and other eye-catching advertising devices in Dutch cities, including Amsterdam, The Hague and Rotterdam (Figures 8.1 and 8.2). And despite the success of the Bond Heemschut, the craze continued, reaching its peak in the 1930s.

In 1936, E. B. W. Schuitema, author of one of the earliest Dutch advertising handbooks, the *Grondslagen van de moderne reclame (Principles of Modern Advertising)*, asserted, in accordance with contemporary Dutch advertising theory, that outdoor advertising was ineffective: 'Generally speaking, all of the factors influencing the preference for a certain product fall just outside the reach of outdoor advertising.'[4] Reality and theory seem to be at odds here, given the actual increase in outdoor advertising in this period. In this essay I will try to shed light on this paradox, primarily by taking a closer look at the development of the theoretical literature on advertising in the period between the two world wars. In doing so I will try to understand the theoretical marginalization of outdoor advertising by considering psychology's role in the development of advertising practice's rationale for influencing the consumer in the 1920s. It should become clear that although advertising concen-

8.1 Amsterdam, Utrechtsestraat in 1898. Photograph by Jacob Olie

Source: Gemeentearchief Amsterdam

8.2 The Hague, Spui, 1929

Source: P. Nijhof, *Buitenreclame in beeld. 50 jaar Alrecon Media 1946–1996*
(Zwolle: Waanders, 1996)

trated on the effectiveness of its subject, it still lacked any real knowledge of how the 'public' functions. In conclusion, I will argue that the way in which advertising practice nevertheless handled the question of how to influence consumer behaviour ruled out the possibilities of outdoor advertising. I hope to show that the struggle for professionalism on the part of people in advertising, most visible in big campaigns and in the development of advertising theory, had a negative impact upon the status of the *illustrated* poster. Resulting from the professionalization of advertising, the interest in its effectiveness and the decline of the status of the illustrated poster as well as of illustrated advertising in general, the importance ascribed to outdoor advertising declined. This became evident in advertising theory of the late 1930s.

The campaign for Blue Band margarine in the 1920s

Advertising in public spaces is the norm in most of Europe and North America. But passing through a Dutch city, an American or a Frenchman might find the dearth of outdoor advertising slightly unnerving. This lack is due to the strict regulation of public space by the Bond Heemschut and other organizations. The Dutch themselves are now much more irritated by the explosion of television advertising in the 1990s. This brings into sharp relief the fact that most of the advertising media which dominate today – television, film, illustrated magazines – did not exist or were not fully developed at the beginning of the twentieth century. But then as now the advertising world turned to any means at hand to convey a message. Perhaps the best example of this is one of the most famous campaigns in Dutch advertising history: the Blue Band margarine campaign begun in 1923.

In that year, the Van den Bergh company of Rotterdam introduced a new product, Blue Band margarine, which had been successful on the British market in the 1910s.[5] Van den Bergh was one of two companies that had successfully established a brand name; together with the Jurgens company, which was based in Oss and Nijmegen, Van den Bergh dominated between 75 and 80 per cent of the market in 1920. By then the number of margarine companies had dwindled to twenty (from seventy in 1880), but the margarine market was still competitive after the First World War. Throughout the 1920s, the two main companies intensified that competition, using a number of tactics to drive competitors from the market. These strategies, which the large companies aimed primarily at one another, included touting their fully modern production techniques (production and packaging had been thoroughly mechanized in 1920), launching new brands, and increasing the number of travel-

8.3 1920s mural for Blue Band margarine in Amsterdam on Van Eeghenstraat
Source: E. van Ravensberg, Amsterdam.

ling salesmen who were sent directly to shops. In 1927, the competition between Van den Bergh and Jurgens grew so fierce that margarine prices dropped below production costs. A merger of the two companies turned out to be the solution and, with the help of the ongoing campaign, the most costly the Netherlands had yet experienced, Van den Bergh & Jurgens completely dominated the market in 1935 with their product, Blue Band margarine.[6]

Van den Bergh hired Coppens' Advies-Bureau (Coppens' Consultation Office) for the advertising campaign in 1923,[7] and the firm drew on an entire range of advertising techniques, both new and old, with impressive results. Han Coppens, the head of the agency, visited the margarine factory in order to understand the company atmosphere, and invented a slogan, 'Blue Band – *versch gekarnd*', which borders on a fabrication, for it suggested that the margarine was 'freshly churned'. The agency also designed long-running and relatively large advertisements, all sorts of outdoor advertising, and materials for the interiors and windows of shops. With one exception, Coppens decided to use the same image in every advertisement: a young red-haired girl, smiling attractively and clad

8.4 The model Norah Walters poses in the Blue Band girl outfit in front of a chalk board with the text 'The Low Country's quality standard' in the early 1920s. Notice on the top right the efforts made to emphasize the (blue) scarf. Insert: Painting of the Blue Band girl.

Source: K. Sartory et al., *De Vierde Vrijheid, zijnde een blik in de historie van het reclamebureau delamar* (Amsterdam: 1955)

in a white dress and hat with blue borders. The very simple package which she emphatically presented to the viewer was designed in the same colours, so that the blue of her dress and hat as well as that of the package reminded one of the brand name (Figure 8.3).

There were also a variety of special forms of advertising, which often required a great deal of effort and attracted a great deal of attention. Among these was the temporary acquisition, in 1924, of the right to print postage stamps and adding 'Blue Band' to them. Real girls in blue and white dresses were sent to visit exhibitions and events specially organized to familiarize people with Blue Band. The brand name was spelled out in light bulbs on the bridge in front of the factory, close to the city centre, and was written on the underside of the wings of a small airplane flying above Rotterdam in 1925.

Coppens neglected nothing; every step appears to have been well thought out. The campaign was not only massive and sometimes sensa-

KOOPT HEDEN

BLUE BAND

VERSCH GEKARND

30 CENT PER ½ POND

8.5   Early 1920s poster for Blue Band margarine by Rie Cramer

Source: Van den Bergh Nederland, Rotterdam

tional, but coordinated in time, place and design. The *unity* of the campaign was evident in the consistent use of the brand name and its visual translation into blue and white, augmented by the appearance of the Blue Band girl. The enormous range of activities, which used any and every means available, was to become typical of advertising from the 1920s on. However, while we have become used to campaigns which maintain a central theme for years, the unity and consistency of Coppens's Blue Band campaign were revolutionary at the time. Since we are dealing here with outdoor advertising and its gradual loss of significance, it is important to remember that outdoor advertising was a significant component of this campaign. The use of light bulbs and airplanes, for instance, was sensational, preceding as it did the widespread use of neon signs in urban areas (which, as we have seen, became massively popular between the world wars).

Among the more standard techniques of the campaign were posters, murals and enamel signs showing the Blue Band girl as originally drawn by an English advertising artist. There was also an 'artistic' poster designed by Dutch illustrator Rie Cramer (Figure 8.5). She had to conform to the specifications of the girl designed by the English artist, including her dress, her posture and the package she held. This is quite remarkable: whereas the illustrated posters, murals and enamel signs, which were central to the campaign, were designed by a foreigner, the art poster designed by a Dutch artist constitutes only one of a whole range of *special* activities. It may have been added to the campaign to satisfy those who tore artistic posters from walls as a cheap way to acquire a piece of art. In the opinion of an advertising professional like Coppens, it seems to have had little use in terms of selling a product. In order to explain this, let us first take a short look at the history of artistic and illustrated posters of that period.

Eye-catching illustration

The differentiation between illustrated outdoor advertising and an exceptional artistic poster is symptomatic of the retreat of outdoor advertising from the centre of strategic advertising theory. This development started with the shift of strategic interests from advertising illustration to advertising message, which, in the Netherlands, occurred after the First World War. This shift was not always easy to see, on account of the continued public enthusiasm for the eye-catching effects of illustrated posters.

Only forty years before the Blue Band campaign began, from the 1880s on, as industrial production gradually moved away from direct forms of distribution and turned to the development of packaged and brand-name products, the main goal of advertising strategy became drawing attention to a brand name and associating it with a product. Posters and murals now tended to be large and impressive.[8] It had become customary to blow up a limited number of words (such as the brand name) to immense size. Variations in font and colour were also typical.[9] In the last decades of the nineteenth century, illustrations were introduced into the poster. Although illustrations *per se* were nothing new, they now became more widespread than before. It had been found that 'visuals', including design and illustration, would attract attention. The illustrated poster appeared to be a perfect way to inform as many people as possible of the emergence of a new brand.

The evolution of the illustrated advertising poster, in its principal form, was a continuation of the well-established tradition of evocative and provocative outdoor advertising. This tradition was a response to the introduction of brand-name products and the consequent growth in competition among advertisements in public spaces. In a more general sense, it was a commercial response to urbanization. Paris, London and

Berlin, where splendid accomplishments in poster art originated, were growing into cities of unprecedented size. Public life in these and many other European cities took place on an immense scale. In order to be seen at all, to reach the attention of the public amidst the confusion of modern urban life and the accompanying multiplicity of visual impressions, posters had to be adapted to new circumstances. A poster had to be eye-catching, which was as true at the turn of the twentieth century as at the turn of the twenty-first. Even in the Netherlands, where the growth of cities had only begun in the last quarter of the nineteenth century, the necessity of eye-catching poster design was evident. The fact that Dutch art critic Willem Steenhoff refers to this necessity in a 1928 text shows how widespread this idea was in the Netherlands:

> The poster is the furniture of the street, of places where the crowd is perpetually gathering and scattering ... It must be seen from afar, peeking between the heads and behind the backs of the chaotic human stream. It must, so to speak, be picked up by the eye in passing. [Posters] shape individually and collectively their own universe – for the rest there is the space in the streets ... If the poster practically and ideally has to adapt to its environment then [it must do so] in accordance with both the workings and the *atmosphere* of contemporary transportation in which people and vehicles always seem just to escape a collision, where, at night, electric light sources shoot out their beams around and among all the disorder of movement.[10]

Between about 1880 and 1920, the design of artistic posters changed from complicated to simple, the most important stylistic shift of that time. The German *Sachplakat* of the 1910s, with its simple forms, clear outlines, bright colours, reduced number of visual elements and concentration on the product and brand name, is generally identified as the apex of this evolution. In the Netherlands, this development proceeded less rigorously than in the surrounding countries. Advertisers seem to have perceived little need to strike the eye of a passer-by with illustrated advertising adjusted to long-distance vision, perhaps because there was so little open space and so few broad streets or blank house walls in city centres. Possibly lower levels of economic pressure from brand competition were influential as well.[11] Whatever the reason, in Dutch cities there were few advertising posters and one relied on the large lettering of brand names on house walls, enamel signs and posters.[12] Furthermore, the format of illustrated posters remained relatively small. Still, the opinion that a good poster must be eye-catching was generally evident.

Therefore, Steenhoff was arguing from a position of strength when in 1928 he fiercely criticized the well-known and greatly admired 1895 art nouveau poster which Jan Toorop had drawn for the Delft edible oils

8.6   A poster for the Calvé company by Jan Toorop, c. 1894–5

Source: M. Le Coultre Laren.

factory (Figure 8.6). From the perspective of an art critic in 1928, the poster no longer met the criteria for an advertising poster. According to Steenhoff, it was a 'sophisticated and intricately styled poster', but it was 'evident that this complicated and somewhat mysterious and richly detailed composition' was only 'suitable to be looked upon in serenity'. There would not be 'any opportunity' for this 'in the midst of the hustle and bustle of the street'.[13]

Steenhoff tried to explain what would be suitable using the example of Cassandre's 1927 poster for the Etoile du Nord, the train between Amsterdam and Paris. According to Steenhoff, the rails expressed the 'impression of velocity, space and distance ... in the most concise way ... at the same time creating the illusion of international railway traffic'. This would be understood even when the poster was attached to 'a car of Van Gend & Loos in motion' (Figure 8.7).[14] In this praise of Cassandre's design we see another requirement for good posters. Cassandre was admired throughout Europe and later in America too, and not only because his designs were eye-catching. They were modernistic, in both in conception and execution, and also in bonding the concepts they illustrated to the products or services advertised. In the

8.7   A poster by Cassandre on the side of a lorry of the Van Gend & Loos transportation company, 1939

Source: Nederlands Spoorwegmuseum

1920s the advertising world had come to believe that only one glimpse of a poster like this could trigger in the public a positive attitude towards the brand, an idea which was thought to be 'modern' as well.[15]

Art and advertising

All artists know that form can never be separated from content. This is especially true for the advertising artists at the turn of the century, for whom form *meant* content. Most of them came from the tradition of symbolism or were on the way towards abstraction and were very much interested in the effects that images alone could have. With their knowledge of, and interest in, the possibility of communicating content solely by composition and abstract form, poster artists found solutions to the combined problems of optimizing the communication possibilities of the poster and adapting its design to the problems of visibility and legibility in an urban context.[16] As Dirk Reinhardt states in his book on German advertising, 'economic innovation went hand in hand with innovation in communication', when a 'brand-new artistic poster appeared ... as an appropriate means of quickly announcing a not-yet-established brand name'.[17] Finally, the poster artist's participation also improved understanding of the ways in which advertising content could be conveyed by illustration.

From the 1880s on, advertising and art collaborated fruitfully in the design of advertising posters.[18] Nevertheless, as we have seen, things seem to have changed in the 1920s: artist Rie Cramer was allowed to design only a special poster; the commission for the design of the Blue Band girl went to a British advertising artist, who designed a fairly straightforward and traditional illustration.[19] Having said this, it is worth looking at the short but quite fierce debate about art and advertising in the Netherlands which had occurred only a few years earlier.

De Bedrijfsreklame (*Corporate Advertising*) was published between 1916 and 1921, and one of the editor's main purposes was to pursue a reconciliation between art and commerce. It was the first Dutch vehicle for professional advertising. After 1921 it continued under the title of *De Reclame* (*Advertising*) and from that time on, remarkably enough, it propounded an explicit contrast to the aestheticism of its predecessor.[20] Hardly had the Dutch advertising world invited the art world into a dialogue through this periodical, when it deliberately rejected that world and started searching for its own niche. During *De Reclame*'s five years of publication much was said, back and forth, by advertising people about art, and by artists about advertising, and there seem to have been quite a few misunderstandings.

The quarrel that started in 1917 on the occasion of the 'Kunst in de Reclame' (Art in Advertising) exhibition at the Stedelijk Museum in Amsterdam was representative.[21] The tone of rejection was set by the well-known artist R. Roland Holst,[22] who was also the author of an introduction to the exhibition catalogue. After the criticism from the *Bedrijfsreklame* editor, J.J.C. van Dokkum, to the effect that the exhibition displayed more art than advertising, Roland Holst expressed his views, delivered in an address in which he decried the level of understanding of what was going on regarding posters in the advertising world.[23] Artist colleague Albert Hahn, summarizing the differences between the opinions of Van Dokkum and Roland Holst, remarked that, to be effective, a poster had to be able to reach people even from a distance, 'so that the hurrying pedestrian can see in a flash what he needs to know'. Artists like Roland Holst, however, devoted to the British Arts and Crafts movement, emphasized the poster's decorative function. That is, a poster had to be in harmony with its environment and it would be 'useless and senseless for it to try to provide the tone for all possible environments'.[24]

The most obvious reason for the subsequent retreat of the advertising world was its rejection by the art world. The advantages advertising people saw in the use of artistic vocabulary could not be brought in line with the ideas about art promulgated by artists like Roland Holst. This is usually held to be the reason for the end of the formal liaison between art and advertising. Nevertheless, it would be wrong to conclude that the collaboration between art and commerce had failed. Through the involvement of artists, those means effective in capturing public attention had gradually been linked with the task of transmitting a message. Yet it seems that from the beginning, advertising professionals, usually without training in the visual arts, did not consciously reflect upon the relation between pictorial form and advertising content. In the Dutch advertising world the relationship of images to texts in advertisements, and the effect of both on the public, did not appear as a topic of discussion until the 1920s.[25] By then the art world and advertising world had become separated and there were very few Dutch artists who classified themselves as professional advertising designers. Those who did, unlike their counterparts in Germany, had to rely largely on their own experience to learn such aspects of their trade as the role which illustration could play in communication. The status to be accorded such experience was a subject of debate in the 1920s and 1930s, and the doubts on this topic affected theories of the effectiveness of various means of advertising, again including illustration.

A turning-point

The period around 1920 can be considered the central turning-point in Dutch advertising history.[26] After 1920 Dutch advertising developed the basic structures necessary for it to function within the interdependent worldwide web which today's consumer industry has become. First of all, since about 1920 the advertising world has claimed to have more knowledge than anyone else and than ever before of the methods that induce the public actually to buy a particular product. The effectiveness of those methods became the keystone of the Dutch advertising world's struggle for recognition as a profession. Furthermore, empirical psychology in the Netherlands discovered that research into the functioning of advertising, and especially the advertisements themselves, would be fruitful. In the course of this research, psychologists released research results in favour of the claim of the effectiveness of methods used in advertising practice. Finally, advertising's alienation from art around 1920 was paralleled by the rise of a new view on the messages of advertising, namely that they should relate to the rational and emotional interests of the public. From this perspective, the alienation from art was primarily the consequence of a lack of knowledge of the public's interests.

In the Netherlands, a more considered approach to advertising became reality during the 1920s as the result of the coincidence of at least two developments. The first of these was the economic changes that followed the First World War: the intensification of market competition, the transgression of traditional regional borders as markets expanded, technological progress, and the need to evaluate sales techniques. Advertisers also wanted to be accepted as professionals, and hoped that businesses would receive them better if advertising were perceived as a science rather than as an art. This was quite different from the situation in the USA, where, in 1917, according to Leiss, Kline and Jhally, 95 per cent of advertising activities lay in the hands of advertising agencies.[27] Even in comparison with contemporary advertising business in England or Germany, the advancement of Dutch advertising agencies toward the point at which companies would naturally turn to them had only just begun. The tasks handed over by the Van den Bergh company to Coppens's Advies-Bureau, for example, were still very few: the bulk of the work was still done by Van den Bergh's own advertising department.[28]

After the First World War it became essential for both the consumer industry and the advertising business to evaluate advertising and selling strategies.[29] First of all, in order to meet the commercial world's growing interest in both advertising and sales, better knowledge of advertising's effect on sales was needed. Theories of how far into the future it would be possible to predict that effect were also of great interest. Overall, ways and means of advertisement had to be considered anew. Although the advertising literature written by leaders in the field did not explain how advertising worked, the tips and instructions it offered, which were based on practical experience, still seemed to be valid. At the very least these 'how-to' books stated affirmatively that advertising worked and proffered a few tricks for successful advertising that could be gleaned from these nineteenth-century success stories.[30] For example, one of the early 'laws of "the science of advertising"' that showed up in advertising literature was 'the principle of repetition'.[31] The Dutch advertising man Abraham De la Mar had also put together a manuscript, entitled 'How to advertise'. It was never published, but in it he confirmed this rule: advertising would be most effective when it was 'steady and regular'.[32] Following the example of P. T. Barnum, whose autobiography had been published in Dutch in 1856, he propounded the belief that advertising had to be used when and where it made sense – hence, for instance, the lettering on the façades of stores.[33]

Advertising professionals held to this advice during the 1920s, although as Merle Curti, considering American publications on advertising between 1890 and 1910, rightly remarks, for 'the relatively few writers of this period who did speak of advertising as a science ... the term meant classification and codification of rules of thumb arrived at by impressionistic observations'.[34] Probably any science starts out that way. Yet in the case of the development of a 'science' of advertising, or at least the growing number of theoretical publications on advertising, it is interesting to see how much of it was related to the worry of some advertising people about their reputation as professionals. This is especially observable in the Netherlands, where writings on advertising theory and psychology were very rare before the First World War, whereas pleas for professionalism were heard just before the war began.

Han Coppens, whose agency was to become responsible for the advertising campaign for Blue Band margarine, was one of the early advocates of the professionalization of advertising. He himself, unusually for that time, was a well-informed advertising professional. He joined his father's firm in 1914, having already studied ad-writing at the British School of Advertising in England, and thus was one of the first Dutch advertising men to have had a real education in the field (Figure 8.8). He did not want his firm to be considered an advertising agency, but rather a consulting office, and himself an 'advertising consultant'. Moreover, he apparently attended lectures on psychology at the University of Amsterdam,[35] most probably in the 1920s; he is said to have audited the lectures of Anton A. Grünbaum, who became the first Dutch advertising psychologist.[36] Later he was to become the chair of the Genootschap for Reclame (Dutch Advertising Association).[37]

By 1914 Coppens was already advocating a more 'scientific' approach. In his contribution to Paul Ruben's famous publication, *Die Reklame – Ihre Kunst und Wissenschaft* (*Advertising – Its Art and Science*),[38] Coppens stressed that it would be useful for advertising people to work scientifically: 'creating advertisements should never be a leap in the dark; it has to be founded on scientific principles, for only thus does it fulfil its purpose ... only thus does one obtain the desired commercial effect'.[39] Five years later in the periodical *De Bedrijfreclame*, joining the ongoing debate on art and advertising, Coppens argued that it would not be enough only to build on art; advertising should above all be interested in the results obtained by the company: 'The great aim of advertising, frankly speaking, should be progress in business matters.'[40]

All this might lead one to the conclusion that the Coppens's work was based on psychological theories, and that the withdrawal from a connection to 'art' was a part of the scientific approach to advertising. But, in fact, it was not the tenets of an advertising 'science' or psychol-

8.8   Advertisement for Coppens' Advies-Bureau, 1914 by J. Proper With the
slogan 'Don't advertise without an expert' and the name of the agency,
Coppens' Advies-bureau (Coppens' Consulting Office), Coppens advertises
his agency as service-oriented and himself as an advertising professional.
The illustration shows a businessman who is broke and an advertising
man entering, but too late ('te laat') as is indicated on the label beneath
the empty safe. The advertising man holds a booklet entitled 'advertising
science' ('Reclame wetenschap'), as a reminder of the fact that Coppens
was an advocate of scientific advertising. An illustrative detail of Coppens's
scepticism regarding art in advertising is to be found on the bookshelf on
the top left side, where on the books standing upright is written 'advertising'
('reclame') contrasting with the books which lean left and right on which
'art' ('kunst') is written.

Source: Paul Ruben (ed.), *Die Reklame: Ihre Kunst und Wissenschaft* (Berlin:
Hermann Paetel Verlag, 1913–14)

ogy that mattered, but the 'scientific' proof of the effectiveness of
advertising. Before the First World War the idea of professionalism
started to tempt some advertising people, including Coppens. And it
may have been the case that, because the Netherlands was not involved
in that war, the Dutch advertising world, by presenting its methods as
being based on scientific research, had a chance to find out how advertising achieved recognition in other countries.

Advertising as applied psychology

Around the turn of the century it had still been enough to ask whether advertising would be noticed, and to what extent it and the brand represented would be remembered by the public. But between roughly 1910 and 1930, as the consumer industry was transformed, it was necessary for advertising professionals to consider and refine certain aspects of advertising effectiveness in reaching and communicating with the public. Advertising professionals started to think more carefully about the interaction of text and image as well as about the function of illustrations within the process of communication. But the rules given in ordinary advertising literature did not discuss ways of ascertaining in advance what would be an effective advertising message or use of imagery, with or without text. I have already mentioned that Dutch artists did not seem to want or to be able to help out with this problem, and furthermore, advertising agencies doubtless claimed expertise in relating text and image within an advertisement.[41]

An illustrative early example of this interest is again found in Coppens's 1914 contribution to *Die Reklame – Ihre Kunst und Wissenschaft*. He noted a change in German advertisements since the nineteenth century, when they had consisted predominantly of text. He then remarked (although this seems a bit at odds with prevailing wisdom), 'However, since the advertising illustration overpowers the text, a direction that appears to be less advantageous, a new trend has just developed which aims at making the text of equal value to the drawing.'[42] Coppens remarks almost casually that securing a balance between picture and text would be the task of professional advertisers: 'In order to achieve this necessary harmony in advertising the German businessman prefers to turn to a professional advertising consultant who, from his own experience, knows how to put text and picture into correct relation with one another.'[43] This was written at the peak of the influence of illustrated poster advertising. As an advocate of the professionalization of advertising, Coppens obviously did not allow other new professions to intrude upon agencies' attempts to become the central resources for companies with advertising needs.

The Dutch advertising world started to look for scientific assistance and evidence of its effectiveness in the second decade of the century, and but not until ten years later, in 1926, did Dutch psychologist A. A. Grünbaum state that 'advertising is applied psychology'.[44] In other countries, psychologists had been involved in evaluating advertising's effectiveness since about 1910. Despite this, research on the psychological effects of advertising was still in its infancy during the 1920s. In the USA, for example, before the First World War, psychologist Henry

Foster Adams had carried out experiments concerning the attention given to print advertising and its relation to colours, geometrical forms and layout, and in 1916 had published his results in *Advertising and its Mental Laws*.[45] Following these studies on the effects of formal elements of advertising, studies on the significance of the emotional appeal of advertising appeared. The ever-present character in this is Walter Dill Scott, author of the famous book *The Psychology of Advertising* (1908).[46] Usually considered the first lengthy study of the psychology of advertising, Scott's book combined both lines of psychological reflection on aspects of advertising.[47]

In the Netherlands the development of advertising psychology started a little later. The booklet entitled *Reclame* (*Publicity*), written by Piet Beishuizen and published around the end of the First World War, is a Dutch case in point.[48] Beishuizen's reference to psychology was still very general and he tried to convince the reader only of the overall utility of psychology in advertising. A few years later we find the first systematic publication on advertising psychology in the Netherlands. This was a series of twenty-one articles entitled 'Psychologie en Psychotechniek van de Reclame' ('Psychology and Psycho-Techniques of Advertising'), written by Grünbaum and published between 1924 and 1928 in the periodical *Administratieve Arbeid. Maandblad voor rationele Werkmethoden* (*Administrative Work. Monthly for Rational Working Methods*).[49]

Grünbaum had studied with Wilhelm Wundt in Germany and was therefore an exponent of experimental psychology and concerned with the processes of perception and memory.[50] This branch dominated both German and Dutch psychology at the time; in Germany it was very important to industrial psychology, and contributed some classical texts on advertising research. Accordingly, Grünbaum's sources were German reports on the application of empirical psychology, and especially experimental psycho-physics, to advertising.[51] Most of the time Grünbaum is not looking at advertising overall. He concentrates on such physical aspects as illustration, text, font, logo and others such as the frequency with which an advertisement might appear. Not surprisingly, since he was a psychologist, he occasionally steps aside and considers the expressive or affective value of pictures and writes about 'physiognomics', which he understood as those creative elements 'expressing one or another psychological attribute',[52] in general and in typography in particular. In attempting to explain how much this had to do with advertising, he also tried to work out a suitable physiognomy for the product offered. In this he had to admit that 'receptive' capacities would be needed; while unsuitable creations could easily be identified, suitable ones were much more difficult to define in advance. Without actually mentioning artists he hoped to do research into that, too. He certainly thought that research into details would make clear how the overall effect came about, writing that the 'physiognomic extends to every aspect – font, text, illustration, borders, distribution, size, etc. – as well as to the total impression and its relation to the actual content of the advertisement'.[53]

Grünbaum's interest in the components of perception is characteristic of experimental psychology. This is also true for his greatest interest, the possibility of simultaneously perceiving and understanding advertisements. At the time, experimental psychology was involved in a theoretical discussion of whether understanding was a mentally delayed process of apperception and the association of elementary physiological sensations, or whether interpretation began with perception.[54] Grünbaum inclined toward the belief that within visual perception there is something akin to understanding, and this is reflected in his writing. Therefore he continually returns to the 'visual unity' of advertising design and to the means of achieving it – contrasts, colours, eye-catching forms, simplicity of design or visual elements that could connect details of an advertisement. That is also the reason why he seems to value the use of illustrations in advertising so highly, noting that illustrations kill two birds with one stone: 'The illustration, whether we want it or not, always reaches the centre of our attention and remains longer in our memory.'[55] He emphasizes that the use of illustrations in advertising has the advantage of 'focusing the attention on the product by the shortest route',[56] and that for the assimilation of an illustration, 'less time is required than for a printed sentence'.[57]

Grünbaum distinguishes 'two large groups' of advertisement: the "formal", and those "effective through their contents"'.[58] The latter would allow advertising to be 'suggestive'. It is stunning to realize the strength of our tendency to believe a psychologist like Grünbaum when he posits that the effects of both form and content of advertisements are tested by empirical means. Basically, however, his only advice concerning the content of advertising is that the brand name and the illustration of the product should be, respectively, clearly legible and visible, and that the connection between illustration and text should be clear. All he has to say about suggestiveness is that it would depend on the combination of pictures and text and the agreement of both with the product advertised. That is, the entirety of the composition should suggest to the public what to buy.

But this again is a comment on form, and still we do not know what the content of the suggestion would be – apart from being consistent with the merchandise. In fact, when Grünbaum mentions suggestion, he is not speaking about emotional appeal in the sense of advertising messages

8.9 Example of a slide used in an experiment on the perception of advertising, published 1938
This example illustrates characteristics of early empirical advertising psychology: the concentration on parts of advertising design (we see the hat of the Blue Band girl); on aspects of human behaviour (e.g. the relation between perception and memory); and on the advertising material itself (first used in 1923). Advertising psychologist Roels uses this example, designed without the help of a psychologist, in an account on the use of psychological knowledge for advertising. He states that anybody would recognize this allusive drawing – an indication of the fame the Blue Band campaign had gained by the late 1930s.

Source: Franciscus Roels, *Psychologie der Reclame* (Amsterdam: H.J.W. Becht, 1938).

appealing to deep or unconscious drives of human behaviour (an idea with which we have been familiar since the 1950s).[59] His idea of suggestion is coloured by the context of the experimental psychology of the late nineteenth century, when suggestion was discussed in terms similar to those of hypnosis. Grünbaum considered suggestion – that is, the narrowing of attention and the exclusion of distracting elements (again, typical of hypnosis) – as consisting of the brand name or picture of the product, and that this alone would induce the public to remember the product.[60]

Nowadays everybody seems able to understand the underlying meaning of dreams and people do not hesitate to comment on the behaviour of others by elaborate 'Freudian' interpretations. But referring to the 'socialized unconscious' was surely no common habit at the beginning of the twentieth century, neither with the general public nor with empirical psychologists. Grünbaum, for example, elaborates on pictorial aids that would effectively advocate, through visual attention, the purchase of the advertised brand. Accordingly, he increases knowledge only of the visual behaviour of human beings. A close look reveals that this is true for most of the contributions to the 'science' of advertising by German and Dutch experimental psychologists during the 1910s and 1920s.[61] These psychologists preferred to focus on observable aspects of human perception and behaviour (see Figure 8.9). Of course, we do find vague interpretations that just pretend to be based on 'empirical' research in their publications too. But the much more complicated problem which the advertising practitioners faced of how to influence the public's willingness to buy a certain product could not be solved by the experimental psychologist's findings concerning the laws of visual perception.

Lacking knowledge about the public

As a reaction to the mass basis of city life and the increase in economic pressure to keep new products or brands on the market over extended periods of time, the question of the effectiveness of advertising was raised around 1920. In brief, the more competitive the situation became in the consumer market, the more advertising aimed at influencing the consumer's buying behaviour, and the more it tried to seem to address customers individually. Attempting to appeal to the masses as a whole was no longer sufficient. Stemming from the desire to provide product and brand differentiation, attracting attention was still relevant but needed to be directed towards much less significant differences in products and brands. The criteria deemed to improve sales should have become core issues from this point on, and the focus of the search for effective advertising methods. For advertising to be effective, the trinity of product quality, communication and audience should have been well balanced, but as we have seen, this was of little concern for somebody like Grünbaum.

Grünbaum's advertising psychology was part of the beginning of an evolution in which the social and psychological sciences gradually became involved in problems of manipulating and regulating large groups of individuals; these are issues typical of the social, political and economic sectors in the twentieth century. Particularly after the First World War, the optimistic notion that it would be possible to regulate people and processes was widespread in a broad range of economic, political and administrative professions. Thinking in these terms seemed to be an answer to the requirements of mass production in industry and in the growth of the social and cultural dimensions of the lives of individuals.[62] Experimental psychology partly turned into applied psychology through working in advertising and its growing involvement in industry.

The connection between the development of applied psychology in industry and the birth of advertising psychology is relevant if we are to understand the character of the first scientific publications on advertising. With the experimental tools needed to do research on various aspects of the relationship of human beings to their surroundings, and with a holistic view of human nature, applied psychologists (psycho-technicians) were able to contribute to the 'science' of advertising. Grünbaum also wrote on themes such as the 'psycho-technique of the typewriter' or the 'fitness of typists'.[63]

Grünbaum constantly repeats that psycho-technical research for advertising was necessary and pleads with admen to take interest in 'theoretically based results',[64] 'careful psychological research',[65] 'psychological experience',[66] and so on. His claim, and that of his colleagues, to conduct studies relevant to the practice of advertising was not completely unfounded. At least the use of illustrations and graphic elements in general was irreversible. That the experimental psychologists paid attention primarily to visual aspects of advertising may have been useful for advertisers: on the one hand they were able to negotiate with the weight of 'science' behind their words when showing advertising designs to the people who commissioned their work, and on the other hand they were able to use their own criteria and jargon when arguing with external artists. Furthermore, here were arguments that elevated the use of imagery above the level of entertainment, helping advertising to feel more confident while flowing with the stream towards a 'visual culture', and thus giving this evolution an extra thrust.

However, when advertisers tried to determine how to present a product in order to appeal most to the consumer, they were still faced with a lack of more detailed insight into subjective motives for buying.[67] To return to Grünbaum, he simply refers to 'typical' personal and social motives for behaviour as criteria by which to create or choose an advertising message: patriotism, pity, thriftiness, self-protection, yearning for power or knowledge, but also curiosity, laziness, vanity.[68] Fourteen years later F. Roels, another Dutch experimental psychologist, published *Psychologie der reclame* (*Psychology of Advertising*).[69] Roels gives a list of attributes similar to Grünbaum's, but differentiates between 'common, human' basic needs to which advertising messages could appeal: 'health, hygiene, protection against illness and accidents, concern for the upbringing of children', and what he calls 'social needs': 'being with others, domesticity, ambition, the urge to imitate' and, again, 'thriftiness'.[70] Whenever Grünbaum refers to the psychological effects of advertising on human behaviour in a more general sense, which is rarely, he only understands that advertising is there to 'create needs'. Therefore, one has to see to it that 'all natural economic brakes' are abolished and that the 'decision to buy' is not only be assured 'for the moment' but also 'for the future'.[71] Roels's thoughts on these questions are only slightly more elaborate. He mentions several strategies for approaching the public, among them suggestion, appealing to an authority, awakening dormant needs, promising that these newly perceived needs will be satisfied, and using only positive arguments.[72]

The history of this kind of thought is well known, and within the context of advertising psychology, we can trace it back to America and the behaviouristic research of H. L. Hollingworth and E. K. Strong in the early twentieth century.[73] Nevertheless, the balance, or lack of balance, between the dearth of coverage of socio-psychological material and the elaborate accounts of experiments concerning human apperception in the publications of Roels and Grünbaum, is at least typical of Dutch advertising psychology. The reception of ideas concerning underlying motives and needs, aspects characteristic of American versions of advertising psychology, was quite restrained. Jaap van Ginneken, Dutch historian of applied psychology, also concludes that the influence of American socio-psychology was only felt around 1930, and that in the following years, the evolution of Dutch advertising psychology actually came to a stand-still.[74] In the Netherlands we find the same phenomenon that Reinhardt observes in Germany: extreme psychoanalytical or psycho-dynamic approaches, with elaborations on sexual instincts, for example, appeared only incidentally.[75]

Nevertheless, it is true that the advertising world started to reflect on its public more thoroughly during and after the 1920s, so that it could become more effective. With regard to Dutch advertising history, it makes more sense to ask about the general impact of the concept of 'human nature' put forth by proponents of American psycho-dynamics than of its presuppositions of a static, heavily emotional core of human beings. In an illuminating article on this matter, Merle Curti stresses that in American advertising at the turn of the century a rationalistic view of the consumer was predominant.[76] In advertising psychology after 1910 the popular conception of human beings shifted towards one that was more emotional, or at least non-rational.[77] Thus, after the crisis of 1929, the flexibility of human behaviour seems to have become of greater interest to both advertising psychologists and American advertising men.[78] I would like to suggest that the aspect of 'flexibility' in the socio-psychological concept of human nature, as it had gradually appeared in American advertising psychology since the 1910s, had a far more comprehensive influence at least on Dutch advertising practice. During the 1920s it made up for a lack of more detailed knowledge about the public, and it fitted into an advertising practice that in the nineteenth century had already learned how effective it would be to deluge the public with advertising.

The public as puppet

In the Netherlands 'psycho-technicans' misunderstood what the essential problems of advertising were during the 1920s. It was only in 1930 that one of them wrote, in the same periodical in which Grünbaum had published his series: 'To be honest, we have to admit that it is exclusively our fault if advertising until now sneered at us when we talked about rationalization ... Advertising is not unscientific, we ourselves act unscientifically.'[79] Further on in this article J. van Gogh, the writer of this admission, discusses the primary advertising strategy of the day, mentioning the crucial difficulty that stood at its base:

> The task [of rational advertising] is to locate and exploit points of contact with the public (as potential buyers). Efficiency in advertising thus corresponds to modulating the advertising to mediate between the merchandise to be propagated, through the means of advertising, and the psyche of the people. Yet because this psyche had never been subject to an absolutely scientific analysis, it seems as if any propaganda work has to build solely on *hypotheses.*[80]

Advertising psychologists, he contends, had concentrated too heavily on details, and on ideas about the background of human behaviour too vague to really be useful in advertising.

It has already been said that early advertising psychology was mainly interested in empirical, experimental and simple behaviouristic notions, and that Dutch advertising practitioners very hesitatingly grasped the possibility of appealing to emotions. All that seems to have reached the ears of advertising practitioners of the 1920s was the idea of the flexibility, or 'malleability', as Curti phrased it in 1967, of human nature. One might even argue that the psychological concept of human nature as generally flexible was one of the most important contributions of psychology to the history of advertising. The scientific confirmation that human nature was apt to change principally in response to external influences must have been of particular interest to the advertising profession, looking as it was for explanations of, and arguments for, the idea that advertising was indeed effective. With this psychological concept of a receptive human being, to aim at influencing the buying behaviour of consumers must have seemed both actually possible and scientifically supported. And, at least in the context of Dutch culture, the idea of a strong emotionality driving human beings to act in a certain way was more believable than one of absolute rationality. Also, because empirical psychology was based on experiments using a broad range of stimuli, it became possible to argue that advertising, seen as a coordinated constellation of stimuli, could have predictable effects. Finally, in the dynamic, or flexible, conception of human nature, a stable centre remained – that is, the emotionality or irrationality of human beings. From the perspective of advertising and selling, any model of human behaviour sufficed. Otherwise it would have been impossible to predict or influence anything – that is, to choose a direction for commercial persuasion that would be effective in the long run.

The basic behaviouristic conception of a flexible human nature was a very broad idea indeed. But because there was no way to look inside the heads of consumers, so to speak, it must have seemed better to cling to visible human behaviour. The only thing that seemed possible and effective was, as Van Gogh observed, to 'locate and exploit points of contact with the public'. The advertising practitioners themselves had come up with what can be called a technical solution to getting closer to the consumer. Scientists (that is, psychologists and sociologists) had not yet found better methods of reducing the distance between human beings and theories of the causes of their behaviour. It was still not possible to adjust the content of advertising text and/or images more precisely to smaller groups of the public. Advertising still had to wait for market research and marketing to get information which would enable a message to be aimed more specifically at the consumer. Market research looking for more information about the relationship between buying habits, advertising messages, and the role of psychological factors only began in the 1930s to bring to light results worth mentioning.[81] Marketers who could have helped to adapt products to the desires of consumers had not yet been found.

Therefore, advertising professionals like Coppens decided to hang on to a more traditional approach. We have seen that he was well informed and even an early defender of more 'scientific' methods of advertising. For the Blue Band campaign he used an attractive, smiling girl, because she would appeal to the consumer; his slogan strongly conveyed the right message. These choices may have been induced in part by earlier American advertising literature, but they surely were not based on a thorough knowledge of the rational or emotional interests that influence people's willingness to buy margarine. What really was modern about this campaign, though, mainly its scale and its consistency, was based on the experiences of half a century of advertising practice. The principles of repetition and of impressiveness were now combined with careful reflection about the possibilities that opened up through the enormous range of new and varied advertising media in the 1920s.

For this reason, the best way to use advertising media for a complex public was to be the foremost subject for 'scientists', or theorists, of advertising, from the 1930s through the 1950s. It is important to note that advertising men, not psychologists, were to write Dutch advertising theory of that period. Obviously, within advertising theory, the expertise of advertising people themselves had again become crucial. One of these people was Schuitema, cited earlier, who held a position at the Philips company. His 1936 book on the principles of modern advertising reflects the turn towards advertising media. He notes that a theory of the advertising media 'is yet to be born'.[82] This is in fact a criticism of the practical uselessness of what psychologists had hitherto contributed to a theory of advertising. Because advertising people who now conceived of themselves as professionals, had solved their main problems by themselves throughout the 1920s, their experiences were an important source for the development of ideas on how to approach the consumer.

To 'think professionally' took on new connotations in the 1920s and 1930s. It no longer meant simply putting a product or brand in the centre of advertising. 'Professional' now included considering, during the planning of an advertising campaign and the selection of the advertising media, how and when the public would receive the advertising. The main remedy for the absence of an exact knowledge of consumer behaviour was literally to surround consumers, using every means imaginable to get a grip on him (or her), whether in the private space of the living room, the semi-public space of the shop and shop window, or the public space of the street. Within this concept of massive campaigning there were remnants of the behaviouristic concept of human nature: the consumer as a programmable puppet, mechanically triggered by advertising that followed him wherever he was.

The possibilities of effective commercial communication through images were given little attention. This resulted in the displacement of the illustrated poster in advertising practice from a central tenet to a peripheral, merely technical and supporting means of advertising. Around the turn of the century, posters had been developed into an advertising tool used to inform an enormous and anonymous audience of the existence of a product or brand. Its goal had been to reach a large group of people without explicitly differentiating among special target groups. An eye-catching and, in the urban environment, competitive and generally attractive visual field had offered the solution for this. In the 1920s and 1930s, when campaigning became commonplace, the illustrated poster was limited to this function.

Illustration in general was already discounted as a useful means of advertising. The experimental psychologists' opinion on the advertising effectiveness of images was ambiguous. Although Grünbaum, for example, frequently elaborated on psychological aspects of advertising imagery, he thought that the use of illustrations as a means to sell a product should be handled delicately. He stated that illustrations 'can fascinate us, they can remind us of the merchandise, yet they will only in a few cases cause us to buy'.[83] He argues even more vehemently that advertising needs to convince the public and that this is the reason why the text for him is the 'soul of advertising'.[84] At best, illustrations could 'arouse attention and feeling, yet not reason and will', which in his opinion were necessary to get people to buy a product.[85]

The increasing concentration of professional advertising practice on campaigning and the opinion that illustrations alone could not adequately communicate combined to marginalize the illustrated poster. During the 1920s, the illustrated poster, along with other types of outdoor advertising, was reduced the role of attention-grabber in the increasing volatility of city life. At last, in the 1930s, as more and more sensational neon signs were installed, and more and more impressive murals competed for attention, advertising people started to understand what some psychologists had attested to: only text and illustration perceived together, as is the case in advertisements, could motivate the consumer to buy. And fifteen years after Roland Holst had suggested that it would be 'useless and senseless for it [the poster] to try to provide the tone for all possible environments' of the city, an advertising man like Schuitema had come to agree. He found a striking, and to us quite paradoxical, argument for those mourning the phased-out poster: '[In] our tremendously sensationalistic time [the consumer] no longer experiences the strength of a simple, contrasting effect as such, since practically every manifestation of daily life already contains so many contrasting elements.'[86] The poster would not be conspicuous any more, and neither would other sorts of outdoor advertising be effective enough. He wrote not only that 'all factors influencing the preference for a certain article fall just outside the reach of outdoor advertising,' but that 'name publicity' was no longer sufficient and that it must always 'be accompanied by advertising statements which point out the attractiveness of the article and arouse consumer appetite and the preference for this brand at the cost of competing ones'.[87] As a consequence, in the following decades the search for more specific information about the public really took off, so that advertising messages could be more persuasive in their content and better presented in print.

Notes

1. This essay, which is part of my dissertation research, was made possible by the support of the Nederlandse organisatie voor Wetenschappelijk Onderzoek (Dutch Organization for Scientific Research) in The Hague. Parts of my account here are based on my chapter on the Dutch advertising theory of images before 1940. I would like to thank my supervisor Prof. Dr J. Stumpel at Utrecht University, Department of Art History, and am very much indebted to P. Buch and P. Wageman for their help in translating the text.

2. M. Huig, 'De kijk op Nederland. Van monumentenzorg naar Heemschut', *Nederland 1913: Een reconstructie van het culturele leven*, edited by J. de Vries (Haarlem: Meulenhoff and Landshof, 1988), 158.

3. W. F. A. M. Gerrese, 'Die buitenreclame van Amsterdam', *Heemschut: Orgaan van de Bond Heemschut* 1 (February 1950), 18–20.

4. E. B. W. Schuitema, *Grondslagen van de moderne reclame*, Handboek der Reclame, edited by F. Roels en E. B. W. Schuitema, vol. 1, (The Hague: H. P. Leopold's UMNV 1936), 142.

5. The details on the history of the margarine industry presented here come from R. D. Tousley's 'Marketing', in *Honderd jaar margarine, 1869– 1969*, edited by Johannes H. Stuijvenberg (The Hague: Martinns Nijhoff, 1969), 231–84; N. Verbeek, *Honderd jaar Nassaukade: De geschiedenis van Ven den Bergh en Jurgens, Nassaukade 1891–1991* (Rotterdam: 1991). There are also English and French editions of the first book: *Margarine: an Economic, Social, and Scientific History, 1869–1969*, edited by Johannes H. Stuijvenberg (Liverpool: Humanities Press International, Inc., 1969); *La margarine: Histoire et Évolution*, edited by Johannes H. Stuijvenberg (Paris: 1969).

6. The campaign seems to have cost 1.8 million gilders in just four months (Wilbert Schreurs, *Geschiedenis van de reclame in Nederland: De ontwikkeling van de reclame in Nederland 1890 tot 1990* (Utrecht: Spin 1989), 68. Tousley stressed that one company could produce an enormous range of different brands, and he accounts for 1,600 margarine brands of which 172 had distinctive packages (Tousley, 'Marketing', 238 and 245).

7. The details on the campaign presented here come from Karel Sartory, *De Vierde Vrijheid, zijnde een blik in de historie van het reclamebureau DelaMar*, published for the occasion of the seventy-fifth anniversary of the N.V. DelaMar (Amsterdam: 1955), 78–80; Schreurs, *Geschiedenis van de reclame in Nederland*, 67–8; N. Verbeek, *Honderd jaar Nassaukade*, 98–100. Schreurs also gives the information on the history of Coppens' agency used here; see especially 66–72.

8. Surely the range of devices and activities to attract attention developed by advertising people in the second half of the nineteenth century was broader. For instructive illustrations and descriptions, see Terence R. Nevett, *Advertising in Britain: a History* (London: Heinemann, 1982).

9. The variety of type occurred in newspaper advertising as well and may have served the same function.

10. W. Steenhoff, 'De reclameplaat', in *De tijd van H. Robbers: Bloemlezung uit Elsevier's Geïllustreerd Maandschrift 1905–1937*, edited by W. J. Simons (Amsterdam, Brussels, 1968), 217–22. With thanks to T. Meedendorp.

11. There is very little research on the evolution of poster advertising in the Netherlands compared to in other European countries. Differences in economic, demographic or urban development are usually relevant, as well as differences in the ways city councils dealt with advertising in public spaces. The explanation given here broadly parallels the reflections of art historian H. L. C. Jaffé on this issue. See Dick Dooijes and Pieter Brattinga, *A History of the Dutch Poster 1890–1960* (Amsterdam, Vaheltema & Holtema 1968), 9–14.

12. P. van Dam, *Een eeuw affichekunst (A Century of Poster Art)* (Amsterdam, 1987), 9–18. P. Nijhoff, (ed.), *De kunst van het verleiden. Geëmailleerde reclame in Nederland* (Zwolle: Waanders, 1991), 7–8.

13. Steenhoff, 'De reclameplaat', 218.

14. Ibid., 222. Van Gend & Loos was the transportation company hired by the Dutch railways.

15. A good history of the early illustrated posters is A. Halter's *Als die Bilder reizen lernten. Zum Umgang mit den Produkten im französischen Warenplakat 1900–1930* (Zürich: Schweizer Rück, 1992).

16. See Martin Henatsch, *Die Entstehung des Plakates: Eine rezeptionsästhetische Untersuchung*, Studien zur Kunstgeschichte 91 (Hildesheim, Zurich and New York: Georg Olms Publishers, 1995), 106–226. On pp. 259–73, Henatsch links the artists' interest and capability to come up with these kinds of solutions to the developments in aesthetics in the nineteenth century. For more on abstract forms in poster design as conveyors of content, see pp. 111–42.

17. Dirk Reinhardt, *Von der Reklame zum Marketing: Geschichte der Wirtschaftswerbung in Deutschland* (Berlin: Akademie Verlag, 1993), 59.

18. For examples see Dooijes and Brattinga, *A history of the Dutch poster 1890–1960* and *The Modern Dutch poster: The First Fifty Years, 1890–1940*, edited by Steven S. Propokoff (Cambridge, London: MIT Press, 1987); P. Van Dam, *Een eeuw affichekunst*; Kees Broos and Paul Hefting, *Grafische vormgeving in Nederland: Een eeuw* (Amsterdam: L. J. Veen, 1995). It is generally known that some of the best and earliest Dutch examples of the collaboration with artists in advertising a particular product are the posters drawn around the turn of the century for Calvé, a factory in Delft that produced edible oils. This represents a special chapter in Dutch advertising history. These advertisements were the result of the enthusiasm for art by an official who oversaw advertising and belong to the history of the art collector as well. The Calvé posters were mainly designed in the art nouveau style and because of them this style in Dutch is known as 'Slaoliestijl', which means, more or less, 'style of edible oils'. For more on the Calvé posters, see P. L. Djie, 'Kunst voor Calvé: Een inventarisatie van het drukwerk gemaakt in opdracht van de Nederlandse oliefabrieken, Delft (1893–1930)', (Master's thesis, Utrecht University, 1994).

19. The historicity of the differentiation between artist and advertising artist is, for the most part, associated with developments in the applied arts in the first half of the twentieth century and has received little scholarly attention until quite recently. One courageous exception is Michele H. Bogart's *Artists, Advertising, and the Borders of Art* (Chicago and London: University of Chicago Press, 1995).

20. *De Bedrijfsreclame: Officieel Orgaan van de Vereeniging ter bevordering*

der Bedrijfsreclame was published in Amsterdam from 1916 until 1921. What applies to *De Bedrijfsreclame* is also valid for its publisher, the Vereeniging ter bevordering der Bedrijfsreclame (Society for Supporting Company Advertising), later to become the Genootschap voor Reclame (Association for Advertising), which still exists. Even earlier, by 1911, *De Ark: Tijdschrift voor Algemeene Reclamekunst* began to be published, although publication ceased after only four numbers. Schreurs, *Geschiedenis van de reclame in Nederland 1870–1990*, 35 (*De Ark*), 49–61 (*De Bedrijfsreclame*), 84–5 (*De Reclame, Vereeniging/Genootschap voor Reclame*). A. I. Conijn, 'De Bedrijfsreclame: Een kunsthistorisch onderzoek naar het eerste Nederlandse reclametijdschrift, 1916–1921', (Master's thesis, Nijmegen University, 1989).

21. The exhibition was organized by the VANK (Vereeniging voor Ambachts- en Nijverheidskunst (Society for Art in Industry and Craft, 1904–42)); Schreurs, *Geschiedenis van de reclame in Nederland 1870–1990*, p. 59. For a short history of the VANK, see A. Martis, 'Enkele organisaties en hun activiteiten', in *Industrie en vormgeving in Nederland 1850–1950* (Amsterdam 1985), 25–6.

22. For a recent account of this affair see Elisabeth P. Tibbe, *R. N. Roland Holst: Arbeid en schoonheid vereend. Opvattingen over Gemeen-schapskunst* (Amsterdam: Architectura and Natura, 1994), 249–51. R. Holst worked for a commercial enterprise as well, the Calvé factory in Delft; H. Saam, 'Roland Holst als Reclamekunstenaar', *Jong Holland* 3, no. 1 (1987), 48–56.

23. Schreurs, *Geschiedenis van de reclame in Nederland 1870–1990*, 59. The speech by Holst was published again later as 'Moderne eischen en artistieke bedenkingen', *Wendingen* 2 (1919), 3–16. When artists like Roland Holst emphasized the decorative function of pictures, they based their assess-ments on two criteria: their own interest in the 'autonomous effect of creative means' as well as the 'ideal of an art having influence on its human environment'. These standards derive from M. Rummens, 'De verleiding van het decoratieve: Twee opstellen over compositie, expressie en abstractie in de theorie en in praktijk van de moderne schilderkunst' (Ph.D. diss., University of Amsterdam, 1991), 179.

24. Tibbe, *R. N. Roland Holst*, 249. Hahn's summary of the discussion was published under the title 'Kreet of mededeling?' *De Socialistische Gids* 2 (1917): 457–65. Hahn was a socialist and designed a great deal of social-ist propaganda; for more on his life, see Marien van der Heijden, *Albert Hahn* (Amsterdam: T. Rap, 1993). He criticized Roland Holst for over-emphasizing the negative aspect of 'shouting'. For him, it was a perfectly adequate means of communication with the public and he believed it possible to make a difference between artistic aims and the needs of advertising; on this see also Dooijes and Brattinga, *A history of the Dutch poster 1890–1960*, 28–29; Schreurs, *Geschiedenis van de reclame in Nederland 1870–1990*, 59–60.

25. Before the 1920s the editors of *De Bedrijfsreclame*, for example, seem mainly to have been interested in art for reasons of aesthetics as well as ethics. Schreurs, *Geschiedenis van de reclame in Nederland 1870–1990*, 54–5; Conijn, 'De Bedrijfsreclame'.

26. In chapter 2 (45–96) of *Geschiedenis van de reclame in Nederland 1870–1990*, Schreurs considers the period between 1914 and 1929 and gives a

number of examples of the change around 1920 and the subsequent developments in the advertising business of the 1920s.

27. William Leiss, Steven Kline and Sut Jhally, *Social Communication in Advertising: Persons, Products & Images of Well-Being*, 2nd rev. edn (London: Routledge, 1990), 135.
28. Schreurs, *Geschiedenis van de reclame in Nederland 1870–1990*, 68.
29. There are also institutional consequences of this fusion of interests of the bigger companies and the increasingly service-oriented advertising agencies. During the First World War, magazine and newspaper editors, together with the association that represented the more established advertising agencies (Vereeniging van Erkende Advertentie-Bureaux (Association of Recognized Advertising Agencies)) had come to agree on the awarding of discounts. After 1919, when the Bond van Adverteerders (Association of Advertisers) was finally founded as well, and because those rules on discounts were not well handled by the media, businesses as well as the advertising companies could work together to control the way in which the growing world of print media handled the matter of advertising. Schreurs, *Geschiedenis van de reclame in Nederland 1870–1990*, 47–49 and 83.
30. Perhaps the first original Dutch publication on advertising is L. Hansma, *Moderne reclame-gids* (Rotterdam: 1894). Before there were only translations of foreign publications or compilations of material taken from those publications. Schreurs, *Geschiedenis van de reclame in Nederland 1870–1990*, 30, 37–8.
31. Merle Curti, 'The Changing Concept of "Human Nature" in the Literature of American Advertising', *Business History Review* 41, no. 4 (winter 1967) 335–57: 343.
32. De la Mar is known to have been an admirer of Thomas Holloway and his agency became the cradle for 'most – if not all – big Dutch advertising agencies'; G. H. van Heusden, *Een eeuw adverteerkunde: De sociaal-economische en psychologische ontwikkeling van het adverteren in Nederlandse kranten*, Bouwstenen voor de kennis der maatschappij, edited by P. J. Bouman, Sj. Groenman, J. A. Ponsioen, vol. 44 (Assen: Van Gorcum, 1962), 124–6; K. Sartory, *De Vierde Vrijheid*, 15–16. See both books as well as Schreurs, *Geschiedenis van de reclame in Nederland 1870–1990*, 24–5, for the early history of De la Mar's agency.
33. P. T. Barnum, *The Life of P. T. Barnum: Written by Himself* (Darby: Arden Library, 1986 (originally published in 1855)). P. T. Barnum, *Leven en avonturen van P. T. Barnum* (Rotterdam: Nijgh, 1856). Henricus Nijgh was partner of what was to become the second forerunner of professional Dutch advertising agencies, Nijgh & Van Ditmar. For the early history of Nijgh & Van Ditmar, see Schreurs, *Geschiedenis van de reclame in Nederland 1870–1990*, 20–24.
34. Curti, 'The Changing Concept of "Human Nature" in the Literature of American Advertising', 343.
35. Schreurs, *Geschiedenis van de reclame in Nederland 1870–1990*, 67.
36. Van Ginneken, *De uitvinding van het publiek: De opkomst van opinie- en marktonderzoek in Nederland*, 32,35 and 206 n. 6.
37. Schreurs, *Geschiedenis van de reclame in Nederland 1870–1990*, 67. In 1927, the Genootschap voor Reclame (Association for Advertising) succeeded the Vereeniging voor Reclame (Society for Advertising), founded

in 1923. It is probable that the first well organised platform in the Netherlands on which advertising specialists could meet had been the Vereeniging ter bevordering der Bedrijfsreclame (Society for Supporting Company Advertising, 1916–1921); Schreurs, *Geschiedenis van de reclame in Nederland* 49–50, 84–5.

38. P. Ruben (ed), *Die Reklame – ihre Kunst und Wissenschaft*, 2 vols (Berlin: Hermann Paetel Verlag, 1913/14).

39. G. Coppens, 'Die Bedeutung der Handelsreklame in unserer Zeit', in *Die Reklame*, vol. 2, edited by P. Ruben (Berlin 1914), 194. It is not entirely clear if the text in Ruben's *Die Reklame* was written by Gerd Coppens, as the letter 'G' for the first name indicates, or by Han Coppens. Schreurs presents this text as written by Han Coppens, but he also informs us that Gerd Coppens was his father; Schreurs, *Geschiedenis van de reclame in Nederland 1870–1990*, 66–7. It is possible, however, that Han used his father's name.

40. H. Coppens, in *De Bedrijfsreclame* 3 (November 1919), 53; cited in Schreurs, *Geschiedenis van de reclame in Nederland 1870–1990*, 67.

41. On the professionalization of advertising agencies in relation to the history of the broadening of the service of De la Mar as well as of Nijgh & Van Ditmar, see G. H. van Heusden, *Een eeuw adverteerkunde*, 119–38.

42. G. Coppens, 'Die Bedeutung der Handelsreklame in unserer Zeit', in *Die Reklame*, 203.

43. Coppens, ibid.

44. Anton A. Grünbaum, 'Psychologie en psychotechniek in de reclame: De vrouw en de reclame', *Administrative Arbeid: Maanblad voor rationele werkmethoden* 4, no. 11 (November 1926), 304.

45. Henry Foster Adams, *Advertising and its Mental Laws* (New York: Garland Publishing, Inc., 1985). A. Uhry Abrams, 'From Simplicity to Sensation: Art in American Advertising, 1904–1929', *Journal of Popular Culture* 3 (1976), 624.

46. W. Dill Scott, *The Psychology of Advertising: A Simple Exposition of the Principles of Psychology in their Relation to Successful Advertising* (Boston: Ayer Company Publishers, Inc., 1979) (originally published in 1908).

47. Leiss et al., *Social Communication in Advertising*, 138.

48. P. Beishuizen, *Reclame* (Amsterdam: n.p., n.d.). Van Ginneken, *De uitvinding van het publiek*, 33. Beishuizen was one of the editors of the periodical *De Bedrijfsreclame*; Schreurs, *Geschiedenis van de reclame in Nederland 1870–1990*, 50.

49. *Administrative Arbeid: Maanblad voor rationele werkmethoden* was founded in 1923. From January 1924 until January 1925 the first thirteen articles were published, and another eight appeared before February 1928. The series amounted to a total of 100 pages. For a discussion of this series as the first 'systematic' advertising psychology in the Netherlands, see van Ginneken, *De uitvinding van het publiek*, 35.

50. Van Ginneken, *De uitvinding van het publiek*, 99. Grünbaum became well known because of a specific testing method and for his research on aphasia and apraxia phenomena; van Ginneken, 203 n. 12. Born in 1885 in Odessa, Russia, he died in 1932 ('In Memoriam Prof. Dr A. A. Grünbaum', *Administrative Arbeid: Maanblad voor rationele werkmethoden* 10, no. 1 (January 1932), 5.

51. Grünbaum points this out himself; see A. A. Grünbaum, 'Psychologie en

psychotechniek van de reclame: Inleiding', *Administrative Arbeid: Maanblad voor rationele werkmethoden* 2, no. 1 (January 1924), 19.

52. A. A. Grünbaum, 'Psychologie en psychotechniek van de reclame: Physiognomische waarde van een reclame', *Administrative Arbeid: Maanblad voor rationele werkmethoden* 4, no. 9 (September 1926), 249.

53. Ibid., 251 and 'Psychologie en psychotechniek van de reclame: De inwerking op het gevoel', *Administrative Arbeid: Maanblad voor rationele werkmethoden* 2, no. 11 (November 1924), 314–18. For similar reflections in German and Dutch advertising psychology see also A. Berliner, 'Atmosphärenwert von Drucktypen: Ein Beitrag zur Psychologie der Reklame', *Zeitschrift für angewandte Psychologie* 17 (1920), 165–72; Th. König, *Die Psychologie der Reklame*, 3rd edn (Würzburg: 1922), 125–42 (font), 180–88 (colour); R. Seyffert, *Die Reklame des Kaufmanns* (Leipzig: 1925), 28–33 (colour); G. Révész, 'De psychologische beteekenis van papier en van de kleuren voor de reclame', *Administratieve Arbeid. Maandblad voor rationeele werkmethoden* 5, nos 3 and 4 (March and April 1927), 66–9, 96–101. G. W. Ovink, *Legibility, atmosphere-value and forms of printing types* (Leiden: A. W. Sijthoff, 1938). Information about Révész, an immigrant from Budapest, can be found in van Ginneken, *De uitvindig van het publiek*, 37, 203 ns 17–21.

54. The summary of the problems and discussions in experimental psychology around the turn of the century, and especially their close relation to the appearance of Gestalt psychology in the nineteenth century, which seemed most convincing to me is that of C. van Campen, 'Gestalt van Goethe tot Gibson: Theorieën over zien van schoonheid en orde' (Ph.D. diss., Utrecht University, 1994).

55. A. A. Grünbaum, 'Psychologie en psychotechniek van de reclame. Het opwekken van behoeften. Iets over illustraties', in *Administrative Arbeid: Maanblad voor rationele werkmethoden* 2, no. 2 (February 1924), 48.

56. Ibid., 50.

57. Ibid., 48.

58. Ibid., 47.

59. Vance Packard, *The Hidden Persuaders* (New York: Pocket Books, 1987, originally published in 1957).

60. The issue of 'suggestion' within psychology is far more complicated than the summary of it presented here. Discussion of it dates back to the late nineteenth century and also belongs to experimental psychology. For a discussion of suggestion, see the work of W. Dill Scott, and for advertising around the turn of the century: D. P. Kuna, 'The Concept of Suggestion in the Early History of Advertising Psychology', *Journal of the History of the Behavioral Sciences* 12 (1976), 347–53. Kuna concludes that Scott's adaptation of the concept of suggestion to advertising made the advertising world recognize the role that psychology could play. According to Kuna, the idea of suggestion lost its real meaning after 1910 (although Curti places the date after 1930), to be reassessed only in the late 1940s; for more on this, see Curti, 'The Changing Concept of "Human Nature" in the Literature of American Advertsing', 335–57. For developments in Europe, see F. Jaspert, 'Werbepsychologie: Grundlinien ihrer geschichtlichen Entwicklung', in *Die Psychologie im 20. Jahrhundert*, Anwendungen im Berufsleben. Arbeits-, Wirtschafts- und Verkehrspsychologie, edited by F. Stoll, vol. 13 (Zürich: 1981), 170–89.

61. For other examples of Dutch advertising psychology, see van Ginneken, *De uitvinding van het publiek*, 30–48. For more on German advertising psychology, see the sources cited by Dirk Reinhardt, *Von der Reklame zum Marketing*, 87–99.

62. E. Jonker, 'De sociologische verleiding: Sociologie, sociaal-democratie en de welvaartsstaat' (Ph.D. diss., Utrecht University, 1988), 42–3. Robert H. Wiebe, *The Search for Order 1877–1920* (New York: Hill & Wang, Inc., 1966), 145–56. C. Hartveld, 'Moderne zakelijkheid: Efficiency in wonen en werken in Nederland, 1918–1940', (Ph.D. diss., University of Amsterdam, 1994). M. Wildt 'Technik, Kompetenz, Modernität', in *Amerikanisierung: Traum und Alptraum im Deutschland des 20. Jahrhunderts*, edited by Lüdtke, Marßolek, Saldern (Stuttgart: Steiner, 1996), 78–95.

63. Important in Europe: Hugo Münsterberg, *Psychologie und Wirtschaftsleben: Ein Beitrag zur angewandten Experimental-Psychologie* (Leipzig: J. A. Barthe, 1912). U. Nienhaus, 'Rationalisierung und "Amerikanismus" in Büros der 20ger Jahre: Ausgewählte Beispiele', in *Amerikanisierung: Traum und Alptraum im Deutschland des 20. Jahrhunderts*, edited by Lüdtke, Marßolek and Saldern (Stuttgart: Steiner, 1996), 73. 'In Memoriam Prof. Dr A. A. Grünbaum', *Administratieve Arbeid. Maandblad voor rationeele werkmethoden* 10, no. 1 (January 1932), 5.

64. A. A. Grünbaum, 'Psychologie en psychotechniek van de reclame: Over de herhaling der reclame', *Administrative Arbeid: Maanblad voor rationele werkmethoden* 2, no. 10 (October 1924), 291.

65. A. A. Grünbaum, 'Psychologie en psychotechniek van de reclame: De "aanschouwelijke" tekst. "Symbolische" illustratie', *Administrative Arbeid: Maanblad voor rationele werkmethoden* 2, no. 7 (July 1924), 215.

66. A. A. Grünbaum, 'Psychologie en psychotechniek van de reclame: Over de zoogenaamde "blikvangers." Illustreerende letters', *Administrative Arbeid: Maanblad voor rationele werkmethoden* 2, no. 3 (March 1924), 83.

67. For further reading on this topic, see Roland Marchand, 'Keeping the Audience in Focus', and 'Abandoning the Great Genteel Hope: From Sponsored Radio to the Funny Papers', both in *Advertising the American Dream: Making Way for Modernity* (Berkeley and Los Angeles: University of California Press, 1985), 52–87, 88–116.

68. A. A. Grünbaum, 'Psychologie en psychotechniek van de reclame: Iets over de tekst', in *Administrative Arbeid: Maanblad voor rationele werkmethoden* 2, no. 6 (June 1924), 184–7. See also A. A. Grünbaum, 'Psychologie en psychotechniek van de reclame: Het opwekken van behoeften. Iets over illustraties', 46–52. On the difficulty of persuading female customers to buy, see Grünbaum, 'Psychologie en psychotechniek in de reclame: De vrouw en de reclame', 301–4.

69. Roels, *Psychologie der reclame*, 2nd rev. edn (Amsterdam: H. J. W. Becht, 1952). More than a quarter of the illustrations in both editions are taken from Grünbaum's series, without clearly referring to him; Van Ginneken also noticed this in *De uitvinding van het publiek*, 48 and 204 n. 28.

70. Roels, *Psychologie der reclame*, 44.

71. Grünbaum, 'Psychologie en psychotechniek van de reclame: Inleiding', 19.

72. Roels, *Psychologie der reclame*, 31–47 and 311–31.

73. The main publications of both authors are Harry L. Hollingworth, *Ad-*

vertising and Selling (New York: Garland Publishing, Inc., 1985 (originally published in 1913)); Edward K. Strong and J. E. Loveless, *Psychology of Selling and Advertising* (New York: 1925). Strong published his research in articles earlier, but this book is more widely used. Grünbaum (1924–28) and Roels (1938) refer to both.

74. Van Ginneken, *De uitvinding van het publiek*, 50.
75. The exception in the Netherlands is A. A. Bosschart, *Theory of Advertising* (The Hague: 1934). This publication is very similar to F. M. Feller, *Psycho-Dynamik der Reklame* (Bern: 1932).
76. Curti, 'The Changing Concept of "Human Nature" in the Literature of American Advertising', 335–57.
77. Compare Kuna, 'Early Advertising Applications of the Gale-Cattell Order-of-Merit Method', *Journal of the History of Behavioral Sciences* 15 (1979), 38–46. See also Curti, 'The Changing Concept of "Human Nature" in the Literature of American Advertsing', 338, 353–7.
78. Landmark texts for advertising psychology concentrating on this aspect of human nature are Albert Poffenberger, *Psychology in Advertising* (New York: McGraw-Hill, 1932); Henry Charles Link, *The New Psychology of Selling and Advertising* (New York: Macmillan, 1934). Schuitema (1936) and Roels (1938) refer to both. Curti compares the development of advertising psychology with the writings of 'admen' in the foremost American advertising periodical *Printers' Ink*. This was an important periodical for Dutch advertising theorists as well.
79. J. van Gogh, 'Speculatieve of rationeele reclame', *Administratieve Arbeid: Maandblad voor rationeele werkmethoden* 8, no. 6 (June 1930), 131.
80. Ibid., 132.
81. Van Ginneken, *De uitvinding van het publiek*, 53–96.
82. Here he talks about the 'Reklamemittellehre' (science of advertising means). Schuitema, *Grondslagen van de moderne reclame*, 68.
83. Grünbaum, 'Psychologie en psychotechniek van de reclame: Iets over de tekst,'. 184
84. Ibid., 185.
85. Ibid., 184–5.
86. Schuitema, *Grondslagen van de moderne reclame*, 147.
87. Ibid., 142.

Select Bibliography

Abrams, A. Uhry, 'From Simplicity to Sensation: Art in American Advertising, 1904–1929', *Journal of Popular Culture* 3 (1976), 620–28.

Adams, Henry Foster, *Advertising and its Mental Laws*. New York: Garland Publishing, Inc., 1985.

Agulhon, Maurice, *Histoire vagabonde: ethnologie et politique dans la France contemporaine*. Paris: Gallimard, 1988.

———, *Marianne au pouvoir: l'imagerie et la symbolique républicaines de 1880 à 1914*. Paris: Flammarion, 1989.

Alessio, Dominic T., 'Capitalist Realist Art: Industrial Images of Hamilton, Ontario, 1884–1910', *Journal of Urban History* 18 (August 1992), 442–69.

Baker, Florence, 'Parisians and their Parks', Ph.D. diss., University of California at Los Angeles, 1994.

Barnum, P. T., *Die Kunst Geld zu machen: Nützliche-Winke und beherzigenswerte Ratschläge*. Berlin: Eulenspiegel Verlag, 1991.

———, *Leven en avonturen van P. T. Barnum*. Rotterdam: n.p., 1856.

———, *The Life of P. T. Barnum: Written by Himself*. Darby: Arden Library, 1986 (originally published in 1855).

Barre-Despond, Arlette, *Jourdain*. New York: Rizzoli, 1991.

Barrows, Susanna, *Distorting Mirrors*. New Haven: Yale University Press, 1981.

Baudrillard, Jean, *The System of Objects*. New York: Verso, 1996. Originally published as *Le système des objets* in 1968.

Beale, Marjorie, Advertising and the Politics of Public Persuasion in France, 1900–1939, Ph.D. diss., University of California, 1991.

Bedarida, François and Anthony Sutcliffe, 'The Street in the Structure and Life of the City: Reflections on Nineteenth Century London and Paris', *Journal of Urban History* 6, no. 4 (August 1980), 379–96.

Benjamin, Walter, 'Das Kunstwerk im Zeitalter seiner technischen Reproduzierbarkeit', *Gesammelte Schriften* 7, no. 1 (1989), 350–84.

Biedermann, Detlev von, *Das Zeitungswesen sonst und jetzt*. Leipzig: Verlag von Wilhelm Friedrich, 1882.

Bluestone, Daniel M., '"The Pushcart Evil": Peddlers, Merchants and New York City's Streets, 1890–1940', *Journal of Urban History* 17 (November 1991), 68–92.

Böbel, Ingo, 'Advertising and Economic Development: The West German Experience during the 1970s', *Journal of Advertising* (1982), 237–52.

Bogart, Michele H., *Artists, Advertising, and the Borders of Art*. Chicago and London: University of Chicago Press, 1995.

Bolten, Jürgen, 'Werbewandel – Wertewandel: Werbegeschichte als Kommunikationsgeschichte', *Universitas* 51 (1996), 127–42.

Borsay, Peter, 'The English Urban Renaissance: the development of provincial urban culture c.1680–1760,' *Social History* 5 (May 1977): 581–603.

Borscheid, Peter, 'Am Anfang war das Wort. Die Wirtschaftswerbung beginnt mit der Zeitungsannonce', in *Bilderwelt des Alltags: Werbung in der Konsumgesellschaft des 19. und 20. Jahrhunderts*, edited by Peter Borscheid and Clemens Wischermann, 20–43. Stuttgart: Franz Steiner Verlag, 1995.

Borscheid, Peter and Clemens Wischermann (eds), *Bilderwelt des Alltags: Werbung in der Konsumgesellschaft des 19. und 20. Jahrhunderts*. Studien zur Geschichte des Alltags, vol. 3. Stuttgart: Steiner, 1995.

Bosschart, A. A., *Theory of Advertising*. The Hague: n.p., 1934.

Bourdieu, Pierre, *La distinction. Critique sociale du jugement*. Paris: Les éditions de minuit, 1979. Translated as *Distinction: a social critique of the judgement of taste*. Cambridge: Harvard University Press, 1984.

Braudel, Fernand, *Civilisation matérielle, économie et capitalisme, XVe–XVIIIe siècle*. Paris: A. Colin, 1979.

Broido, Lucy, *The Posters of Jules Chéret*. New York: Dover Publications, 1992.

Broos, Kees and Paul Hefting, *Grafische vormgeving in Nederland. Een eeu*. Amsterdam: L. J. Veen, 1993.

Brune, Silke, '"Lichter der Großstadt": Werbung als Signum einer urbanen Welt', *Bilderwelt des Alltags: Werbung in der Konsumgesellschaft des 19. und 20. Jahrhunderts*, edited by Peter Borscheid and Clemens Wischermann, 90–115. Stuttgart: Steiner, 1995.

Buchli, Hanns, *6000 Jahre Werbung: Geschichte der Wirtschaftswerbung und der Propaganda*. 3 vols. Berlin: n.p., 1962–66.

Chatterjee, Partha, *The Nation and Its Fragments*. Princeton: Princeton University Press, 1993.

Clausen, Meredith, *Frantz Jourdain and the Samaritaine*. Leiden: E. J. Brill, 1987.

———, 'Toward a redefinition of the Art Nouveau', *Gazette des beaux-arts* (September 1985).

Cleven, Esther Erika, *Image bedeutet Bild: Eine Geschichte des Bildbegriffes in der Werbetheorie am Beispiel der Niederlande, 1917–1967*.

Clifford, Helen, 'Parker and Wakelin: the Study of an Eighteenth Century Goldsmithing Business with Particular Reference to the Garrard Ledgers 1770–1776'. Ph.D. diss., Royal College of Art, 1989.

Collins, Bradford, 'Jules Chéret and the Nineteenth-Century French Poster'. Ph.D. diss., Yale University, 1980.

Conijn, A. I., 'De Bedrijfsreclame: Een kunsthistorisch onderzoek naar het eerste Nederlandse reclametijdschrift, 1916–1921', Master's thesis, Nijmegen University, 1989.

Coquery, Natacha, 'L'hôtel aristocratique. Le marché du luxe à Paris au XVIIIe siècle' (Paris: Publications de la Sorbonne, 1998.

Cowen, Tyler, *In Praise of Commercial Culture*. Cambridge, Mass.: Harvard University Press, 1998.

Crary, Jonathan, 'Unbinding Vision: Manet and the Attentive Observer in the Late Nineteenth Century'. In *Cinema and the Invention of Modern Life*, edited by Leo Charney and Vanessa N. Schwartz, 46–71. Berkeley and Los Angeles: University of California, 1995.

Cross, Gary, *Time and Money: the Making of Consumer Culture*. London: Routledge, 1993.

Curti, Merle, 'The Changing Concept of "Human Nature" in the Literature of American Advertising', *Business History Review* 41, no. 4 (winter 1967), 335–57.

Dam, P. van, *Een eeuw affichekunst*. Amsterdam: n.p., 1987.

Davis, Dorothy, *A History of Shopping*. London: Routledge, 1966.

Defoe, Daniel, *The Complete English Tradesman*. New York: Burt Franklin, 1970.

Djie, P. L., 'Kunst voor Calvé: Een inventarisatie van het drukwerk gemaakt in opdracht van de Nederlandse oliefabrieken, Delft (1893–1930)'. Master's thesis, Utrecht University, 1994.

Dodanthun, Alfred, *Des Affiches électorales: étude de droit public*. Paris: n.p., 1903.

Dooijes, Dick and Pieter Brattinga, *A History of the Dutch Poster 1890–1960*. Amsterdam: Vaheltema & Holtema, 1968.

Douglas, Mary, *Purity and Danger*. New York: Praeger, 1966.

Duara, Prasenjit, *Rescuing History from the Nation*. Chicago: University of Chicago Press, 1995.

Elias, Norbert, *The Court Society*. Oxford: Basil Blackwell, 1983.

Englund, Steven, 'The Ghost of Nation Past', *Journal of Modern History* 64 (June 1992), 299–320.

Ewen, Stuart, *Captains of Consciousness: Advertising and the Social Roots of the Consumer Culture*. New York: McGraw-Hill, 1976.

Fitzgerald, Robert, *Rowntree and the Marketing Revolution, 1862–1969*. Cambridge: Cambridge University Press, 1995.

Fourié, Abbé, *De l'affichage politique; conseils pratiques pour la rédaction, l'apposition et la protection des affiches*. Paris: 1903.

Freedberg, David, *The Power of Images*. Chicago: University of Chicago Press, 1989.

Gérin, Octave-Jacques and Camille Espinadel, *La Publicité suggestive: théorie et technique*. Paris: 1911.

Gerlach, Siegfried and Dieter Sawatzki, *Grands magasins oder Die Geburt des Warenhauses im Paris des 19. Jahrhunderts*. Dortmund: Harenberg, 1989.

Gold, Philip, *Advertising, Politics and American Culture: From Salesmanship to Therapy*. New York: Paragon House, 1987.

Goldstein, Robert Justin, *Censorship of Political Caricature in Nineteenth-Century France*. Kent, Ohio: Kent State University Press, 1989.

Gries, Rainer, Volker Ilgen, Dirk Schindelbeck, *'Ins Gehirn der Masse kriechen!' Werbung und Mentalitätsgeschichte*. Darmstadt: Wissenschaftliche Buchgesellschaft, 1995.

Haas, Stefan, 'Die neue Welt der Bilder: Werbung und visuelle Kultur der Moderne', in *Bilderwelt des Alltags: Werbung in der Konsumgesellschaft des 19. und 20. Jahrhunderts*, edited by Peter Borscheid and Clemens Wischermann, 64–77. Stuttgart: Steiner, 1995.

————, 'Psychologen, Künstler, Ökonomen: Das Selbstverständnis der Werbetreiben zwischen Fin du Siècle und Nachkriegszeit', in *Bilderwelt des Alltags: Werbung in der Konsumgesellschaft des 19. und 20. Jahrhunderts*, edited by Peter Borscheid and Clemens Wischermann, 78–89. Stuttgart: Steiner, 1995.

Halter, A., *Als die Bilder reizen lernten. Zum Umgang mit den Produkten im französischen Warenplakat 1900–1930*. Zürich: Schweizer Rück, 1992.

Hartveld, C., 'Moderne zakelijkheid: Efficiency in wonen en werken in Nederland, 1918–1940', Ph.D. diss., University of Amsterdam, 1994.

Henatsch, Martin, *Die Entstehung des Plakates: Eine rezeptionsästhetische Untersuchung*. Studien zur Kunstgeschichte, vol. 91. Hildesheim, Zürich, New York: Georg Olms Publishers, 1995.

Hollingworth, Harry L., *Advertising and Selling*. New York: Garland Publishing, Inc., 1985.

Homburg, Heidrun, 'Werbung – "Eine Kunst, die gelernt sein will." Aufbrüche in eine neue Warenwelt 1750 – 1850', *Jahrbuch für Wirtschaftsgeschichte* 1 (1997), 11–52.

Horkheimer, Max and Theodor Adorno, *Dialektik der Aufklärung: Philosophische Fragmente*. Amsterdam: Querido, 1947.

Huysmans, Joris Karl, 'L'Etiage', *Oeuvres complètes* 8 (Paris, 1928), 137–40.

Jamakorzian, Roussignann, *De la publicité commerciale en France*. Paris: 1911.

Jaspert, F., 'Werbepsychologie: Grundlinien ihrer geschichtlichen

Entwicklung', in *Die Psychologie im 20. Jahrhundert. Anwendungen im Berufsleben. Arbeits-, Wirtschafts- und Verkehrspsychologie*, ed. F. Stoll, vol. 13, 170–89. Zürich: 1981.

Jeffreys, J., *Retail Trading in Britain 1850–1950*. Cambridge: Cambridge University Press, 1954.

Knies, Karl, *Der Telegraph als Verkehrsmittel: Mit Erörterungen über den Nachrichtenverkehr überhaupt*. Tübingen: Verlag der H. Laupp'schen Buchhandlung, 1857.

König, Th., *Die Psychologie der Reklame*. Würzburg: 1922.

Koshar, Rudy, '"Against the Frightful Leveler": Historic Preservation and German Cities, 1890–1914', *Journal of Urban History* 19 (May 1993), 7–29.

Kroeber-Riel, Werner, *Konsumentenverhalten*. 4th edn. Munich: Vahlen, 1990.

Krünitz, Johann Georg, 'Kauf-Laden', in *Oekonomisch-technologische Encyclopädie*. Vol. 36. Edited by Johann Georg Krünitz, 482–86. Berlin: Joachim Pauli, 1786.

Kuna D. P., 'The Concept of Suggestion in the Early History of Advertising Psychology', *Journal of the History of the Behavioral Sciences* 12, (1976), 347–53.

Lamberty, Christiane, '"Die Kunst im Leben des Buttergeschäfts": Geschmacksbildung und Reklame in Deutschland vor 1914', *Jahrbuch für Wirtschaftsgeschichte* 1 (1997), 53–78.

Langholz-Leymore, Varda, *Hidden Myth: Structure and Symbolism in Advertising*. London: Heinemann Educational, 1975.

Lassalle, Ferdinand, *Die Feste, die Presse und der Frankfurter Abgeordnetertag: Drei Symptome des öffentlichen Geistes. Eine Rede gehalten in den Versammlungen des Allgemeinen deutschen Arbeiter-Vereins zu Barmen, Solingen und Düsseldorf*. Düsseldorf: Schaub'sche Buchhandlung, 1863.

Latour, Bruno, *Wir sind nie modern gewesen: Versuch einer symmetrischen Anthropologie*. Berlin: Akademie Verlag, 1995.

Le Men, Segolène, *Seurat & Cheret : le peintre, le cirque et l'affiche*. Paris: CNRS éditions, 1994.

Lehmann, Hartmut, 'The Rise of Capitalism: Weber versus Sombart', in *Weber's 'Protestant Ethic': Origins, Evidence, Contexts*, edited by Hartmut Lehmann and Guenther Roth, 195–208. Washington, DC: German Historical Insitute and Cambridge: Cambridge University Press, 1993.

Leiss, William, Steven Kline and Sut Jhally, *Social Communication in Advertising: Persons, Products and Images of Well-Being*. Toronto and New York: Methuen, 1986.

Lenger, Friedrich, *Werner Sombart, 1863–1941: Eine Biographie*. Munich: Beck, 1994.

Léon, Pierre, *Histoire économique et sociale du monde*. Paris: Armand Colin, 1977.

Levin, Miriam, 'Democratic Vistas – Democratic Media: Defining a Role for Printed Images in Industrializing France', *French Historical Studies* (spring 1993), 82–108.

————, *Republican Art and Ideology in Late Nineteenth-Century France*. Ann Arbor: University of Michigan Press, 1986.

Link, Henry Charles, *The New Psychology of Selling and Advertising*. New York: Macmillan, 1934.

Lysinski, Edmund, *Psychologie des Betriebes*. N.p., 1923.

Maindron, Ernest, *Les Affiches illustrées*. Paris: H. Launette, 1886.

Marchand, Roland, *Advertising the American Dream: Making Way for Modernity 1920–1940*. Berkeley and Los Angeles: University of California Press, 1985.

Marcuse, Herbert, *One-dimensional Man: Studies in the History of Advanced Industrial Society*. Boston: Beacon Press, 1964.

Martin, Marc, *Trois siècles de publicité en France*. Paris: Odile Jacob, 1992.

Marx, Roger, *L'Art Social*. Paris: Bibliothèque-Charpentier, 1913.

Mass Observation, *Browns and Chester: Portrait of a Shop 1780–1946*, edited by H. D. Willcock. London: Drummond, 1947.

Mataja, Victor, *Die Reklame: Eine Untersuchung über Ankündigungswesen und Werbetätigkeit im Geschäftsleben*. Leipzig: Duncker & Humblot, 1910.

————, 'The Economic Value of Advertising', *International Quarterly* 8 (1903–4), 379–98.

Mathias, Peter, *Retailing Revolution*. London: Batsford, 1967.

McKendrick, Neil, John Brewer and J. H. Plumb, *The Birth of a Consumer Society*. London: Europa Publications, 1982.

Mermet, Emile, *Guide Mermet: la publicité en France*. Paris: n.p., 1878.

Merriman, John, 'Images of the Nineteenth Century French City', in *French Cities in the Nineteenth Century*, edited by John M. Merriman. New York: Holmes & Meier, 1981.

————, *The Margins of City Life*. New York: Oxford University Press, 1991.

Miller, Daniel, *Material Culture and Mass Consumption*. Oxford: Blackwell, 1987.

Miller, Michael B., *The Bon Marché: Bourgeois Culture and the Department Store, 1869–1920*. Princeton: Princeton University Press, 1981.

Moch, Leslie Page, 'Pushing at the Margins of French Urban History', *Journal of Urban History* 22 (March 1996), 377–83.

Mohrmann, Ruth E., 'Stadtfahrung und Mentalität', in *Stadt und Verkehr im Industriezeitalter*, edited by Horst Matzerath, 261–75. Cologne, Weimar and Vienna: Böhlau, 1996.

Mui, Lorna and Hoh-cheung Mui, *Shops and Shopkeeping in Eighteenth Century England*. Montreal: McGill-Queen's University Press, 1989.

Müller, Wendelin G., *Interkulturelle Werbung*. Konsum und Verhalten, vol. 43. Heidelberg: Physica/Verlag Rudolf Liebing, 1997.

Münsterberg, Hugo, *Psychologie und Wirtschaftsleben: Ein Beitrag zur angewandten Experimental-Psychologie*. Leipzig: J. A. Barth, 1912.

Nayrac, Jean-Paul, *Physiologie et psychologie de l'attention*. Paris: F. Alcan, 1905.

Nevett, Terence R., *Advertising in Britain: a History*. London: Heinemann, 1982.

Nienhaus, U., 'Rationalisierung und "Amerikanismus" in Büros der 20ger Jahre: Ausgewählte Beispiele', in *Amerikanisierung. Traum und Alptraum im Deutschland des 20. Jahrhunderts*, edited by Alf Lüdtke, Inge Marßolek, and Adelheid von Saldern. Stuttgart: Steiner, 1996.

Nijhoff, P. (ed.), *De kunst van het verleiden: Geëmailleerde reclame in Nederland*. Zwolle: Waanders, 1991.

Nijhof, P. *Buitenreclame in beeld. 50 jaar Alrecon Media 1946–1996*. Zwolle: Waanders, 1996.

Nord, Philip, *Paris Shopkeepers and the Politics of Resentment*. Princeton: Princeton University Press, 1986.

Norris, James D., *Advertising and the Transformation of American Society, 1865–1920*. New York and London: Greenwood Press, 1990.

Nye, Robert, *The Origins of Crowd Psychology*. London and Beverly Hills: Sage Publications, 1975.

Packard, Vance, *The Hidden Persuaders*. New York: Pocket Books, 1987.

Paneth, Erwin, *Entwicklung der Reklame vom Altertum bis zur Gegenwart: Erfolgreiche Mittel der Geschäfts-, Personen und Ideenreklame aus allen Zeiten und Ländern*. Munich and Leipzig: R. Oldenbourg, 1926.

Parrot, Nicole, *Mannequins*. Paris: Editions Colona, 1981.

Poffenberger, Albert T., *Psychology in Advertising*. New York and London: McGraw-Hill, 1932.

Pomian, Krzysztof, *Collectionneurs, amateurs et curieux*. Paris: Gallimard, 1987.

Postman, Neil, *Amusing Ourselves to Death: Public Discourse in the Age of Show Business*. New York: Viking Press, 1985.

Propokoff, Steven S. (ed.), *The Modern Dutch Poster: the First Fifty Years, 1890–1940*. Cambridge, London: MIT Press, 1987.

Reinhardt, Dirk, 'Beten oder Bummeln? Der Kampf um die Schaufensterfreiheit', in *Bilderwelt des Alltags: Werbung in der Konsumgesellschaft des 19. und 20. Jahrhunderts*, edited by Peter Borscheid and Clemens Wischermann, 116–25. Stuttgart: Steiner, 1995.

————, 'Vom Intelligenzblatt zum Satellitenfernsehen. Stufen der Werbung als Stufen der Gesellschaft', in *Bilderwelt des Alltags: Werbung in der Konsumgesellschaft des 19. und 20. Jahrhunderts*, edited by Peter Borscheid and Clemens Wischermann, 44–63. Stuttgart: Steiner, 1995.

————, *Von der Reklame zum Marketing: Geschichte der Wirtschaftswerbung in Deutschland*. Berlin: Akademie Verlag, 1993.

Ribot, Théodule, *La Psychologie de l'attention*. Paris, 1889.

Richards, Thomas, *The Commodity Culture of Victorian England: Advertising as Spectacle, 1851–1914*. Stanford: Stanford University Press, 1990.

Riesman, David, Renel Denney and Nathan Glazer, *The Lonely Crowd: A Study of the Changing American Character*. New Haven: Yale University Press, 1950.

Riotor, Léon, *Le Mannequin*. Paris, 1900.

Roche, Daniel, *The People of Paris: an Essay in Popular Culture in the Eighteenth Century*. Berkeley and Los Angeles: University of California Press, 1987.

Roche, Daniel, *Le Peuple de Paris*. Paris: Aubier Montaigne, 1981.

Roels, Franciscus, *Psychologie der Reclame*. Amsterdam: H. J. W. Brecht, 1938, 2nd rev. edn. Amsterdam: H. J. W. Becht, 1952.

Ronte, Dieter and Holger Bonus, *Werbung*. Münster; 1993.

Ruben, Paul (ed.), *Die Reklame: Ihre Kunst und Wissenschaft*. 2 vols. Berlin: Hermann Paetel Verlag, 1913–14.

Rummens, M., 'De verleiding van het decoratieve. Twee opstellen over compositie, expressie en abstractie in de theorie en praktijk van de moderne schilderkunst'. Ph.D. diss., University of Amsterdam, 1991.

Sartory, K. et al., *De vierde vrijheid, zijnde een blik in de historie van het reclamebureau delamar*. Amsterdam, 1955.

Schaufenster: Die Kulturgeschichte eines Massenmediums. Edited by the Württembergischer Kunstverein. Stuttgart: Dr Cantz'sche Druckerei, 1974.

Schirner, Michael, *Werbung ist Kunst*. Munich: Klinkhardt and Biermann, 1988. With an introduction by Hans Ulrich Reck.

Schmidt, Hans-Walter, 'Schaufenster des Ostens: Anmerkungen zur Konsumkultur der DDR', *Deutschland-Archiv* 27 (1994), 364–72.

Schmidt, Siegfried J., Detlef Sinofzik and Brigitte Spieß, 'Wo lassen Sie leben? Kulturfaktor Werbung – Entwicklungen und Trends der 80er Jahre', in *Aufbruch in die Neunziger*, edited by Christian W. Thomsen, 142–70. Cologne: DuMont, 1991.

Schmölder, Robert, *Das Inseratenwesen: Ein Staatsinstitut*. Leipzig: C. Reissner & Ganz, 1879.

———, *Wie können die Schäden unserer periodischen Presse dauernd geheilt werden?* Barmen: n.p., 1880.

Schmoller, Gustav, *Zur Geschichte der deutschen Kleingewerbe im 19. Jahrhundert: Statistische und nationalökonomische Untersuchungen*. Halle: Buchhandlung des Waisenhauses, 1870.

Schramm, Christine, *Deutsche Warenhausbauten: Ursprung, Typologie und Entwicklungstendenzen*. Aachen: Shaker, 1995.

Schreurs, Wilbert, *Geschiedenis van de reclame in Nederland: De ontwikkeling van de reclame in Nederland 1870 tot 1990*. Utrecht: Spin, 1989.

Schröter, Harm G., 'Die Amerikanisierung der Werbung in der Bundesrepublik Deutschland', *Jahrbuch für Wirtschaftsgeschichte* (1997), 93–115.

Schudson, Michael, *Advertising, the Uneasy Persuasion: Its Dubious Impacts on American Society*. New York: Basic Books, 1984.

Schuitema, E. B. W., *Grondslagen van de moderne reclame*. The Hague: H. P. Leopold's U.M.N.V., 1936.

Schulze, Gerhard, *Die Erlebnisgesellschaft: Kultursoziologie der Gegenwart*. Frankfurt a.M. and New York: Campus, 1993.

Scott, W. Dill. *The Psychology of Advertising: A Simple Exposition of the Principles of Psychology in their Relation to Successful Advertising*. Boston: Small, Maynard & Company, 1908.

Sennett, Richard, *The Conscience of the Eye: the Design and Social Life of Cities*. New York: Alfred A. Knopf, 1990.

Seyffert, R. *Die Reklame des Kaufmanns*. 3rd edn. Leipzig: n.p., 1925.

Silverman, Debora, *Art Nouveau in Fin-du-Siècle France*. Berkeley and Los Angleles: University of California Press, 1989.

Sombart, Werner. *Der Bourgeois: Zur Geistesgeschichte des modernen Wirtschaftsmenschen*. Munich and Leipzig: 1920.

———, 'Die Reklame', *Morgen: Wochenschrift für deutsche Kultur* 6 (March 1908), 281–6.

Spiekermann, Uwe, *Basis der Konsumgesellschaft: Entstehung und Entwicklung des modernen Kleinhandels in Deutschland 1850–1914*. Munich: C. H. Beck, 1998.

———, 'Elitenkampf um die Werbung: Staat, Heimatschutz und Reklameindustrie im frühen 20. Jahrhundert', in *Bilderwelt des Alltags: Werbung in der Konsumgesellschaft des 19. und 20. Jahrhunderts*, edited by Peter Borscheid and Clemens Wischermann, 126–49. Stuttgart: Steiner, 1995.

————, 'Medium der Solidarität: Die Werbung der Konsumgenossenschaften 1903–1933', in *Bilderwelt des Alltags: Werbung in der Konsumgesellschaft des 19. und 20. Jahrhunderts*, edited by Peter Borscheid and Clemens Wischermann, 150–89. Stuttgart: Steiner, 1995.

————, 'Theft and Thieves in German Department Stores, 1895–1930: A Discourse about Morality, Crime, and Gender', in *Cathedrals of Consumption*, edited by Geoffrey Crossick and Serge Jaumain. Aldershot: Ashgate, 1999.

————, *Warenhaussteuer in Deutschland: Mittelstandsbewegung, Kapitalismus und Rechtsstaat im späten Kaiserreich*. Frankfurt a.M.: Peter Lang, 1994.

Stearns, Peter N., 'Stages of Consumerism: Recent Work on the Issues of Periodization', *Journal of Modern History* 69 (1997), 102–17.

Steenhoff, W., 'De reclameplaat', in *De tijd van H. Robbers: Bloemlezung uit Elsevier's Geïllustreerd Maandschrift 1905–1937*, edited by W. J. Simons, 217–22. Amsterdam, Brussels: n.p., 1968.

Strong, Edward K. and J. E. Loveless, *Psychology of Selling and Advertising*. New York: 1925.

Styles, John, 'Manufacturing, Consumption, and Design in Eighteenth Century England', in *Consumption and the World of Goods in the Eighteenth Century*, edited by John Brewer and Roy Porter, 527–54. London and New York: Routledge, 1993.

Sutcliffe, Anthony, *The Autumn of Central Paris: the Defeat of Town Planning, 1850–1970*. London: Edward Arnold, 1970.

Tenefelde, Klaus, 'Klassenspezifische Konsummuster im Deutschen Reich', in *Europäische Konsumgeschichte. Zur Gesellschafts- und Kulturgeschichte des Konsums, 18.-20. Jahrhundert*, edited by Hannes Siegrist, Hartmut Kälble and Jürgen Kocka, 245–66. Frankfurt and New York: Campus, 1997.

Treitschke, Heinrich von, *Politics*. Vol. 1. Translated by Blanche Dugdale and Torben de Bille. London: Constable and Company Ltd, 1916.

Van der Heijden, Marien, *Albert Hahn*. Amsterdam: T. Rap, 1993.

Van Heusden, G. H., *Een eeuw adverteerkunde: De sociaal-economische en psychologische ontwikkeling van het adverteren in Nederlandse kranten*, Bouwstenen voor de kennis der maatschappij, vol. 44. Assen: Van Gorcum, 1962.

Varnedoe, Kirk and Adam Gopnik, *High and Low: Modern Art and Popular Culture*. New York: The Museum of Modern Art, 1990.

Väth-Hintz, Henriette, *Odol: Reklame-Kunst um 1900*. Gießen: Anabas, 1985.

Verhagen, Marcus, 'The Poster in Fin-du-Siècle Paris: That Mobile and

Degenerate Art', in *Cinema and the Invention of Modern Life*, edited by Leo Charney and Vanessa N. Schwartz, 103–29. Berkeley and Los Angeles: University of California Press, 1995.

Walker, R. B., 'Advertising in London Newspapers 1650–1750', *Business History* 15 (1975), 112–30.

Walsh, Claire, 'Shop Design and the Display of Goods in the Eighteenth Century', Master's thesis, Royal College of Art/V&A, 1993.

———, 'Shop Design and the Display of Goods in Eighteenth-Century London', *Journal of Design History* 8, no. 3 (1995), 157–76.

Weatherill, Lorna, *Consumer Behaviour and Material Culture in Britain, 1660–1760*. London and New York: Routledge, 1988.

Wehle, J. G., *Die Reclame: Ihre Theorie und Praxis: Uebersichtliche Darstellung des gesammten Ankündigungswesens*. Vienna, Pest, Leipzig: A. Hartleben, 1880.

Weiss, Jeffrey, *The Popular Culture of Modern Art: Picasso, Duchamp, and Avant-Gardism*. New Haven: Yale University Press, 1995.

Wicke, Jennifer, *Advertising Fictions: Literature, Advertisement and Social Reading*. New York: Columbia University Press, 1988.

Wiebe, Robert H., *The Search for Order 1877–1920*. New York: Hill & Wang, Inc., 1966.

Wiener, Alfred, *Das Warenhaus: Kauf-, Geschäfts-, Büro-Haus*. Berlin: Ernst Wasmuth, 1912.

Williams, Rosalind H., *Dream Worlds: Mass Consumption in Late Nineteenth-Century France*. Berkeley and Los Angeles: University of California Press, 1982.

Wilson, William H., 'The Billboard: Bane of the City Beautiful', *Journal of Urban History* 13 (Aug. 1987), 394–425.

Wischermann, Clemens, 'Der kulturgeschichtliche Ort der Werbung', in *Bilderwelt des Alltags: Werbung in der Konsumgesellschaft des 19. und 20. Jahrhunderts*, edited by Peter Borscheid and Clemens Wischermann, 8–19. Stuttgart: Steiner, 1995.

———, 'Grenzenlose Werbung? Die gesellschaftliche Akzeptanz der Werbewelt im 20. Jahrhundert', in *Bilderwelt des Alltags: Werbung in der Konsumgesellschaft des 19. und 20. Jahrhunderts*, edited by Peter Borscheid and Clemens Wischermann, 372–407. Stuttgart: Steiner, 1995.

———, 'Werbung zwischen Kommunikation und Signifikation im 19. und 20. Jahrhundert', in *Kommunikationsrevolutionen im Vergleich. Die neuen Medien des 16. und 19. Jahrhunderts*, edited by Michael North, 191–202. Köln/Weimar/Wien: Böhlau, 1995.

Wities, Bernard, 'Das Wirkungsprinzip in der Reklame: eine psychologische Studie', *Zeitschrift für Philosophie und philosophische Kritik* 128 (1906), 138–54.

Zola, Émile, *The Ladies' Paradise*. Translated by Brian Nelson. Oxford: Oxford University Press, 1995.

Index

Aachen, retailing in 147
Action française (journal) 121
Adam, Paul 126
Adams, Henry Foster 188
Adorno, Theodor W. 17
advertising
    beginnings and development of 1–
        15, 58–61, 80–82
    psychology and 15, 16–17, 60,
        183–97
    social science and 15–25
        communications models 17–20
        'hidden myths' 20–22
        'hidden persuaders' 16–17
        signifying power of advertising
            22–5
    view from twenty-first century 25–
        7
aestheticization 59–60
Agence Dalziel 115
Agence nationale d'achiffage 115
Agulhon, Maurice 128
Alexandre, Arsène 122
Allgemeine Deutsche Arbeiterverein
    (General German Workers'
    Association ADAV) 33–4
L'Ami des monuments et des arts
    parisiens et français 129
Amsterdam 172
Anglomania 107–9
anonymity in cities 62–5
anti-clericalism 127–8
architectural advertising 64–5
Arson (furrier) 104
art
    advertising and 13, 116, 182–3
    French court society and 96–109
    posters 117–23
    developments in 60
    French court society and advertis-
        ing art 96–109
Art moderne (journal) 121
Arts and Crafts Movement 182
Ascher & Münchow (department
    store) 150–51
d'Avenel, Vicomte Georges 113
awnings 156

balls 123
bargaining 88, 102–3
Barnou (haberdasher/embroiderer)
    108
Barnum, P. T. 33, 42, 184
Barthes, Roland 56
Baudrillard, Jean 20
bazaars 149
Beaulard (fashion merchant) 100,
    107
Beauvais, Ibert 104, 108
Bedrijfsreclame (journal) 182, 185
behavioural research 18
behaviourism 15
Beishuizen, Piet 188
Bellepanne (fireworks manufacturer)
    107
Berlin
    advertising as *Kulturkampf* in
        Berlin and Vienna 32–50
    illuminated advertising in 68
    regulation of street advertising 70
    retailing in 142–3, 145–7, 154, 159
Berliner Tageblatt 39–40
Berliner Volkszeitung 36
Bernhard, Lucien 69
Bernheim, Hippolyte 126
Bernstein (editor of *Berliner
    Volkszeitung*) 36
Bertin (fashion merchant) 107, 108
Besnard, Albert 122
Biermer, Magnus 40, 41
Billard, Estelle (embroiderer) 107
Bismarck, Otto von 34
blinds 156
Blue Band margarine 174–8, 182,
    184, 195–6
Bond Heemschut 172, 174
Bonnot (haberdasher) 108
books 81, 82
Bordeaux, posters in 115
Bouchot, Frédéric 131
Boulanger, Georges 128
Bourdieu, Pierre 13, 14
Bourgeois, Léon 122
Bracquemond, Félix 122
Brand, Horst 18

brands, development of 62, 80
Brentano, Lujo 41–2
Briscoe, Stafford 85, 86
British School of Advertising 185
brochures 101, 106
Broerman, Eugene 130
Bücher, Karl 36, 47
Budapest 64
Buffault (silk merchant) 102, 108
Burty, Philippe 122
Büsser, Otto 59

Cabinet des Modes (magazine) 98–9
Calteau (glover/perfumer) 107
Campbell (cabinetmaker) 84, 85
carnivals 122–3
Carrier-Belleuse, Albert Ernest 122
Carrière, Eugène 122
Cassandre 180, 181
Certeau, Michel de 56
Chaniaud (saddler) 108
Charcot, Jean-Marie 126
Chasles, Philarète 124
Chéret, Jules 116–23
cinema, control of advertising for 70–
    71
cities
    mental models of cities and the
        emergence of commercial
        advertising 54–75
    development of advertising 58–
        61
    early advertising strategies and
        anonymity in cities 62–5
    end of unregulated advertising
        under National Socialism
        72–4
    from *flâneur* to patchworker 74–
        5
    sources and methods 56–8
    struggle for the city 69–72
    taking over the cities 65–9
poster and urban territory in 19th
    century France 113–33
    city and state 126–9
    contaminating advertisement
        123–4
    critiques of the will 124–6
    naturalist criticism 115–23
    preservation 129–30
    quarantine 131–2

Clement (stoneware merchant) 104
clocktowers 68
cognitive paradigm 19
Commission du vieux Paris 129, 130
commodity culture 22
communications theories 17–20
competition on prices 1, 155
consumer goods
    advertising and marketing in
        eighteenth century London
        79–93
        history 80–82
        newspaper advertising versus
            marketing through the shop
            87–92
        surveys 82–7
consumerism 97
cooperatives 46, 152–3
Coppens, Han 175–7, 178, 185–6,
    187, 195
Coppens Advies-Bureau 175, 184,
    186
Courbet, Gustave 121
court society 4
    advertising art in eighteenth
        century Paris and 96–109
Cramer, Rie 177, 182
Crary, Jonathan 125
crime, depiction of 131–2
Crystal Palace (Great Exhibition
    1851) 23, 24
Curner-Neilson (hosier) 107
Curti, Merle 185, 193, 194

Dalou, Jules 122
Davis, Nathalie Zemon 132
De la Mar, Abraham 184
Degournay (silver-plater) 103–4
Delaroue (fashion merchant) 107
Demachy (pharmacist) 103
Denney, Renel 16
department stores 10, 62
    German 66, 149–52, 159–64
    Paris 5, 6–7, 22–3
Dernburg, Mitzi 39
Desperrelles (hatter) 107
Détaille, Edouard 119, 130
Deutsche Werbung (journal) 58
Devaux (innkeeper) 108
Dhercourt, Gillebert 131
Dickens, Charles 45

Dillmann, Christian Heinrich von 43–5
Dokkum, J. J. C. van 182
Douglas, Mary 132
Dupon, Chafanel 101, 103, 106

Eclair (journal) 119
economic approach to advertising 60–61
Edison phonographs 41
education, posters and 118
Egalité (journal) 119
employment of women in advertising 47
Esders & Dyckhoff (department store) 159, 160
Estampe et l'affiche (journal) 118
Etzel 69
Exner, Robert 57
expressionism 71, 72

fashion 8
in England 79, 84
magazines 98–9
Paris and 4, 96–109
Féderation lithographique 119
Fénéon, Félix 119
Fernandez et Joly (haberdashers) 107
Ferry, Jules 127
Firardin (fabric merchant) 107
Fould, Georges Achilles 124–5
Fourié, Abbot 128
Fragonard, Jean Honoré 120
France
posters in 113–33
city and state 126–9
contaminating advertisement 123–4
critiques of the will 124–6
naturalist criticism 115–23
preservation 129–30
quarantine 131–2
regulation of competition in 1
state control of advertising in 3
see also Paris
France illustrée (journal) 124

Garnier, Charles 129
Geffroy, Gustave 118
Genootschap for Reclame 185

Germany
American influence in 25–6, 33, 38, 41, 66–7
department stores 66, 149–52, 159–64
development of advertising in 10, 58–61
display windows and window displays in German cities of the nineteenth century 139–65
after 1900 158–65
before 1835 140–41
development 1835–70 141–8
development 1870–1900 148–58
Jewish influence in 33, 36
mental models of cities and the emergence of commercial advertising 54–75
development of advertising 58–61
early advertising strategies and anonymity in cities 62–5
end of unregulated advertising under National Socialism 72–4
from *flâneur* to patchworker 74–5
sources and methods 56–8
struggle for the city 69–72
taking over the cities 65–9
press
advertising as *Kulturkampf* 32–50
degeneration of 34, 35–9
politics and 44
social change and 35
state control of 34–5
state control
advertising 3, 36, 48
press 34–5
see also Berlin
Gérôme, Jean Léon 118
Gerson, Hermann 145
Gill, André 127
Ginneken, Jaap van 193
Glazer, Nathan 16
Gobelins tapestries 122
Gogh, J. van 194, 195
Granchez (jeweller) 103, 107, 109
Grand-Carteret, John 119
Grande encyclopédie 126

Grare (cloth merchant) 108
Grünbaum, Anton A. 185, 187, 188–93, 194, 197
Guesnier (silk merchant) 108

Hague, The 172
Hahn, Albert 182
Hamburg, retailing in 143, 144, 145
handbills see posters and handbills
Hayet (fabric merchant) 103
Heimatschutz 70, 172
Hertzog, Rudolph 145, 159
Hodd, Fred 68
Hollingworth, H. L. 193
Holst, R. Roland 182, 197
Homburg, Heidrun 3
Höniger, Dr 70
Horkheimer, Max 17
Huysmans, Joris-Karl 116, 122

illumination see lighting
Intelligenzblätter (journal) 36, 48
interior design 89–91, 92, 159–62
International Advertising Association 47
International Quarterly 45
invoices 97, 99–109

Jahnke, Karl 72
Jhally, Sut 184
Jordan, Heinrich 159
Jourdain, Frantz 121
Journal des arts 118, 121
Joyce, James 45

Kaisers Kaffeegeschäft 153
Kander (department store) 151, 152
Kersten & Tuteur (department store) 159–60, 161
Kline, Steven 184
Knies, Karl 42–3, 48
Kroeber-Riel, Werner 19
Kulturkampf, advertising as Kulturkampf in Berlin and Vienna 32–50

La Briere (merchant) 107
labels 97
Lacan, Jacques 20, 21
Lacoste (fashion merchant) 107
Lamouroux, Adrien 129

Landsberger, Louis 145
Langholz-Leymore, Varda 20–21
Lassalle, Ferdinand 32–7, 39, 43, 47, 49
Latour, Bruno 139
Le Bégue (dyes merchant) 108
Le Duc, Viollet 129
Le Havre, posters in 115
Le Normand et Cie. 101, 108
Leipzig 3
Leiss, William 184
Lemaître, Jules 122
Leroux et Delasalle (fabric merchants) 107
letterheads and invoices 97, 99–109
Levée, François 130
Lévi-Strauss, Claude 20
lighting
    illuminated advertising 66, 67–8, 172, 173, 176
    interior 160
    window displays 156–7, 163, 164
Lille, posters in 115
Lilly, Charles 88
Lingner, Karl August 62
Livre et l'image (journal) 118
London
    consumer goods advertising and marketing in eighteenth century London 79–93
    history 80–82
    newspaper advertising versus marketing through the shop 87–92
    surveys 82–7
    Crystal Palace (Great Exhibition 1851) 23, 24
    economic supremacy of 3
    origins of advertising in 3–4
    shopping streets 7
Lyons, posters in 115, 131, 132
Lysinski, E. 13

McKendrick, Neil 79
mail-order selling 80
Mandelbaum, S. 67
manipulation theories 16–17
mannequins 116, 156
Manoli brand 69
market research 15, 195
markets 80, 92, 140

Marlboro advertisements 25–6
Marseilles, posters in 115
Marx, Roger 118, 119–20, 122
Masefield's (wallpaper/papier mâché seller) 90
mass culture 13–15
Mataja, Victor 39, 45–8
medicines 81–2
Mercier, Sébastien 107, 118
Michel (fabric merchant) 108
Michelet, Jules 118
Mignot (glover) 109
Mithouard, Adrien 130
Mitteilungen des Verbandes der Reklamefachleute (journal) 57–8
Montassier (hosier) 107
monuments and landmarks, posters and 129–30
Morel (silk shop) 103
Morgen (journal) 40, 41
Mosse, Rudolf 39, 40
Mui, Lorna and Hoh-cheung 88

Nantes, posters in 115, 131, 132
National Socialism, state control of advertising and 72–4
Nayrac, Jean-Paul 125
Neheon, Lucas de 141
Netherlands
    advertising theory in the 1920s and 1930s 172–97
    advertising as applied psychology 187–91
    art and advertising 181–3
    Blue Band margarine in the 1920s 174–8, 182, 184, 195–6
    eye-catching illustration 178–81
    lacking knowledge about the public 191–4
    public as puppet 194–7
    turning point 183–6
New Institutional Economics 20
newspapers see press
Normand, Charles 129

Odol brand 62, 69
official culture 13
Organisation (journal) 41

Packard, Vance 16, 18, 20

Pannelier, Victor Louis 130
Paris
    Anglomania in 107–9
    court society in 4
        advertising art and 96–109
    cultural supremacy of 3
    department stores 5, 6–7, 22–3
    expositions 11
    fashion and 4, 96
    illuminated advertising in 66
    posters in 113, 114, 122–3, 128, 129–30, 131, 132
    transformation of 10
Père peinard (journal) 119
photography 47
pillars, advertising 8, 61
Poculla, Max 59
pointillism 60
politics
    advertising and 71–2
    press and 44
Pompeii 1
posters and handbills 91, 97, 178–81, 197
    Blue Band campaign 177–8, 182
    poster and urban territory in nineteenth century France 113–33
        city and state 126–9
        contaminating advertisement 123–4
        critiques of the will 124–6
        naturalist criticism 115–23
        preservation 129–30
        quarantine 131–2
Pradel & Co. 104
pre-industrial advertising 1
press
    advertising in 3, 9, 10
        consumer goods advertising and marketing in eighteenth century London 79–88
        as Kulturkampf in Berlin and Vienna 32–50
    degeneration of 34, 35–9
    fashion magazines 98–9
    politics and 44
    professional advertising journals 56–8, 182
    social change and 35
    state control of 34–5

prices
  bargaining 88, 102–3
  competition 1, 155
  fixed 85, 102, 155
Propaganda (journal) 57, 65
Provost (button maker) 107–8
psychology, advertising and 15, 16–
    17, 60, 183–97
pub signs 1
public lavatories 131
Publicité moderne (journal) 115
puffing 83–4

Quid'beuf, Léon 126

Rambaud, Alfred 119
Ravoise (confectioner) 107
ready-made clothing 9
Reclame (Dutch journal) 182
Reinhardt, Dirk 181–2, 193
Reklame (German journal) 57, 72
religion, anti-clericalism 127–8
representation 22
reputation 91
  Parisian merchants at the end of
    the eighteenth century 96–109
retailing *see* shops and shopkeepers
Ribot, Théodule 125
Richards, Thomas 22, 23, 25
Richter, Eugen 152
Riesman, David 16–17
Rigonot (hosier) 107
Robert (fabric merchant) 108
Roels, Franciscus 190, 192–3
Roland, Wilhelm 58, 65
Roll, Alfred Philippe 122
Rops, Félicien 122
Rosipal (department store) 149–50
Rotterdam 67
Rouen, posters in 115
royalty, patronage of 105, 107
Ruben, Paul 185

St Louis, World's Fair (1904) 47
Saloman, E. 64
sandwich boards 68
Sauvan (fashion merchant) 108
Savary des Bruslons, J. 99
Schmidt, Hermann 69
Schmidt, Siegfried J. 19
Schmölder, Robert 47

schools, posters and 131
Schopenhauer, Joanna 89
Schuitema, E. B. W. 172, 196, 197
Schulze, Gerhard 26
Scott, Walter Dill 188
sensationalism 9–10
Sharpe, W. 56
shops and shopkeepers 4–6, 7
  consumer goods advertising and
    marketing in eighteenth
    century London 79–93
  history 80–82
  newspaper advertising versus
    marketing through the shop
    87–92
  surveys 82–7
  department stores 5, 6–7, 10, 22–3,
    62, 66
  interior design 89–91, 92, 159–62
  reputation of Parisian merchants at
    the end of the eighteenth
    century 96–109
  see also window displays
signifying power of advertising 22–5
signs 1, 97
Silverman, Deborah 117
Sinofzik, Detlef 19
Smith, Adam 22
Smuda, Manfred 56
social science
  advertising and 15–25
    communications models 17–20
    'hidden myths' 20–22
    'hidden persuaders' 16–17
    signifying power of advertising
      22–5
Société des amis des monuments
  parisiens 129
Société générale de publicité 115
Sombart, Nicolaus 39
Sombart, Werner 33, 37–42, 47, 49
Spiess, Brigitte 19
standardization 8, 80
Stanton, John 83
state control
  advertising 3, 36, 48, 70–72
    National Socialism and 72–4
  press 34–5
Steenhoff, Willem 179, 180
stimulus-response 15, 18, 19
Stockman, Fréd 116

Strong, K. 193
subliminal advertising 16, 18

Tempé (embroiderer) 107
Thumb, General Tom 33, 42
Tietz, Hermann (department store)
    151
Tissot (ribbon merchant) 108
Toorop, Jan 179–80
Towsey, E. and S. 84
trade cards 91
Treitschke, Heinrich 33, 37, 39, 43,
    47, 49

United Kingdom
    Anglomania in France 107–9
    price competition in 1
    see also London
United States of America 13, 15
    advertising in 66–7, 184
    influence
        in Germany 25–6, 33, 38, 41,
            66–7
        in Netherlands 193–4
    psychology of advertising in 15,
        16–17
urban areas see cities
urinals 131

Vachon, Marius 122
Vallès, Jules 121
Van den Bergh's Blue Band margarine
    174–8, 182, 184, 195–6
Vaugeois (toy merchant) 102, 105
Verband Deutscher Illustratoren 72
Verein der Reklamefachleute 70
Verein für Handelsgeographie 43

Verein für Socialpolitik 38, 40
Veuillot, Louis 128
Vienna, press advertising in 38, 42
Viollette, Maurice 131
Voltaire 96

Walker, R. B. 81, 82
wall advertising 9, 14
Walters, Norah 176
wartime 63
    regulation of advertising during
        70–71
Watteau, Antoine 120, 121
Weddy-Pönicke (department store)
    160, 161
Wedgwood, Josiah 83–4, 85
Wertheim (department store) 151
Wiener, Alfred 66
Willrab, Willy 64–5
window displays 10, 11, 65–6
    display windows and window
        displays in German cities of
        the nineteenth century 139–65
    after 1900 158–65
    before 1835 140–41
    development 1835–70 141–8
    development 1870–1900 148–58
Wollock, L. 56
women, employment in advertising 47
Wundt, Wilhelm 188

Zola, Emile
    'A Victim of Advertising' 123–4
    Au bonheur des dames (The
        Ladies' Paradise) 6–7, 10, 22–
        3, 123
Zucca, O. 115